British History
1760 – 1914

Elizabeth M M Tucker M Sc (Econ)

Edward Arnold

First published 1982
by Edward Arnold (Publishers) Ltd
41 Bedford Square, London WC1B 3DQ

British Library Cataloguing in Publication Data

Tucker, Elizabeth M. M.
   British history 1760-1914
   1. Great Britain—History—19th century
   2. Great Britain—History—20th century
   I. Title
   941.07   DA470

   ISBN 0-7131-0601-8

Printed by Butler & Tanner Ltd
Frome and London

Preface

A study of the period 1760 – 1914 provides a background which is essential for anyone wishing to understand life in Britain today. This short volume is confined to the major issues of this eventful period of history. Inevitably the process of selection may have led to over-simplification in some areas but the aim of the book is to provide an insight into the most important events of the period.

The book is intended for 'O' level students although it can be used to provide an introduction to 'A' level. Each chapter is followed by a summary, drawing the main strands together and emphasizing what has been discussed. In addition, questions, typical of those found in 'O' level examination papers, have been included at the end of each chapter. They should be particularly useful for revision purposes.

Acknowledgments

The Publishers' thanks are due to the following for permission to reproduce copyright photographs:

Science Museum, London: pp 24, 272;
Mansell Collection Ltd: pp 38, 63, 64, 138t & b, 170, 230;
British Museum: p 90;
BBC Hulton Picture Library: p 133, 200

Contents

Maps and Diagrams

Tables

Illustrations

1
Britain in 1760

1 The System of Government

When George III came to the throne in 1760 he was determined to rule in a different manner from the first two Hanoverians. He wanted the British government to be based on patriotism and purity, free from the corruption and sectional interests which had characterized the reigns of the first two Georges. He did not wish to use any more power than his grandfather. However, believing that he knew best how the country should be governed, he looked with suspicion on those who opposed him. In a settled era he would probably have succeeded in carrying out his aim of pursuing a national policy. Unfortunately for George III great issues arose in England and America which upset his plans. They placed a strain on the political system, causing it to work in a way which he had not foreseen.

In 1760 the civil administration, or civil service as we call it today, was regarded as the king's government which he should run for himself and pay for himself. So long as each civil servant worked within his means he was allowed to manage his department as he pleased. Parliament did not concern itself with the operation of the civil service unless it threatened to deprive MPs of their independence.

Like his predecessors George III chose his own ministers to carry out the government of the country. Their duties included conducting foreign policy, collecting taxes and running the court. In 1760 few MPs were anxious to hold ministerial posts. Two types of men might become ministers. In one category might be included men of influence and family connections such as Bute (1713–92), Grenville (1712–70), Newcastle (1693–1768), Rockingham (1730–82), Shelburne (1737–1805), Grafton (1735–1811) and North (1732–92). In a second category were men of ambition from less exalted backgrounds who hoped to improve themselves in political service. Such men did not usually gain the highest offices but they were able and efficient.

On George III's accession he found ministers quarrelling amongst themselves. Since the death of Henry Pelham in 1754 it had been difficult to find a team of ministers who could work together for longer than a few months. The Pitt – Newcastle combination which George III inherited had arisen in response to the dangers of war. The fact that it had existed for three years did not mean that it was as stable as appearances might suggest. It did not last long in the new reign. The decade following 1760 was one of ministerial instability with opposing groups unable to form a lasting administration.

Political parties as we know them today did not-exist in the eighteenth century. There were Whigs and Tories but most MPs did not belong to either of these groups. These labels only applied to certain families and in certain parts of the country. Originally the Tories had supported the Stuart kings and opposed the accession of the Hanoverian George I, whilst the Whigs had opposed the Stuarts and supported the accession of George I. By 1760 the labels of Whig and Tory served little purpose. There has been much talk of the existence of a government party or a party known as the 'King's Friends' created by George III. However, although he did build up a body of supporters in the Commons, the group was not sufficiently large or powerful to carry the king's ministers through periods of unpopularity.

There were 558 MPs in the House of Commons. Unlike today the House of Lords was a powerful force in the country's government. In the 1760 House of Commons there were 92 members for counties, 417 for borough seats; four University members and 45 Scottish MPs. The uneven distribution of parliamentary seats gave more representation to the south-east and south-west areas of the country. Few people had the vote and the franchise was not uniform. This was the era of rotten and pocket boroughs (see pp 116 – 17) and of self-made men eager to buy themselves a seat in Parliament. Elections were noisy and rough. Voting was conducted in the open and accompanied by bribery, corruption and intimidation. Since elections were expensive politicians preferred, where possible, to avoid a contest. The 1761 election was typical of the age — out of 315 constituencies polling in that year only 48 seats were contested.

Most MPs believed that their role in the House of Commons was to represent their constituency which they regarded almost as an independent community. They were suspicious of the power of central government and held the view that the best government was the least government. To them local affairs were all important. They found proceedings at Westminster tedious and time-consuming.

In 1760 local government was carried out with little interference from London. In the counties the Lord Lieutenant was the leader of

the justices of the peace and the head of the armed forces. JPs had to
be men of an estate worth at least £100 per year. As well as enforcing
the law they dealt with the maintenance of roads and public buildings and the administration of the poor law. In the towns municipal
corporations regulated local affairs.

2 The Economic Framework

In 1760 the population of England and Wales was approximately
6,500,000. Scotland's population was 1,250,000 and there were
about 3,250,000 people in Ireland. The birth and death rates were
both high. However, the death rate was just beginning to decline.
Improvements in medical care, together with higher nutritional
levels, were responsible for this trend, and by the end of George III's
reign in 1820 the population had almost doubled.

There were only two cities in England with a population of over
50,000. Bristol had 60,000 and London 750,000. Towns were
beginning to provide a few basic facilities such as street paving but
for the most part they were dirty and often dangerous places. The
bulk of the population lived in small market towns, ports and
villages. There was little labour mobility and if people moved away
from their birth place it was usually only a short distance.

Britain was endowed with rich farmland and in 1760 most people
worked on the land. Revolutionary changes were taking place in
agriculture (see Chapter 2). Enclosures were followed by the adoption of new techniques, machinery and crops and experiments in
animal husbandry. For many people the changes led to hardship,
but society remained stable.

To supplement their income from agriculture many families
engaged in the domestic system of industry, manufacturing goods
on a part-time basis in their homes. Most woollen cloth was produced in this way. Many families who engaged solely in industrial
production also worked at home. In the Midlands nail and pottery
producers lived in rows of cottages which amounted to sub-divided
factories. Factories sprang up where an industry demanded heavy
equipment or water power. Britain possessed rich mineral deposits.
Iron and steel works depended on supplies of water and coal. Mining
communities tended to be rather isolated. In 1760 British industry
was prosperous but it had not yet experienced revolutionary changes
nor did it act as a magnet for the rural population.

Industrial and agricultural progress requires capital investment.
Only limited banking facilities were available in 1760. One survey
showed that there were little more than twelve 'banking shops'

outside London. By 1793 there were 400. Entrepreneurs sought funds from local merchants and land tax collectors. There were few insurance facilities and no limitation of liabilities to protect them when their ventures failed although this did not stop enterprising businessmen.

As well as capital, industrial and agricultural expansion requires an adequate transport network. In 1760 the canal age was only just beginning and an improvement in the condition of roads had not yet reached its peak. It was not unusual for villages to be cut off from the rest of the world in winter when the surrounding roads became impassable. However, water transport flourished. Few areas of the country were more than a day's journey from navigable water. England's ports and rivers were thriving avenues of trade.

By 1760 Britain had a long tradition as a trading nation. In the early years of George III's reign MPs were far more interested in problems of trade than in those of industry. Merchants engaged in trade with India, South America, the West Indies, the Baltic countries, North America, most European countries and even Greenland. In 1760 Britain imported goods valued at £11,000,000 whilst exports stood at £16,000,000. The most important trade route was the Atlantic triangle. England exported manufactured goods to Africa. She took slaves from Africa to the West Indies. From the West Indies she imported sugar.

3 British Society

British society was stable when George III ascended the throne. The class structure was fixed although there was some room for social mobility. At the top the upper ranks of society lived in sumptuous surroundings, whilst at the bottom the poor did little more than exist in conditions of great hardship and squalor. Ownership of land was the key to a position in society and the possession of political rights. Beneath the landowning upper classes were the lesser gentry. Many were squires who dominated village life. They often worked on their own farms but considered themselves superior to members of the professions and wealthy industrialists. In turn the city merchant considered himself superior to the shopkeeper and skilled craftsman. For social climbers it took three generations to rise from tradesman to landed gentry.

Most people in Britain were members of the Church of England. In 1760 this church was the subject of criticism for it contained many abuses. The higher clergy, bishops, deans and canons, were appointed by the Crown. They were well paid with ample leisure time. On the other hand the incomes of country clergy were often deplorably low. Amongst the clergy there were many absentees and pluralists — men who held more than one living or parish. The clergy often neglected their spiritual duties. In many parishes confirmation and communion services were rarely held. It is not surprising that men like John Wesley (1703–91), the Methodist, sought to reform this sorry state of affairs. On the positive side, the church tried to bring standards of decency into everyday life.

Today we have a number of welfare services to help those in need. This was not the case in the eighteenth century. However, each parish was responsible for its own poor. An overseer was appointed to administer poor relief. Usually the less the overseer spent the more successful he was considered to be. Schools and hospitals for the poor were set up by charitable means. Many rich people believed that they had an obligation to administer charity to the poor. The squire and his family would help the local poor by supplying them with baskets of food and clothing. Only the 'deserving' poor were recipients of charity. A clear distinction was made between those who had fallen on hard times through no fault of their own and the wastrels and scoundrels who did not deserve any compassion.

Many people in 1760 received no formal education. Unlike today, attendance at school was not compulsory and secondary education was a luxury reserved for those who could afford to pay fees or were clever enough to win a scholarship. However, there were some schools for the poor funded by charity. The Society for the Promotion of Christian Knowledge, an Anglican organization founded in 1698, supported schools which taught children reading, writing and the Christian religion. On a higher level grammar schools provided a narrow classical education. Above the grammar schools were public schools, like Eton and Winchester, which educated the country's future leaders. Boys from grammar and public schools could progress to the universities of Oxford and Cambridge where their social life was often more important than their studies.

Life in England in 1760 was violent. It could almost be said that riots and disorders were national pastimes. Riots helped to break the monotony in the lives of the poor and violent demonstrations were practically the only way the poor could attract attention. They were a safety valve — a release for pent-up emotions and energy. Violence was taken for granted and the authorities did little to prevent the outbreak of riots.

Throughout the eighteenth century there was a considerable crime rate. Most criminals went unpunished. Roads were infested with robbers and in the towns there was no effective police force and the parish watch-men fought a losing battle against crime. Criminals who were caught received savage punishments. The death penalty was imposed for a theft of five shillings from a shop or forty shillings from anywhere else. By the end of the century over 200 crimes were punishable by death. Prisoners who escaped the death penalty could be transported to America or Australia. Another form of punishment was a public flogging which was often administered by the local hangman. Criminals sentenced to terms of imprisonment served their sentences in overcrowded, filthy conditions. Many died from 'gaol fever' before they had completed their sentences.

The violence of eighteenth-century life was reflected in the pastimes of rich and poor alike. Cruel sports such as cock-fighting and bull and bear-baiting were very popular. Prize-fighting, where the boxers fought without gloves, attracted a great deal of support and was accompanied by heavy gambling. Fox-hunting and shooting occupied the wealthy in the countryside. Other popular open-air pursuits included bowls, fives, skittles, football and cricket. For those who preferred to stay indoors there was dancing, eating and drinking. Fashionable London society could be seen at masked balls and the theatre or strolling in the Vauxhall pleasure gardens. When rich living took its toll the wealthy would travel to spas to 'take the waters' and be rejuvenated.

Summary
In 1760 Britain's government was neither democratic nor efficient. At every level of government amateurs were responsible for the smooth running of the country. Britain's economic potential was enormous for the country had an adequate supply of labour and was endowed with rich farmland and mineral deposits together with a transport and financial network. Whilst the government and economy were in a state of change in 1760 British society was stable. Life was not always pleasant. Violence, crime and ignorance were widespread. This did not stop people at every level in society from finding ingenious ways of enjoying themselves.

Exercises
1. What is democracy? In what respects was Britain's government undemocratic in 1760?
2. What indications were there in 1760 that Britain might become a wealthy nation?
3. How did the rich and poor amuse themselves in their leisure time?

2
The Agricultural Revolution

Britain's agricultural revolution took place during the second half of the eighteenth century when significant changes in the organization of farm land and the development of better crops and livestock occurred. These changes took place over a long period of time and they marked a transition from the old-style subsistence method of farming to a more capital-intensive approach to agriculture.

The Open Field System

At the beginning of the eighteenth century approximately half of all the arable land in Britain was farmed under the open field system. The land in an open field village was divided into large fields which were subdivided into long, narrow strips. Most of the villagers owned or leased several strips of land and their animals grazed on the common or in the hay meadow. All farming activities in the open field village were regulated by the manorial court. There was a three-year crop rotation of wheat, barley or oats and a fallow field. Farm implements were primitive and communal. Tasks such as sowing, reaping and harvesting had to be carried out by all the villagers on the same date. Although the open field system of farming was inefficient it had satisfied England's needs for many centuries. It was not until the eighteenth century that critics of the system began to raise their voices.

The Need for Change

During the eighteenth century there was a dramatic increase in Britain's population, leading to an increased demand for food. Increased demand highlighted the defects of the open field system which was wasteful of time and energy and tended to stifle initiative. Unless agriculture adapted to the rise in population, by increasing output, there was a danger that there might be widespread starvation, especially in the newly developing towns. This danger was intensified by the series of poor harvests from 1760 onwards and by the French Wars, 1793 – 1815, which forced Britain to try to become self-sufficient in food. These factors led farmers to work marginal land which had hitherto been considered unprofitable. At the same time rising prices encouraged farmers to invest in their land and seek ways of increasing output.

1 Enclosures

Enclosure means the consolidation of scattered strips of land and common rights into a single compact farm, separated from other farms by a hedge or ditch. The pace of enclosing land, which had begun in Tudor times, quickened after 1750. Three methods of enclosing land were adopted. A number of enclosures were carried out by mutual agreement with adjacent strips of land being exchanged until each farmer had a small-holding. Enclosure was also carried out by obtaining a private Act of Parliament. Finally, in 1801, a General Enclosure Act was passed which simplified and standardized the process of enclosure. By the end of the first quarter of the nineteenth century most of the open field arable land was enclosed.

The Process of Enclosure

Before land could be enclosed Parliament had to be petitioned by a majority of the landowners (by acreage) of the open field to be enclosed. Parliament could not consider the petition unless those who signed it owned at least three quarters of the land to be enclosed. Opponents of enclosure could submit a counter-petition. Once sufficient local support had been obtained there was usually no difficulty in securing the passage of an Act of Enclosure at Westminster.

The Act of Parliament appointed commissioners to redistribute the land in compact farms. The commissioners were land agents or surveyors. They visited the village and made a map of it. Then there came the division of the land. A second map was drawn up and on this there was allotted to every owner exactly the same amount of arable land as he held before plus a share of the common, waste and meadow land. On the second map all the land was in compact holdings. The Act of Parliament ordered hedges or fences to be put around each farm. It was the commissioners' job to settle all disputes which might arise over the woodland and waste, customary rights and fencing costs.

Enclosure was expensive. Legal fees had to be paid, together with fees to the commissioners and their surveyors. New roads had to be built. These costs varied from five shillings per acre to five pounds per acre; the average was twenty five shillings per acre. In addition farmers had to pay for fences or hedges, new outbuildings, stock, seeds and equipment.

The Economic Effects of Enclosure
There is general agreement that the economic effects of enclosure were beneficial. Enclosures led to an increase in the land under cultivation and were followed in most cases by the adoption of improved methods of farming, leading to increased output. Enclosures helped Britain's export trade; livestock and grain were exported to several countries, providing Britain with increased wealth.

The Social Effects of Enclosure
There is no doubt that rich landowners benefited from enclosures and usually became even more wealthy. However, the effects of enclosure on those who were not rich has been the subject of controversy. Some historians believe that enclosure brought nothing but suffering to the small cultivator in the form of eviction, degradation and unemployment. Others believe that although the short-term results of enclosure might have been harsh their long-term effects were beneficial.

It has been argued that small landowners suffered at the time of enclosure. They were faced with a comparatively large bill for hedges, ditches and roads. In return they were given a minute holding, too small to carry crops and livestock at the same time. In addition, they had to buy implements and supply horses or oxen. For many the burden became too great and they were forced to sell their land. They used the money to become a tenant farmer or to establish businesses in one of the new towns and face all the upheavals associated with this change of life-style.

Less is known about the fate of tenant farmers. Enclosures led to increased rents and landlords often wished to consolidate some small tenancies into one large farm, evicting the smaller tenants. However, soon after enclosure had taken place it was not easy to find tenants for large farms, and so there were still many landlords willing to take on small tenant farmers.

Cottagers and squatters often suffered at the time of enclosure, particularly those who had relied on customary rather than legal rights of pasture and cultivation. Some cottagers hired themselves out as labourers, others had to rely on poor relief, whilst others left the countryside for the towns.

Enclosures alone did not cause rural depopulation and until 1815 villages continued to grow at almost the same rate as towns. Most people benefited from the increased quality and quantity of food produced and the standard of nutrition began to improve.

2 New Farming Techniques

Enclosures laid the foundation of the agricultural revolution. Once enclosed, the separate farms could employ their land in whatever way they chose. Enclosures permitted a degree of specialization and experimentation previously impossible. A number of farmers were responsible for introducing new agricultural methods which characterized the agricultural revolution.

Jethro Tull (1674 – 1741)

Jethro Tull farmed in Berkshire where he experimented with many new ideas. He is remembered for the invention of the seed drill. Under the open field system seeds had been scattered broadcast by hand which was wasteful. Tull discovered that seed grew best at definite depths and intervals which were different for each crop. He invented a horse-drawn drill which sowed the seed in rows at a fixed depth. This method of sowing made hoeing possible and Tull invented a horse-drawn hoe which kept down the weeds between the rows of seed and ventilated the soil. These two inventions produced a startling increase in the output of crops. Tull's inventions were not widely used until the second half of the eighteenth century.

Lord Townshend (1674 – 1738)

The Norfolk four-course rotation, which is linked with the name of Lord Townshend, was another important improvement in farming. It consisted of a four-year sequence of crops — clover, wheat, turnips, and barley — which eliminated the wasteful fallow field. Turnips had the added advantage that they could be used as winter fodder for cattle which would otherwise have been slaughtered. Townshend also greatly improved the fertility of his estates by adopting the process of marling.

The new methods introduced by Tull and Townshend led to better cultivation. It is estimated that between 1750 and 1800 the yield of wheat per acre in Britain increased by one third.

Robert Bakewell (1725 – 95)

Robert Bakewell carried out valuable experimental work with cattle and sheep which helped to put an end to the scraggy livestock associated with the common. Bakewell farmed an estate at Dishley in Leicestershire where he specialized in the breeding of sheep and cattle. By the careful selection of the finest types of cattle for his experiments he paved the way for modern stock breeding. Bakewell aimed to produce high quality wool, meat and milk. As his ideas spread there was a steady improvement in the quality and quantity of cattle sold at Smithfield market and English cattle were frequently exported to start new herds abroad. (See Table 1, figures for cattle and sheep at Smithfield.)

Table 1 Figures for Smithfield Cattle and Sheep

Year	Cattle (000's)	Sheep (000's)	Combined Meat Index
1761–70	82	614	102
1766–75	86	607	104
1771–80	95	649	114
1776–85	99	686	119
1781–90	98	687	119
1786–95	104	771	125
1791–1800	114	756	135
1796–1805	120	799	142
1801–10	128	886	154
1806–15	133	939	161
1811–20	131	952	161

3 Publicity for the New Techniques

The Board of Agriculture

With the help of Sir John Sinclair (1754–1835) Arthur Young (1741–1820) secured the creation of a government commission known as the Board of Agriculture. He became its first secretary in 1793. The Board sponsored agricultural research and helped to publicize new farming techniques.

Several farmers learned a great deal from the Board of Agriculture. They were anxious to raise their incomes and prepared to apply the new profitable measures of agriculture. However, they were the exceptions and widespread propaganda was needed before the advantages to be derived from the new techniques were widely recognized. A few outstanding farmers helped to educate hundreds more.

Thomas Coke (1752–1842)

Much useful instruction was given by Thomas Coke who owned an estate at Holkham in Norfolk. He sought to increase the rent from his estate by controlling the farming methods of his tenants. Under the terms of their leases Coke's tenants were obliged to adopt crop rotations carefully adapted to the needs of the particular soils on their farms. The quantity of seeds to be used was laid down and hoeing and manuring were further conditions of the tenancy agreements. Every year Thomas Coke held a sheep-shearing competition which provided an occasion for spreading successful ideas amongst the farmers. Prizes were awarded and gradually the annual meeting became an agricultural show.

King George III (1760–1820)

Agriculture became fashionable amongst the nobility. King George III took a keen interest in the new developments. He set up a model farm at Windsor and regularly sent exhibits to agricultural shows.

Arthur Young

Arthur Young probably did more than anyone else to publicize the new farming techniques. Having failed as a farmer, he began to write about agriculture. From 1767 onwards he travelled extensively in England and Europe and was extremely observant, noting improvements wherever he saw them. From 1784 he edited a journal entitled *The Annals of Agriculture* to which even George III subscribed. With Sir John Sinclair he planned a series of surveys of every county in England and Scotland and wrote many of them himself. He was a keen supporter of enclosures but was aware of the hardships which could result from them.

Summary

Between 1760 and 1850 the narrow strips, characteristic of open field villages, gave way to compact, enclosed farms. Two million extra acres of land were brought under cultivation during this period as a result of enclosure. This increased acreage, coupled with the adoption of new farming techniques, led to a massive increase in the output of agricultural products. It is generally agreed that the benefits which resulted from the agricultural revolution outweighed the hardships felt by some farmers at the time of enclosure.

Exercises

1. What were the defects of the open field system?
2. Describe the process of enclosure.
3. Examine the effects of enclosures on rural life in England.

4. What new techniques were introduced into British farming in the eighteenth century?
5. How did the changes in British agriculture benefit the country?

3
The Industrial Revolution

Britain's industries had been expanding steadily since the sixteenth century. However, in the second half of the eighteenth century the pace and scope of industrial growth was so great that the term 'industrial revolution' has been applied to the changes of that era. Inventions and new methods of production transformed the textile, coal and iron industries and made Britain the 'workshop of the world'.

The Pre-Conditions of Industrial Growth
Before industrial expansion can take place certain pre-conditions must exist. Britain was fortunate in possessing many of the pre-requisites for industrial growth. Her population increased dramatically in the eighteenth century, creating an increased labour supply to work in the new industries and increasing demand in the domestic markets. There was also increased demand from overseas for British goods. There was an increase in the availability of Britain's supply of raw materials to correspond with growing demand. At the same time there was an increase in the amount of capital which could be invested in industry and this process was helped by developments in banking and insurance. The country also possessed the makings of an adequate transport system. Britain's political situation was stable and this peaceful atmosphere allowed scientific progress to flourish. Inventions were numerous and Dr Johnson (1709–84) declared, 'the age is running mad after innovation'. Throughout the eighteenth century and for most of the nineteenth century Britain was the only thoroughly developed industrial state, the sole supplier of many manufactured goods and the cheapest manufacturer of others.

1 Textiles

The Domestic System

In 1700 Britain's major industry was the manufacture of woollen cloth. The output of cotton was insignificant. Where cotton was produced it was usually mixed with wool or linen. Both spinning and weaving were slow processes, carried out in the home and dependent upon a great deal of human labour.

The entire family played a part in this domestic system of industry. Women and children were employed in the carding process to produce the yarn. Next came the spinning process which was usually performed by women. Weaving was the final stage in cloth production and this was done by men. In its simplest form the domestic system operated as follows: the worker bought his raw materials each week and made the cloth with his own implements; at the end of the week he sold the finished product and with the money he obtained from the sale he bought his raw materials for the next week.

From 1730 onwards a series of inventions revolutionized the manufacture of cloth. In all cases the inventions were adopted first in the cotton industry which expanded rapidly in Lancashire; only later did they spread to other branches of cloth manufacture. The inventions hastened the development of the factory system and the domestic system gradually died away.

John Kay (c1700-64)

In the early eighteenth century spinning was a laborious process; ten spinners were required to supply sufficient yarn to occupy a single weaver. Before output could increase an invention was needed to speed up the spinning process. Ironically, the first invention in the textile industry helped to accelerate the weaving process.

In 1733 John Kay, a Lancashire cloth weaver, invented a flying shuttle which passed the shuttle automatically from side to side of the cloth. Only one weaver was now needed to produce even the widest broad-cloth. Although Kay's invention was a valuable step forward it created a bottle-neck in the manufacture of cloth and focused attention on the need to speed up spinning.

James Hargreaves (c1720-78)

Between 1764 and 1767 James Hargreaves, a weaver and carpenter from Blackburn, invented a spinning machine which he named the 'jenny'. This machine enabled a woman to spin eight threads at once and large models with up to 80 spindles soon followed.

However, the yarn spun on the jenny was weak and suitable only for the cross threads (weft) of the fabric.

Richard Arkwright (1732 – 92)
In 1769 Richard Arkwright, another Lancashire man, patented the water frame. This was a water-powered machine which produced a cotton thread strong enough to be used in the longitudinal threads (warp) in a piece of cloth. In 1775 Arkwright patented a second machine which speeded up the carding process. His rotary carding machine made the mass-production of cotton yarn possible.

Samuel Crompton (1753 – 1827)
In 1785 Samuel Crompton, a Bolton weaver, introduced a device which was regarded as a cross between the jenny and the water frame and was called the 'mule'. It produced a fine, strong yarn suitable for both warp and weft. Later models of the mule were driven by water power and towards the end of the eighteenth century the steam engine was also used to drive spinning machines.

Edmund Cartwright (1743 – 1823)
It took several years before steam or water power was applied to the loom because the complicated motions of a loom made it difficult to harness the machine to a single shaft. However, in 1784 the Reverend Edmund Cartwright designed a power loom. It was not widely adopted until the nineteenth century.

The Factory System
The inventions in the textile industry revolutionized the production of cotton and led to the development of the factory system. The first cotton mills or factories were built in Nottingham, but by the nineteenth century the cotton industry was concentrated in Lancashire towns with hundreds of workers employed in large factories. The factory system led to an enormous increase in the output of cotton goods. In 1764 Britain imported 4,000,000 pounds of raw cotton; by 1833 she imported more than 300,000,000 pounds and was responsible for 60 per cent of the world's cotton production.

The growth of factories had a dramatic effect on the life-styles of textile workers. Carrying out their trade at home was no longer possible as they could not compete with large-scale manufacturers and so the textile workers sought jobs in the towns. During the first 30 years of the nineteenth century the population of Bolton, Blackburn, Oldham and Manchester increased three-fold. Factories dominated these towns and the workers spent most of their waking lives in monotonous and often dangerous jobs.

2 Coal

Coalfields and Coalmines

In 1700 coal was mined in north-east England, in the valleys of the Tyne and Wear, in south Yorkshire, south Lancashire, Derbyshire, the Midlands, Nottinghamshire, the Forest of Dean and in Somersetshire near Bristol. Since coal was not easily transported by land, mines without easy access to water transport could only sell to a restricted market.

Before the industrial revolution pits were small, seldom employing more than 50 miners. They rarely penetrated deep into the ground for deep mines were dangerous and beset with many problems which made them unprofitable. The difficulties which had to be faced in the deep mines were the dangers associated with flooding, explosions and collapsing roofs. Further difficulties emerged with lighting and with hauling and hoisting the coal. From 1760 onwards these difficulties were gradually overcome, largely by inventions which revolutionized mining and helped to make it a safer, highly profitable industry.

The Problem of Flooding

Before the industrial revolution miners were prevented from working in deep seams because of the danger of flooding. This problem was overcome by the use of the steam engine, an invention of the greatest importance to the coal industry. The first workable mine pump was invented by Thomas Savery (1650 – 1715) in 1698; it was known as the 'Miners' Friend'. However, it was not efficient enough to cope with the quantity of water to be raised from deep mines and wasted an enormous amount of steam. It was superceded in 1708 by Thomas Newcomen's (1663 – 1729) atmospheric steam engine which was cumbersome and inefficient but was widely adopted. Finally, in 1769 James Watt (1736 – 1819) patented his steam engine. It was first used to pump water from a coal mine in 1784. Watt's engine was so efficient that by 1800 30 engines were at work in mines, making them safer for the miners.

Explosions in the Mines

When the problem of flooding was overcome, enabling miners to penetrate deep underground, they were faced with dangerous gases such as fire-damp (an inflammable methane gas) and choke-damp (or carbon monoxide). Various ventilation systems were adopted in the eighteenth century in an attempt to disperse the gases but most were unsatisfactory. Eventually, ventilation was greatly improved by John Buddle (1773 – 1843) who invented the exhaust fan. This drew out the foul air and blew fresh air into the mines.

Lighting in the mines was closely associated with the problem of explosions — candles and rushlights could not be used underground because they caused frequent explosions. The difficulty of providing an adequate and safe method of lighting led to the formation of an association which invited ideas for a safety lamp. George Stephenson (1781 – 1848) invented several lamps, one of which, the 'Geordie', became popular. In 1815 Sir Humphry Davy (1778 – 1829) invented a safety lamp which was widely adopted. It enabled mining to be carried out in seams previously too dangerous to work.

The Problem of Collapsing

Another difficulty facing miners in the eighteenth century was the problem of collapsing, caused by inadequate methods of roof support. Until the end of the century pillars of coal were left uncut by the miners to support the roof but it was not until the introduction of wooden pit props in the nineteenth century that safety improved. With the introduction of iron and steel girders in the mid-nineteenth century the problem of collapsing ceased to be a major worry for miners.

Haulage and Hoisting

Several methods of hauling coal to the shaft bottom were in use before the industrial revolution. In the northern coalfields barrowmen dragged wooden sledges laden with coal from the face to the shaft. In other mines women and boys dragged the coal in trucks to the bottom of the shaft. Haulage was a slow and tiring process. It was revolutionized by the introduction of iron rails along which wooden trucks could be pulled. Later, miniature railways were used to carry the coal from the face to the shaft.

Before the industrial revolution coal was carried to the surface in baskets strapped onto women's backs. The women climbed ladders or walked up sloping shafts to the surface. It was not until the beginning of the nineteenth century that cages were introduced to carry coal and miners to the surface. These lifts were operated by steam engines and were first introduced in mines in 1794.

The Uses of Coal

The revolution which took place in the coal industry led to an enormous increase in the output of coal. (See table 2, Nineteenth-Century Coal Output.) This had implications for Britain's other key industries. Coal was used in steam engines which were widely adopted as a source of power. It was also used in railway engines and steam ships. Coal was used in the manufacture of iron and steel and continued to be used for domestic purposes.

Table 2 Nineteenth-Century Coal Output

Year	Total U.K. output (millions of tons)	Value at pithead (£m.)	Proportion of output exported (%)
1800	11·0	2·8	2·0
1816	15·9	5·2	2·5
1820	17·4	5·7	1·4
1825	21·9	6·9	1·4
1830	22·4	6·9	2·2
1835	27·7	7·6	2·7
1840	33·7	8·8	4·8
1845	45·9	9·2	5·5
1850	49·4	10·3	6·8
1855	61·5	16·1	8·1
1860	80·0	20·0	9·2
1865	98·2	24·5	9·3
1870	110·4	27·6	13·4
1875	131·9	46·2	13·5
1880	146·8	62·4	16·3
1885	159·4	41·1	19·3
1890	181·6	75·0	21·3
1895	189·7	57·2	22·6
1900	225·2	121·7	25·9

3 Iron and Steel

The Early Iron Industry

Before the industrial revolution the manufacture of iron was a long and expensive process. Iron ore was smelted in a blast furnace using charcoal as fuel. Some iron goods could be cast directly from the blast furnace (cast iron) but most of the iron was run off into sand moulds as pig iron for further treatment. Repeated reheating and hammering removed the impurities from the pig iron and produced bar iron from which a whole range of iron ware could be made.

In the first half of the eighteenth century the iron industry was dispersed throughout the country. The centres of intensive iron production were south Wales, the Forest of Dean, Shropshire, the Midlands, the Weald, south Yorkshire and Derbyshire, the Furness district of north Lancashire and Newcastle. (See Fig. 1, The Iron Industry in 1760.) The industry supplied less than half of the country's requirements and bar iron was imported from Sweden and Russia. The major reason for the inadequacy of the English supply was that charcoal was scarce and expensive. Before the iron industry could advance a substitute fuel would have to be found.

Abraham Darby (1677–1717)

The first successful production of iron using coked coal instead of charcoal as the fuel in the blast furnace was achieved in c1709 by Abraham Darby at Coalbrookdale in Shropshire. The gases released from coal made iron too brittle, but coke did not have this effect and was therefore an adequate substitute for charcoal. At first the iron produced by Darby was only suitable for casting, but his son gradually improved the process until it was possible to make pig iron with coke, which was suitable for refining into bar iron at the forge.

As the practice of smelting by coke spread, the location and scale of the iron industry altered. The industry shifted to areas where coal and iron were found together. Such areas became new industrial centres — the Midlands, south Wales, Tees-side, Tyneside and the Scottish Lowlands.

Henry Cort (1740–1800)

In spite of the improvements introduced by the Darbys the forging of pig iron into bar iron was still a slow process and this hampered the development of the iron industry. A breakthrough was made by Henry Cort who patented processes for rolling and puddling in 1783 and 1784. By using the puddling process impurities were removed from the pig iron whilst it was still molten and, on cooling, the purified iron was rolled into bars. These two inventions led to an enormous increase in the output of bar iron and made Britain less dependent on imports.

John Wilkinson (1728–1808)

John Wilkinson played a vital role in helping to popularize the use of iron. He owned several furnaces and foundries in the Midlands

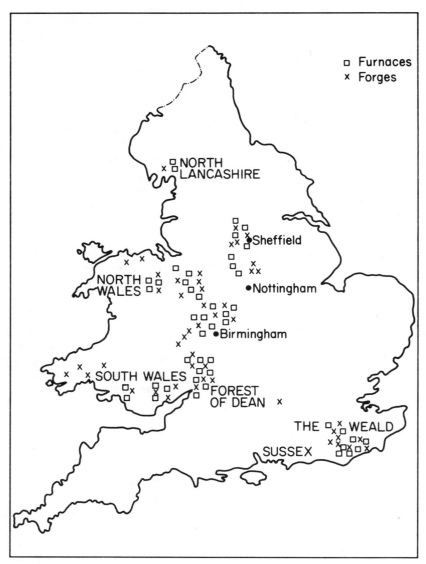

Fig. 1 The Iron Industry, 1760

and was the first to apply steam power to the blast furnace in 1776. In co-operation with the third Abraham Darby he built the first iron bridge near Coalbrookdale in Shropshire. He produced cannons for use in the Napoleonic wars. Wilkinson built the first iron boat which, contrary to most expectations, did not sink. He supplied 40 miles of pipes for the Paris sewers. He slept in an iron bed and, in keeping with his principles, he was buried in a cast-iron coffin under a cast-iron obelisk at his lonely mansion on the north Lancashire coast. By the early nineteenth century, thanks to the work of Wilkinson, there was a huge increase in demand for iron for steam engines, boats, rails, bridges, boilers and a wide range of machinery.

James Neilson (1792–1865)
In 1828 James Neilson invented the hot blast process allowing the use of raw coal in the furnace. Instead of using the bellows to produce a blast of cold air for the furnace, Neilson heated the blast to several hundred degrees centigrade. The result was an immense saving of fuel and a consequent reduction in the cost of iron.

The Early Steel Industry
Before the industrial revolution steel was made in two different ways; both were slow and costly processes. A steel furnace took three weeks to convert 10 tons of iron into steel. It then required repeated forging to produce the metal in a useable form. Steel was expensive and its quality was poor but it was tougher than wrought iron and more flexible than cast iron.

Benjamin Huntsman (1704–76)
Benjamin Huntsman was a Quaker clock-maker from Doncaster who made a valuable contribution to the steel industry. In 1740 he invented the crucible process of steel making which produced steel of a high quality but did nothing to reduce its price. For this process he took bar iron, which had been heated in a furnace for 12 days, causing it to harden, and melted it in a small crucible placed in a coke furnace where the heat was so intense that all the impurities were burned away. Huntsman tried to keep the details of his process a secret and its use remained limited until well into the nineteenth century.

Henry Bessemer (1813–98)
In 1856 Henry Bessemer announced details of a new process of steel making. He produced a converter, a cylindrical vessel, into which

molten pig iron was poured. A hot blast was then driven through the converter to burn out the impurities. This was followed by the addition of the appropriate amount of carbon. His pneumatic method enabled many tons of steel to be produced from molten iron in a process which lasted for only 20 minutes. However, steel produced in the Bessemer converter had two defects — it was brittle and good steel could not be obtained from iron containing phosphorus.

Robert Mushet (1811-91)
Robert Mushet, a metallurgist, helped to overcome the problem of brittleness in steel. He discovered that the addition of a small quantity of manganese to the molten pig iron remedied this fault. However, the second weakness was not so easily overcome. Soon Britain's only non-phosphoric ore field in Cumberland was exhausted.

William Siemens (1823-83)
The next important development in steel making came in 1867 when Siemens invented the open-hearth method of production. In this process the hot blast was brought to a very high temperature by passing through regenerating chambers on its way to the furnace. The source of heat was provided by gas which meant that any type of coal could be used and the temperature could be easily regulated. This process made it easier to regulate the quality of finished steel and it made possible the extensive use of scrap in steel making. However, it did nothing to solve the problem of steel making from phosphoric iron.

Sidney Gilchrist Thomas (1850-85)
The problem of phosphorus was not solved until 1878. In that year Sidney Gilchrist Thomas discovered that by lining the steel furnace with dolomite limestone the phosphorus was extracted from the pig iron and good steel was produced. The phosphorus was not wasted for it proved to be a valuable fertilizer.

In spite of the many advances in steel making in the nineteenth century progress in the industry remained slow. It was not long before the steel industries in other rapidly developing countries overtook the British steel industry.

4 The Development of Power

Until the eighteenth century man had to rely on natural sources of power. He could use muscle power or harness his animals to help him perform heavy tasks. In addition the power of wind and flowing water was harnessed to provide energy. By 1700 water was the most important source of industrial power in Britain. During the next hundred years water power was gradually superceded by steam power.

The Steam Engine

Thomas Savery patented the first steam pump in 1698. This engine used atmospheric pressure, created by condensing steam in a cylinder, to draw water up a pipe to drain mines. In Thomas Newcomen's steam pump, invented in 1709, steam from a boiler was condensed in a cylinder by an injection of cold water. This contraction of the condensed steam drew down a piston which was linked to a rocker arm and operated the rod of a pump. Newcomen's engine was inefficient and consumed a great deal of fuel but as it was used to drain coal mines this was of little importance. James Watt, a laboratory mechanic at Glasgow university, was given a Newcomen engine to repair. Watt quickly realized that the reheating of the cylinder between each stroke of the piston was wasteful and he devised a separate cylinder into which the steam from the main cylinder could be drawn to be condensed by cold water. By avoiding cooling the main cylinder fuel was saved and operating costs reduced. Watt patented his invention in 1769. In 1784 Watt patented parallel motion which enabled machinery to be driven by steam power and in 1787 he invented a centrifugal governor which controlled the steam engine at a constant speed. (See the photograph of Watt's rotative beam engine.)

New Uses for Steam Power

Although steam engines are usually associated with the coal, railway and textile industries they were used in a wide variety of other industries. They were used in tanneries to drive machines which beat and rolled hides. After 1814 newspaper printing was done on steam-powered cylinder machines. Steam engines were used in the pottery industry to mix clay and grind flints for glazing. They were also used in glass making, soap making and brewing. As the century progressed the steam engine was gradually replaced by machinery driven by electricity and by the internal combustion engine. (see p.260 and p.268)

Boulton and Watt's rotative beam engine, 1788

5 The Results of the Industrial Revolution

Economic Effects
The changes which revolutionized British industry were not adopted immediately by other countries. This lack of competition increased Britain's export trade and made her the richest nation in Europe. Wealth gave Britain power and the ability to endure a long war against France.

   Although the industrial revolution was not a primary cause of the dramatic increase in Britain's population which occurred in the second half of the eighteenth century, it certainly stimulated the migration of the population from the countryside to the towns. In the new towns a few businessmen made vast fortunes but most people were not so fortunate. For many years historians have engaged in debate asking, 'did the standard of living rise or fall at the time of the industrial revolution?' Many aspects of the standard of living controversy continue to be debated but there is general agreement that, whilst the industrial revolution did not bring immediate prosperity to everyone, in the long run it raised the general standard of life.

Social Effects

The economic benefits which resulted from industrialization were not achieved without cost. Rapid industrialization was accompanied by social hazards. As industry expanded workers were herded together in slum towns, the victims of new problems created by urban growth. Conditions in the factories were grim; the workers toiled for long hours in squalid, dangerous conditions and were subjected to the tyranny of the overseers. It is not surprising that, whilst factory owners extolled the advantages of industrial progress, factory workers often yearned for a return to pre-industrial times.

Summary

During the second half of the eighteenth century there were sweeping changes in British industry. Goods were no longer made by hand at home but were mass-produced in factories. Mechanization was introduced in all Britain's major industries. The most fundamental change was the substitution of steam power for muscle power. In 1700 Britain was predominantly agricultural but by 1831 only 25 per cent of all families were engaged in agriculture. In that year too, one quarter of Britain's population lived in large towns of 20,000 inhabitants or more. Britain was the first industrial nation and she did not relinquish this position until the end of the nineteenth century.

Exercises

1. What do you understand by the phrase industrial revolution?
2. Explain how the textile industry was revolutionized in the eighteenth century.
3. What problems had to be overcome before the coal industry could expand?
4. Describe the changes which revolutionized the output of iron and steel in Britain.
5. How did the application of steam power help to revolutionize British industry?
6. How did the changes in British industry benefit the country?
7. Why might certain sections of the population have resented the rapid process of industrialization?

4
King George III and his Ministers, 1760–82

George III came to the throne in 1760, aged 22, and reigned for 60 years — the longest span of all British kings. He was the only sober and virtuous Hanoverian monarch. Unlike his Hanoverian forbears he loved England. He was nick-named 'Farmer George' for his love of the countryside and his interest in the agricultural revolution. He was also interested in botany, prison reform, Sunday schools and the Arts — all things which helped to enhance the quality of English life. He was a hard-working monarch, devoted to his royal duties, and he led a simple domestic life with Queen Charlotte and their 15 children.

Few monarchs laboured harder to be a good king. Yet George III is remembered as the king who tried to impose a system of personal government in the early years of his reign. He has been criticized for his dealings with John Wilkes. He is remembered as the king who lost the American colonies and as the man who went up to an oak tree and greeted it as the king of Prussia. Dubbed the 'mad monarch', the last 10 years of George's life were spent in what appeared to be total madness. Recent discoveries have shown that the King was suffering from porphyria. This was, in fact, a physical disease which caused pain and abnormal skin pigmentation but in the later stages of the illness its symptoms were akin to those of madness. George III was neither a great king nor a great man but he helped to bring stability to Britain in an age of great upheaval.

The King's Government
At the time of George III's accession he intended to make significant changes in government and to clean up political life by eliminating corruption. However, his plans did not come to fruition partly because he was very young and inexperienced and chose to rely on the advice of Lord Bute who was also inexperienced. He took his royal duties seriously and was determined to be more effective than the first two Georges. This has led to the criticism that George III was trying to increase his power at the expense of the power of

Parliament. Since the King's exact motives have not been discovered the debate about his role in the constitution continues.

In 1760 George III inherited his grandfather's ministers who were already on uneasy terms with one another before the change of sovereign further disrupted matters. Pitt (1708 – 78), at the pinnacle of his career, was Secretary of State. Holderness (1718 – 78) was the other Secretary. The Duke of Newcastle was First Lord of the Treasury and Legge (1708 – 64) was Chancellor of the Exchequer. The Pitt – Newcastle combination was three years old and seemed stable, but its existence was dependent upon the state of emergency created by the Seven Years' War.

In March 1761 George III's favourite, Lord Bute, replaced Holderness as Secretary of State. Bute controlled 45 Scottish MPs, was very wealthy and had the support of the King. With so many advantages it is difficult to see how Bute could fail to help the King to establish a strong, stable government.

The Seven Years' War, 1756 – 63
When George III became king Britain had been at war with France since 1756. Britain's ally, Prussia, fought French troops in Europe whilst British soldiers attacked the French in India, Canada and the West Indies. In spite of British success, after four years of conflict the country was war weary. The war was costly and very damaging to trade. Whilst the King and Bute contemplated peace Pitt was planning to widen the war. He believed that France was seeking Spanish support and he wanted to extend the war by attacking Spain. When Bute opposed this Pitt, who could not bear to have his views contradicted, resigned on 5 October 1761. Later, in May 1762, Newcastle resigned when most of his cabinet opposed the payment of a subsidy to Prussia. Bute became First Lord of the Treasury. By the end of 1762 he had come to an agreement with France on the main terms of a peace treaty.

The Peace of Paris, 1763
The terms of the Peace of Paris, proclaimed in March 1763, were a recognition of Britain's victory in the Seven Years' War. From France, Britain gained the entire province of Canada, all Louisiana east of the Mississippi river, Cape Breton and the islands in the St Lawrence. In the West Indies Britain gained St Vincent, Tobago, Dominica, and the Grenadines. She retained Senegal on the African coast and recovered Minorca. France was to demilitarize Dunkirk. In India, although French trading stations were restored, France was forced to recognize the supremacy of the British East India

Company. Britain gained Florida from Spain which was forced to restore all conquests to Portugal. To France, Britain returned Martinique, Guadaloupe, Desirade, St Lucia and Mariegalante in the West Indies. On the African coast Goree was returned. Britain also returned Belle Isle and allowed French fishing rights in the St Lawrence. Manila and Cuba were returned to Spain.

In spite of the magnificent gains the Peace of Paris was bitterly criticized in Britain where it was argued that Bute had given away too many conquests. Pitt was the most outspoken critic of the treaty. He was seen as a national hero who had gained a string of victories in the war only to be cast aside by men who had let his conquests slip away. In a Common's speech lasting three and a half hours Pitt denounced the treaty. He attacked the government for making too many concessions to France and for deserting Prussia, a move which left Britain without an ally in Europe. For most people the peace was not glorious but it was widely recognized that an end to hostilities was a financial necessity. In the Commons the vote in favour of the peace was 319 with 65 opposing votes. Although there were stories that Bute and Fox (1705 – 74), the leader of the court party in the Commons, had used bribes to obtain this favourable vote there is no evidence of bribery or intimidation being used to persuade MPs to support the peace.

Ministerial Instability, 1763 – 70

By January 1763 Bute was already weary of the political struggle and was talking of resignation. In April 1763 when peace was made and new problems were arising Bute resigned. Popular opinion condemned the Peace of Paris. Bute's unpopularity was increased by his decision to impose a tax on cider and wine to pay for the costs of war. In addition his relationship with George III's mother roused opinion against him. Bute enjoyed power but could not bear abuse and so he withdrew, much to the despair of the young King.

The King searched for a new chief minister. He had offended both Pitt and Newcastle, the two most likely candidates for the post. There followed a succession of weak, short-lived ministries. Grenville (1763 – 5) was followed by Rockingham (1765 – 6) and by Pitt, now Lord Chatham (1766 – 8) and by Grafton (1768 – 70). During this period a group of about 60 MPs, who were nick-named the 'King's Friends' because they supported him in Parliament, tried to bring firm government to the country. Their patriotism was no match for the two problems which plagued George's ministers — the revolt of the American colonies (see Chapter 5) and the campaign of John Wilkes.

John Wilkes, (1727 – 97)

John Wilkes, MP for Aylesbury and a colonel in the Buckingham-shire militia, led a reckless life, flouting the accepted eighteenth-century code of behaviour. He was a member of the Hell Fire Club and, although extremely ugly, he had a reputation as a ladies' man. In the 1760s he gained a more widespread reputation as a 'champion of liberty'.

In 1762 Wilkes founded the *North Briton* newspaper, in which articles appeared implying that Bute and George III's mother were lovers. In number 45 of the *North Briton*, published on 23 April 1763, Wilkes criticized the Peace of Paris, declaring that the King had not spoken the truth when he described the treaty as 'honour-able to my crown and beneficial to my people'. Several ministers decided to put an end to Wilkes' campaign before the government was damaged any further. On 30 April the Secretary of State, acting in a magisterial capacity, issued a general warrant (which was not directed to a named person) for the arrest of all those concerned with the production of the *North Briton*.

When Wilkes appeared in the Court of Common Pleas in May he defended himself by arguing that general warrants were illegal, that the Secretary of State did not have the power to act as a magistrate and that as an MP he was immune from arrest. He broadened the issue and appealed to the emotions of everyone in the country by declaring that 'the liberty of all peers and gentlemen and that of the middling and inferior set of people is in my case this day to be finally decided upon'. Since MPs could only be arrested for treason, felony or a breach of the peace Wilkes was released. He gained more than his release, for shortly afterwards general warrants were declared illegal and Wilkes was awarded £1000 damages. He had successfully challenged the government's high-handed methods.

George III and his ministers were not prepared to see so dangerous a critic at large. They feared his slogan 'Wilkes and Liberty' and his ability to manipulate the London mob. Parliament voted that number 45 of the *North Briton* contained seditious libel and ordered it to be burnt. The Commons also accused Wilkes of obscen-ity for producing an obscene poem entitled *The Essay on Woman*. In December 1763 Wilkes travelled to France. In the following month he was expelled from membership of the House of Commons. As he did not appear at his trial for seditious libel and obscenity in February 1764 he was outlawed nine months later.

In 1768 Wilkes returned from France and, even though he was still an outlaw, stood as a candidate for Middlesex in the general election. The 40-shilling freeholders of Middlesex were an independent electorate and Wilkes, the enemy of the established order, had no difficulty in gaining the highest number of votes. When the election was over he insisted on being arrested for his former crimes. On 10 May 1768 troops of the Scots Guards clashed with a mob of Wilkes' supporters around his prison. During the skuffle William Allen, a spectator, was killed by the troops. His death was immediately portrayed as an attempt by the Scottish Bute to murder the liberties of Englishmen.

Parliament hastened to expel Wilkes and called for another election in Middlesex. But Wilkes was re-elected a second and then a third time. The elections took place at a time of economic depression and were accompanied by widespread unrest. The needy and angry focused on Wilkes as a champion of the underdog who was prepared to oppose a tyrannical government. Finally, the government declared that Wilkes' opponent had been elected MP for Middlesex even though Wilkes had gained a large majority of the votes.

Eventually, in 1774, Wilkes was allowed to take his seat for Middlesex. His campaign had discredited the government and distracted attention from the growing troubles in America. Thanks to Wilkes people who had previously ignored Parliament began to take an interest in government. Their interest was heightened when Wilkes won the right to report parliamentary debates.

Lord North

George III was delighted when Lord North, a Tory, became Prime Minister in 1770. Lord North has been condemned as a parliamentary Trojan Horse, a vehicle for the King who continued to threaten the country's political liberty by wishing to establish a personal government. Nevertheless, North was able to achieve the three things necessary for success in eighteenth-century politics: he secured a majority in the House of Commons, the loyalty of a large enough group of competent colleagues and the support of the King. Consequently he remained in office for 12 years until defeat in the American War forced him to resign.

In 1772 North steered the Royal Marriages Act through Parliament. It forbade members of the royal family to marry without the King's consent unless they were over 25 years old and had given a year's notice to the Privy Council. This Act was designed to preserve the dignity of the royal family and to prevent a repetition of the problems caused when two of the King's brothers had married commoners. The Act was used by the opposition to indicate that Lord North was too subservient to the crown.

Lord North's Regulating Act, 1773, gave the government a

degree of control over the East India Company (see p.247). The Quebec Act, 1774, granted an official position to the Roman Catholic church there in the interests of stable government. In 1778 the Roman Catholic Relief Bill was introduced to abolish some of the severe restrictions from which British Roman Catholics had suffered. A proposal to extend this moderate toleration to Scotland in 1779 led to riots in that country. In the following year Lord George Gordon (1751 – 93) led a mob to Parliament to petition for the repeal of the Relief Act. The mob rioted and the number of people killed or wounded was 458. Fifty-nine rioters were sentenced to death and 21 suffered the penalty.

Lord North faced another difficulty in 1780. On 6 April John Dunning (1731 – 83), an Opposition leader, moved a resolution in the Commons 'that the influence of the Crown has increased, is increasing, and ought to be diminished'. His resolution was carried by 233 to 215 votes. It was partly North's fault that George III was blamed for exercising too much royal authority, for whenever anything went wrong the Prime Minister constantly lamented that he was forced to stay in office against his will. However, North's position was not threatened since there was no real alternative to him.

Even before hostilities had begun in America in 1775 North had shown signs of wishing to retire. As the war developed this wish became a growing anxiety. In the Commons, while the war made its disastrous progress, North constantly faced cries of 'Resign! Resign!' He eventually resigned in March 1782 (see p.44).

Summary

George III came to the throne with his mother's advice ringing in his ears. She told him 'George, be a king'. Since then historians have criticized him for taking his mother's advice too literally and trying to establish a personal system of government which would deprive Parliament of its traditional powers. However, in the first 10 years of his reign, far from establishing a strong, stable government, George III was faced with the stresses and strains of ministerial instability and the ridicule of John Wilkes. When he found in Lord North a minister capable of holding office for more than a few months his problems did not come to an end. His American subjects began to disrupt the British government and they finally led the King to contemplate abdication.

Exercises

1.   What evidence is there to suggest that George III tried to impose a personal government on Britain between 1760 and 1782?

2. Did George III succeed in ruling Britain personally? Give evidence to support your answer.
3. Describe three achievements in the career of John Wilkes for which he deserves the title 'a champion of liberty'.
4. Describe how Lord North dealt with the government of a) Britain, b) India.

5
The American War of Independence

By 1763 Britain possessed a large number of colonies in the New World. In addition to areas of Canada and the West Indies, she governed 13 colonies on the Atlantic shore of America. These colonies confirmed Britain's wealth and power and enabled her to maintain a dominant position in the world. When the Americans sought independence the British government and people were shocked. They were even more disturbed when it became apparent that all the wealth, political experience and military might of England failed to bring the American colonists to heel. Defeat abroad dealt a harsh blow to George III's prestige and kindled the desire for far-reaching changes at home.

1 The Causes of the War

There were several causes of the American War of Independence. Some sources of grievance dated back almost to the foundation of the colonies; these underlying causes had their roots in the colonial system of administration.

Trade Regulation
Britain regulated American trade by three ordinances which had been introduced in the seventeenth century. They were based on the belief that the colonies were the property of the mother country and existed solely for her benefit. The first ordinance appointed 15

commissioners to regulate colonial trade. The second expressed the view that England's colonies 'are, and ought to be, subordinate to and dependent upon her'. Lastly, the Navigation Act, 1651, laid down that all colonial trade must come through England and be carried in English or colonial ships. Furthermore, the colonists were not allowed to develop industries which might compete with the production of goods in Britain.

These restrictive policies were not considered selfish. It was thought that the Americans would benefit from their economic association with England. In addition, the colonists knew that they could always rely on the British navy for protection. It was argued that the system brought mutual benefits to the colonies and the mother country. However, trading restrictions annoyed many colonists; this irritation led to smuggling and a desire to be rid of regulation.

Colonial Government
Colonial administration was controlled by the British government at Westminster. Each American colony had a governor and an elected assembly but the system was not uniform. Three types of colonial government existed. Firstly, the two 'charter colonies', Connecticut and Rhode Island, elected a Governor each year to run the colony. Secondly, there were the 'proprietary colonies', Maryland, Pennsylvania and Delaware, whose proprietor appointed the Governor of the colony, subject to the approval of the Crown. The remaining eight were 'crown colonies', the Governor being appointed by the King.

It was not unusual for governors to clash with assemblies on matters of policy and this was a constant source of friction. Over the years the colonial assemblies had succeeded in establishing their right to be consulted about laws and taxes. They could initiate legislation. They considered that they knew more about their colony than the politicians in London. The assemblies were jealous of their rights and privileges and resented interference from England. (See Fig. 2, The Thirteen Colonies.)

Social Differences
A fundamental difference between England and the 13 colonies was social. The difference in outlook on the two sides of the Atlantic was the natural product of a difference in life-styles. In England classes were settled and accepted; social mobility was slow. In America fortunes were swiftly made and lost. There were no fixed ranks and classes. Where Englishmen despised the disunity and lawlessness of

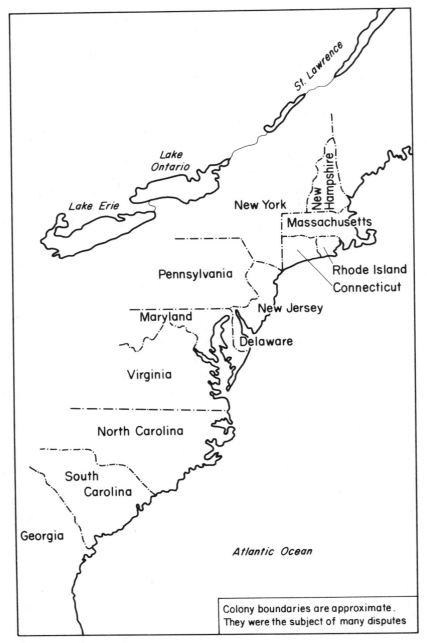

Colony boundaries are approximate.
They were the subject of many disputes

Fig.2 The Thirteen Colonies, 1763

America, the colonists were filled with pride in making a new life for themselves. With two societies so different in habits and situation it was impossible for one to continue to interfere with the other without causing trouble.

American Strength

By 1763 the American colonies were well-populated, rich in natural resources and expanding rapidly in agriculture and industry. After the Seven Years' War they no longer needed British protection against the French. When the colonies had been founded they were dependent upon England for support; by 1763 they were becoming increasingly resentful of British attempts to enforce this dependence. As Tom Paine (1737 – 1809) wrote in his pamphlet *Common Sense* in 1776, 'to know whether it be the interest of this continent to be independent we need only ask this easy, simple question; is it the interest of a man to be a boy all his life?'

In spite of America's increasing strength the colonists lacked unity. However, disunity could give way to a temporary unity if the colonists were sufficiently provoked. This occurred in 1764 when Grenville, appointed Prime Minister in 1763, introduced financial measures which outraged the Americans.

Grenville's Financial Measures

Britain's national debt had doubled as a result of the Seven Years' War and British landowners were heavily taxed. By contrast, the colonies had few debts and were lightly taxed. In these circumstances the British government adopted the view that the Americans should contribute to their own defence. This view hardened after the Pontiac uprising of May 1763, when Indians massacred 2000 colonists. It was decided that 10,000 troops should protect the American frontiers at a cost of £400,000 a year.

Grenville's first financial measure was the Sugar Act, 1764. An Act introduced in 1733 had placed a duty of sixpence a gallon on foreign molasses imported into America for the manufacture of rum. This duty was considered too high and was constantly evaded. Grenville decided to reduce the duty to threepence but to make sure that it was paid in future. This decision created a storm of protest in America for most colonists believed that it would ruin the rum trade. Tight control was kept on smuggling and this angered colonists who were engaged in the coastal trade. However, Grenville argued that he had reduced the duty by half and Americans knew that the British government had the right to regulate colonial trade.

Grenville's second measure, the Stamp Act, 1765, produced a

much greater outcry. The Act placed a stamp duty on a large selection of papers and documents, ranging from official and legal documents to liquor licences, pamphlets and newspapers. It was calculated that it would raise £60,000 a year, all of which was to be spent for American purposes.

The colonists considered the Stamp Act an outrage. It was taxation for the sake of revenue not trade regulation. The Americans argued that the only bodies qualified to levy internal taxes were the assemblies. The greatest cry of all — 'No taxation without representation' — could be heard throughout the colonies. Rioting and mob violence broke out in opposition to the Act. In October 1765 a Stamp Act Congress met and sent a petition to London, registering a strong protest against the Stamp Act.

The Declaratory Act, 1766

The Stamp Act was repealed in 1766, thanks to a campaign carried out by Chatham. In an emotional speech he argued that the Act should be repealed 'absolutely, totally and immediately'. Repeal was accompanied by a Declaratory Act, passed to appease politicians who did not agree with Chatham and who viewed repeal of the Stamp Act as a sign of weakness. The Declaratory Act stated that the British Parliament 'had, hath, and of right ought to have full power and authority to make laws and statutes of sufficient force and validity to bind the colonies and people of America, subjects of the Crown of Great Britain, in all cases whatsoever'.

The Revenue Act, 1767

By 1767 the annual cost to Britain of defending America was £700,000 to which the colonists contributed nothing. For this reason, in spite of the example of the Stamp Act, and in spite of the knowledge that taxation was a sore point in the colonies, Lord Townshend, Chancellor of the Exchequer, introduced a Revenue Bill. He argued that it fell into the category of external taxation and therefore the Americans could not object to it.

The Revenue Act imposed duties on tea, glass, paint, lead and paper imported into the colonies. Once more mob violence broke out. Administration broke down and the courts were powerless to deal with the situation. Troops were sent to Boston, but the British government shrank from violent action, and in 1770 all duties were removed except for that on tea.

Political Instability in Britain

The first 10 years of George III's reign witnessed the rise and fall of five chief ministers — Bute, Grenville, Rockingham, Chatham, and Grafton (see p.28). These changes, coupled with ministerial irresolution, led the colonists to believe that they had the upper hand.

The Boston Massacre, 1770
In March 1770 an event occurred which embittered the American citizens against the British. A guard of soldiers was sent to protect a sentry at a customs house in Boston who was being abused by the mob. The soldiers met the mob in King Street; a skuffle took place and soldiers fired on the mob. Five people were killed and several others wounded. Such hostility was aroused that the military was eventually forced to move all troops from the city of Boston. The colonists regarded this removal as a great victory. (See the print of the Boston Massacre.)

The Gaspée, 1772
Hostility to England, once aroused, did not die away. In 1772 the revenue ship, *Gaspée*, aground off Rhode Island, was burned and its young commander, Lieutenant Dudington, was wounded. Opinion in England was exasperated, but Lord North preferred to let the matter rest.

The Boston 'Tea Party', 1773
The Boston 'Tea Party' ended the working arrangement which Lord North had tried to foster with America. It is testimony to the complete gulf between the two worlds that the immediate cause of the war seems out of proportion to its results. The 'Tea Party' occurred in 1773 when the East India Company was allowed to send tea direct to America instead of via England. On 16 December several radicals, disguised as Red Indians, boarded three ships in Boston harbour and threw their cargo of tea overboard in protest against the duty which still remained on tea. Cargoes of tea in other harbours suffered the same fate. The Boston 'Tea Party' was an insult to British authority. British politicians believed that if they did not take strong action imperial rule in America would be destroyed.

The Co-ercive Acts, 1774
Following the Boston 'Tea Party' the British government introduced a number of Co-ercive Acts designed to bring the colonists to heel. The first Co-ercive Act, known as the Boston Port Act, 1774, closed the port of Boston until compensation was paid to the East India Company for the loss of its tea. It also decreed that the government

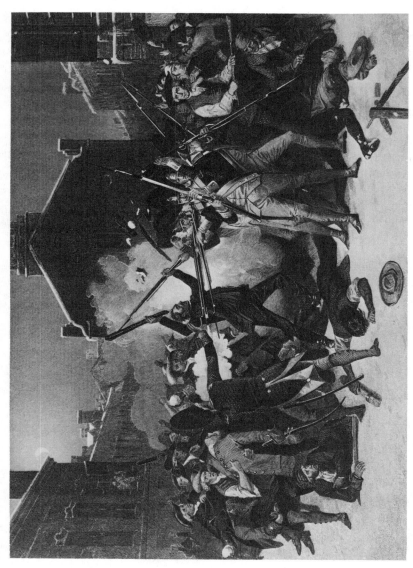

A contemporary print of the Boston massacre, 1770

of Massachusetts and its custom houses were to be removed from Boston to Salem. The Massachusetts Bay Regulating Act, 1774, amended the charter of Massachusetts, replacing the elected assembly with one nominated by the Crown. The Governor's power was increased and town meetings were restricted to one a year. The aim of the Act was to tighten royal control of the colony. The third Co-ercive Act, the Quartering Act, 1774, empowered the Governor of Boston to quarter troops in private dwellings if this became necessary. General Gage (1721 – 87) was given the task of enforcing the Co-ercive Acts. The punishment of Massachusetts by the Co-ercive Acts led to resistance in most of the colonies. The other colonists realized that it was only a matter of time before their own charters and privileges would be threatened.

The Quebec Act, 1774
This Act added to American grievances. It gave Roman Catholics in Quebec the right to hold public office and provided for government by a Governor and nominated council. Quebec's frontier was established west of the New England colonies, preventing the possibility of expansion inland. This Act gave the Americans further evidence that Britain was attempting to reduce colonial independence.

The First Continental Congress, 1774
Throughout the colonies there was widespread support for the defiant action taken by the people of Massachusetts. In September 1774 a congress of representatives from all the colonies, except Georgia, met at Philadelphia. It produced a declaration of rights and listed all the colonial grievances. The congress sent a petition to George III, demanding that the grievances should be redressed and stating that the colonies would resist together until their demands were met. Britain refused to negotiate with the illegal congress and the situation became desperate as the colonies prepared to fight for their liberty.

The Battle of Lexington, 1775
In April 1775 General Gage was ordered to put down the rebellion in Massachusetts. He decided to capture the rebels' supplies at Concord, 18 miles from Boston. On the march to Concord British troops met a band of colonists at Lexington; a fight followed and eight colonists were killed. When he arrived at Concord Gage found that the stores had been moved. On the march back to Boston the British suffered 273 casualties from snipers. The colonists converged on Boston, trying to surround the British troops.

The Battle of Bunker Hill, 1775
When reinforcements arrived from England General Gage felt confident that he could rout the colonists. On 17 June 1775 he attacked the American position on Breed's Hill and Bunker Hill outside Boston. The colonists were only dislodged at the third attempt. Britain suffered over 1000 casualties and the battle of Bunker Hill, although technically a victory, was a great blow to British morale. Boston remained under siege. The British government realized that the suppression of the colonies now required a full-scale war.

2 The War of Independence

Lord North was appalled at the thought of the responsibility and effort involved in the direction of a war. He knew he could not make a success of it and handed over responsibility to the Secretary of State for the colonies, Lord George Germain (1716 – 85). The colonies were 3000 miles from Britain and this, together with the awkward terrain in America, made the conduct of war difficult. George Washington was appointed commander-in-chief of the Americans and most of the colonists supported him. The loyalists, who did not, were never sufficiently numerous or well organized to provide the help that the British government hoped for.

The Siege of Boston, 1775 – 6
In the early stages of the war British troops, led by General Gage, concentrated on Boston and tried to subdue New England. Failure led General Gage to be replaced by General Howe (1729 – 1814) but he had no more success. In March 1776 Washington cut off his supply lines and he was forced into a hasty retreat from Boston, leaving much valuable equipment behind. The New Englanders tried to take advantage of Britain's defeat and seize Canada but General Carlton rebuffed the attack.

Mercenaries
From the start of the war Britain was hampered by a lack of troops. The only answer was to hire foreign soldiers. In January 1776 a treaty with the German states of Hesse-Cassel and Brunswick provided Britain with the services of 18,000 well-trained mercenary troops. Even so, a shortage of transport ships and difficulties in providing equipment and supplies continued to plague the British army.

The Declaration of Independence, 1776
In May 1775 the second Continental Congress met in Philadelphia

to review the colonies' political position. The colonies were strong enough to survive without the help of Britain and in the renewed struggle that was to come they would need help from Britain's enemies, especially France. Only as an independent state could the colonies make an alliance with France and disregard British restrictions on foreign shipping in American ports. A series of resolutions were passed by the Congress in June and July; these were embodied in the Declaration of Independence passed on 4 July 1776.

The Campaign of 1776

In 1776 General Howe launched an attack on the middle colonies. He won a battle on Long Island and entered New York unopposed. Washington was driven out and Britain was in possession of both New York and Rhode Island. However, at the end of 1776, Washington succeeded in raising the morale of his troops. On Boxing Day he attacked the German troops stationed at Trenton. They were surprised by the sudden attack and 1000 men surrendered. This success renewed patriot faith in Washington and provided an irritating end to what had been a successful campaign season for Howe.

Saratoga, 1777

In 1777 General Burgoyne (1722–92) formulated an ambitious plan to subdue the middle colonies. The king was impressed by his energy and self-confidence and appointed him to the command. The plan was for a march from Lake Champlain in Canada to Albany on the Hudson. At the same time it was agreed that General Howe should capture Philadelphia early in the year and then march to join Burgoyne at Albany before the winter. (See Fig. 3, General Burgoyne's Strategy.)

Various delays prevented Howe from leaving New York until July. He landed troops in Chesapeake Bay, defeated Washington at Brandywine and captured Philadelphia. Washington tried to capture British troops at Germantown but failed and went into winter quarters at Valley Forge. However, in spite of this apparent success, Howe also failed, for two weeks later Burgoyne met disaster at Saratoga.

At the start of his campaign Burgoyne had been successful. He destroyed the American flotilla on Lake Champlain and recaptured Ticonderoga from the colonists. Once he left the lake, however, difficulties set in. It took him 10 weeks to cover 50 miles from Ticonderoga to Saratoga. Burgoyne failed to break through south of

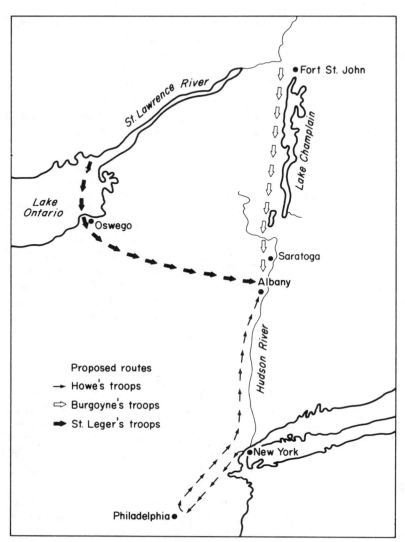

Fig.3 General Burgoyne's Strategy, 1777

Saratoga, reinforcements from Howe did not appear, and on 14 October negotiations were opened for surrender.

The War Widens
Saratoga was a turning point in the war. It gave the Americans confidence and brought them new allies. By September 1777 a

Franco-American treaty of friendship and commerce was approved by Congress and after Saratoga France recognized America as an independent power. Britain declared war on France in June 1778. In June 1779 Spain declared war on Britain. When Dutch merchants continued to carry supplies to Britain's enemies, despite strong protests, Britain declared war on Holland in December 1780. In 1780 the 'League of Armed Neutrality' was formed. This was an alliance of Sweden, Denmark, and Russia to prevent Britain from damaging their trade during the war. Operations against these continental powers took place mainly at sea and in the colonies in India, the West Indies and West Africa. In Europe a French attack on Jersey failed. Gibraltar was gallantly defended but a Spanish attack on Minorca succeeded.

The Attack on the Southern Colonies, 1779

After Saratoga the British military command changed. General Clinton (1738–95) became the new commander-in-chief. In 1778 the British launched no major attack and abandoned Philadelphia. In 1779 they decided to concentrate on the southern colonies. On 29 December 1778 British troops captured Savannah and by February 1779 Georgia was under British control. For the next two years Clinton concentrated on a full-scale campaign to win over the south.

In February 1780 he landed in South Carolina and in April forced the surrender of Charleston. In May he returned to New York to meet the threat of the French fleet, leaving his second-in-command, Cornwallis (1738–1805), to carry on the campaign. Cornwallis invaded North Carolina and in 1781 decided to attack the rebels in Virginia. He was unable to crush all resistance and Clinton ordered him to retire to a fortified base at Yorktown on Chesapeake Bay.

Yorktown, 1781

Washington and the French concentrated all their efforts against General Cornwallis at Yorktown. Cornwallis had a difficult position to defend against a land attack but it would be possible to relieve Yorktown by sea, provided the British fleet retained control of Chesapeake Bay. Britain let this control slip into French hands. When a British force arrived at Chesapeake Bay in September 1781 they found 24 French ships with 1400 guns. The British failed to dislodge the French fleet and suffered severe losses. Cornwallis was now hemmed in by sea as well as by land. He made a desperate attempt to evacuate his force across the York river but rough weather prevented this. On 18 October Cornwallis was forced to surrender.

The Fall of Lord North

When Lord North heard the news of Yorktown he cried, 'Oh God, it is all over'. The King wanted to continue the war and when he realized that the country no longer supported this policy he threatened to abdicate. On 20 March 1782 Lord North resigned. The new ministry, headed by Lord Rockingham, immediately entered into negotiations for peace.

The Peace of Versailles, 1783

The Versailles Treaty brought the American War of Independence to an end. Britain recognized the independence of the 13 colonies and the boundary with Canada was pushed northwards near its present position along the Great Lakes. Debts contracted before 1775 were to be honoured by both sides. Loyalists were guaranteed liberty and the right to emigrate. American fishing rights were also guaranteed. Senegal, St Lucia and Tobago went to France and Florida and Minorca to Spain.

3 Why did Britain Lose the War?

Many reasons have been given to account for Britain's loss of the American colonies. A weak, bungling government, inadequate military commanders, and the intervention of foreign powers, all played their part in Britain's defeat. In the end Britain lost because the colonists were no longer prepared to take part in an out of date, tyrannous system of government and were prepared to fight indefinitely for their freedom.

The Difficulty of Obtaining Supplies

The colonies lay 3000 miles across the ocean from Britain. A good voyage lasted five weeks, a bad one five months. In the winter of 1775 – 6 of the 40 ships sent from Britain only eight reached Boston in safety. Even when supplies reached America it was not easy to transport them across the mountains and forests of the interior.

Guerilla Warfare

The British army was trained to fight conventional warfare, whereas the Americans adopted guerilla tactics. The British soldiers, carrying 60 pounds of equipment, could not compete with the swift-marching colonial troops. The colonists were fighting on their own ground amongst their own people. Thus for the most part the British were fighting not merely an army but an entire people as well.

The Direction of the War

At the beginning of the war British war aims were uncertain. Britain should have crushed the colonists before they had time to organize themselves. This was not done because at first the British government was anxious to come to terms with the Americans. The generals blamed the government for their failure. They declared that, in trying to direct the war from offices in London, the government was bound to come to grief.

Inefficient Commanders

If the war strategy was at fault, more blame rests with the generals than the government. General Howe was cautious and predictable. He always used a flanking movement and the colonists were quick to realize this. Clinton lacked flair and imagination and did not inspire his troops with confidence. Burgoyne was reckless and failed to recognize the importance of sea power. By contrast, George Washington made the most of his opponents' mistakes. He was successful with a badly disciplined, ill-trained, poorly equipped army even though he won no glorious victories.

Foreign Enemies

French and Spanish intervention in the war meant that British defeat was only a matter of time. The British navy was not equal to the combined fleets of France and Spain and loss of control of the sea made defeat inevitable. Britain had no allies and the fight against the American colonies, France, Spain and Holland was too much for her resources.

The Effects of the War on Britain

In 1783 Britain lost her 13 colonies in America. This was a great blow to Britain's prestige and it led to difficulties at home. The ideas of the Declaration of Independence led to a period of liberal inquiry into the defects of the British political system (see p.117). This was abruptly ended with the outbreak of the French revolutionary wars. Ireland, following the American example, demanded self-government but the Act of Union, 1800, put an end to Irish hopes (see p.70). Britain compensated for her losses by acquiring territory elsewhere. Her industrial revolution raised Britain to new heights of power and wealth in the nineteenth century. The short-term effects on Britain of the loss of her 13 colonies were therefore small.

Summary

In 1763 Britain possessed 13 colonies on the Atlantic shore of America. She expected to reap rewards from the colonies in return for providing them with protection and aiding their development. By 1783, following a bitter war, Britain had lost her colonies and suffered the humiliation of defeat. In a state of shock, George III believed that he was to blame, that the loss was his fault, that he had failed in his duty. It was not so simple. The Americans found that they had less and less in common with Britain. They wanted freedom and were prepared to go to any lengths to obtain it. It was beyond Britain's power to suppress indefinitely this desire for independence.

Exercises
1.   Identify four grievances of the Americans which help to explain why they rebelled against the British government.
2.   What actions did the Americans take to oppose the British from 1773 to 1776?
3.   What mistakes by British generals contributed to American victory in the war?
4.   Apart from military mistakes, select and describe three reasons why Britain lost the war with America.
5.   In what ways was the war important for a) Britain, b) America?

6
William Pitt the Younger: the Years of Reconstruction, 1783 – 93

Chancellor of the Exchequer at 23, Prime Minister at 24, William Pitt (1759 – 1806) will always be remembered for the rapidity of his rise to power. Pitt's career was a classic case of a son following in the footsteps of a famous father. Yet the qualities that made Pitt great were very different from those of his flamboyant father, the Earl of Chatham. Pitt the Younger was austere, remote and dedicated to his profession. His administrative and financial skills formed the basis of his remarkable achievements. Within eight years of taking office Pitt had increased the government's revenue by 50 per cent, attacked jobbery and corruption and launched the economy on a new phase of expansion and prosperity.

Pitt's Early Life

William Pitt was born in 1759, the second son of the great William Pitt. Pitt the Elder did not approve of public schools — he once declared that boys were cowed for life at Eton — and so his son was subjected to a harsh regime of home lessons and private tutors. The lonely years of his boyhood made him tough and reserved. On 8 October 1773, accompanied by his tutor, William arrived at Pembroke College, Cambridge, an unhealthy-looking boy of 14. He took a degree at the age of 17, availing himself of the provision which allowed noblemen's sons to dispense with the demeaning business of actually sitting an examination. After Cambridge Pitt went to Lincoln's Inn but soon decided that he would rather be a politician than a lawyer. In 1781 he entered Parliament as the representative for the pocket borough of Appleby.

1 William Pitt and the Whigs

Pitt began his political career as a Whig and always claimed to hold Whig principles. Yet it is safer to say that he stood above party, relying on his own achievements and regarding himself as a national leader. When Pitt took his seat in the Commons in 1781 Lord North was discredited for his mishandling of the American War of Independence and he resigned in 1782. This forced George III to look to the Whigs to form a new ministry which was easier said than done since the Whigs were by no means a united party. There were three divisions amongst them — the Rockingham group, the Fox group and the Shelburne group. Pitt attached himself to the Shelburne group since he believed that it came nearest to representing the views held by his father.

The Rockingham Ministry, March – June 1782

The Rockingham group of Whigs was deeply opposed both to the King's American policy and to his desire to increase the influence of the monarchy. Lord Rockingham was elderly; he drew his support from most of the great Whig aristocratic families. Edmund Burke (1729 – 97) was one of his supporters.

Lord North's resignation led to the formation of the Rockingham ministry in March 1782; it included Charles James Fox (1749 – 1806) and Lord Shelburne. During this ministry Pitt supported the

Economical Reforms Bill which abolished many of the royal sinecures and thereby reduced the patronage and power of the King. However, when Pitt introduced a proposal for electoral reform, which the Rockinghams had appeared to support whilst in opposition, he received a very cool reception from the new administration. Burke attacked Pitt for wanting to 'overturn the constitution' and his Bill was defeated.

The Shelburne Ministry, 1782

Lord Shelburne wanted to form a national party, similar to the ones which exist today. His supporters believed in patriot politics — a cause to serve, a programme to believe in — rather than a clique of friends who simply wished to help each other.

When Rockingham died suddenly on 2 July 1782 George III chose Shelburne to succeed him. This dissolved the temporary union of the Whigs. Fox and Burke resigned rather than work under Shelburne. William Pitt was appointed to the post of Chancellor of the Exchequer. The Shelburne government did not have a majority in Parliament and was therefore always weak. Shelburne ended the American War of Independence and was responsible for drawing up the Treaty of Versailles. When the terms were made public Shelburne was roundly criticized in Parliament for giving too much away. The Tories and Foxite Whigs argued that although peace had to be made with America, Britain should have dealt severely with France and Spain. In February 1783 Shelburne was forced to resign by an opposition party led by Fox and his new-found ally, Lord North.

The Fox–North Coalition, 1783

For six weeks after Shelburne had resigned the King, who detested Fox, looked in vain for a way to avoid a Fox – North administration. Charles James Fox was a gay and dissolute figure who usually preached allegiance to party and supported radical reforms. Fox was discredited by his coalition with North, whose views he had always opposed, and this gave the King hope that he would soon be rid of the man he despised.

Fox and North concluded the Treaty of Versailles and were unable to obtain better terms than those they had criticized. The coalition was unpopular in the country where it was regarded as a cynical administration which cared little for principle. In November 1783 Fox introduced his India Bill which provided for seven commissioners to supervise the political activities of the East India Company. The commissioners had the power to appoint many officials;

this gave them immense powers of patronage. In the Commons William Pitt attacked this plan as 'absolute despotism' and 'gross corruption'. On 11 December 1783 the King let it be known that any peer who supported the India Bill would be considered his enemy. This statement of the King's intentions served its purpose and on 17 December the House of Lords threw out the Bill. George III then dismissed the Fox – North coalition and appointed William Pitt as First Lord of the Treasury and Chancellor of the Exchequer.

2 Prime Minister Pitt, 1783

When William Pitt first became Prime Minister, Fox was the leader of a majority in the House of Commons against him. In the end Pitt scraped together seven colleagues who agreed to form a ministry with him; as well as being peers, they were also either Tories or nonentities. Nevertheless, Pitt carried on the government for three months until, in 1784, George III dissolved Parliament. Elections were held and Pitt secured a majority of over 200 in the new Parliament. In spite of his success at the polls there were many jokes directed at Pitt's youth. Byron wrote:

A sight to make surrounding nations stare:
A Kingdom trusted to a schoolboy's care.

Pitt quickly began work on what he called the most important task of his political life — 'to unite and connect what yet remains of our shattered empire'. This demanded hard work and Pitt was equal to the task. Unlike his father, he was proud to be 'a proposer of plans' and an overseer of planners. He created an entirely new kind of administrative machine. In the field of politics he replaced an age of talk with an age of work.

The Prime Minister and the Political Parties

William Pitt's victory was not a triumph for a particular party or set of policies. His administration contained none of the great Whig or Tory leaders. Instead he was supported by the rank and file of both parties. As the years progressed most of Pitt's support came from the Tories or from the Whigs who had decided to adopt Tory principles. The Whigs who remained true to their principles, an ever-decreasing number of men, were led by Fox.

Pitt's Financial Reforms

As Prime Minister William Pitt was the First Lord of the Treasury and he decided to be his own Chancellor of the Exchequer. He set to work to rebuild the country's economy which was in a state of collapse following the American War of Independence. In the summer of 1784 the national debt was £240,000,000; interest on the debt was £8,000,000 which was well over half the government's annual revenue. Expenditure exceeded revenue and Britain was on the verge of bankruptcy. Pitt adopted several ingenious methods to stabilize the country's economy.

He turned his attention to customs and excise. Pitt decided to lower the levels of indirect taxation, not merely to further the cause of international free trade, but also as a means of increasing the total yield of government income. He calculated, correctly, that lower rates of duty would cut smugglers' profits and in the end kill smuggling far more effectively than harsh penalties and vigilant revenue officers could ever do. The duty on tea was nearly halved by the Commutation Act, 1784. It became possible to buy tea legally at a lower price than had previously been charged for smuggled tea. Once duties were reduced to a level where they neither crippled trade nor encouraged smuggling, they were collected in a way that minimized fraud, evasion and administrative costs.

To maintain revenue whilst waiting for the expansion of trade Pitt imposed extra taxes on luxury items. Windows, servants, horses, playing cards, hair powder, sporting dogs, clocks and watches were all heavily taxed. Pitt was accused of being a prudish young spoilsport who taxed other people's innocent pleasures, but such accusations did not bother him.

Pitt also set up a sinking fund into which the government paid £1,000,000 a year. Six commissioners purchased national stock with the money; the interest from the stock was invested in turn. It was hoped that the profits from the fund would catch up with and redeem the national debt.

Pitt helped the government to save money by reducing the number of sinecure posts. Sinecures were jobs which were usually undemanding but which brought in large fees to their holders. Pitt made a great impression on the Commons by refusing such a post for himself which would have given him an income of £3000 a year. He let sinecures wither quietly away; when their holders died the offices were suppressed instead of being given to somebody else.

Pitt's methods worked. The Prime Minister not only abolished old offices, he also created new ones which did not drain the country's resources. Gentlemanly amateurs were replaced by professional civil servants. These men were often of humble origin, dependent upon their wages. They were paid salaries rather than fees. At long last the government of England was becoming a job to be done rather than an opportunity to be exploited.

Pitt continued to use the accepted channels for raising loans, with the financiers on the Treasury list as agents. But he strengthened the competitive element by requiring offers to be made by sealed tender. He launched the national lottery in 1784, using the receipts to meet the government's temporary shortages of cash and thereby reduce the issue of Exchequer bills.

Pitt's financial measures were a success. By 1793 he had reduced the national debt by £10,000,000. However, once Britain was at war with revolutionary France, her national debt began to rise again and soon reached mammoth proportions.

Naval Reforms

At the end of the American War of Independence the British navy was in a sorry state. Many ships had been lost; the rest were either old and leaky or they were new and had been built with unseasoned timber which soon rotted. Pitt appointed Admiral Lord Howe (1726-99) as First Lord of the Admiralty in 1783. He cut down waste and corruption and soon built up a powerful fleet. However, little was done to improve sailors' living and working conditions.

Free Trade

In his book *The Wealth of Nations* Adam Smith (1723-90) put forward the idea of free trade, indicating that it would make Britain prosperous. William Pitt supported these ideas, but when he tried to put Smith's theories into practice he met with great opposition. Pitt's proposals for free trade with Ireland were accepted by the Irish Parliament in Dublin in 1785, but they encountered such fierce opposition in England that they had to be dropped.

A grandiose scheme for free trade with Europe came to nothing. Pitt had to settle instead for a commercial treaty with France alone which was signed in 1786 and came into force in the following year. By this treaty nearly all tariffs between the two countries were reduced. There were drastic reductions on the duty on French wine coming into England and on English manufactured goods exported to France. Pitt favoured the introduction of free trade with America but public opinion was against this. It was not until 1787 that he was able to take the first real step to re-opening the American trade by setting up free ports in the British West Indies to act as *entrepôts*.

Parliamentary Reform

William Pitt had always been interested in the question of parliamentary reform. However, when his radical friends brought forward a reform motion in 1784 he voted for it but told them that it was 'greatly out of season at this juncture'. By April 1785 Pitt felt he had time to deal more adequately with the problem. On 18 April he introduced a Bill for the purchase of 36 rotten boroughs, paying compensation to those who suffered from this move, and then redistributing the seats amongst London and the counties. Moderate though it was, the proposal was defeated by 74 votes.

The Slave Trade

William Wilberforce (1759 – 1833) convinced Pitt of the need to abolish the slave trade. Pitt arranged for the Privy Council to investigate the trade, and when Wilberforce fell ill in the spring of 1788 the Prime Minister himself agreed to move the Common's resolution against the trade. In the summer of 1788 Pitt helped to carry a Bill in the Commons making improvements in the conditions on board the slave ships. When some of his cabinet colleagues in the Lords threatened to throw the measure out Pitt declared that if they did so he would resign. The threat worked and the Bill became law. Pitt continued to support the total abolition of the slave trade and prohibited the import of slaves from Guiana but he carefully avoided any more cabinet crises. By the time the slave trade was abolished in 1807 Pitt was dead (see p.122).

The Regency Question, 1788–9

In November 1788 King George III lapsed into delirium, terrifying the dinner guests at Windsor by foaming at the mouth and charging at the Prince of Wales. For many weeks it seemed that he would either die or remain permanently insane. The question of appointing a Regent arose. The Prince of Wales, a friend of Fox and the Whigs, was the only possible choice of Regent. During the critical months of the King's illness nobody could be sure whether Pitt would be hurled from office as a result of the King's death or prolonged insanity, or whether Fox would fall from his new powerful position in the event of a royal recovery. Pitt played for time, insisting that a regency could only be set up by Act of Parliament. His Regency Bill was ingenious. It divided power between the Prince and the Queen and prevented the Prince from doing things which his father would not be able to undo in the event of his recovery. In the midst of this, in February 1789, the King regained his sanity, resumed his power and thanked his ministers for their loyalty.

Toleration for Roman Catholics, 1791

In 1791 Pitt secured the passages of an Act which granted Roman

Catholics official religious toleration. But the Act did not abolish various restrictions on their political activity.

Warren Hastings' Trial, 1788–95

Apart from the regency crisis, the parliamentary opposition could find few issues on which to attack Pitt. They were therefore delighted when the question of corruption in India presented itself. In 1785 the East India Company's first Governor General, Warren Hastings (1732 – 1818), arrived back in London. There were ugly rumours about the atrocities he was alleged to have committed and the vast sums of money he was supposed to have obtained by extortion. He challenged his opponents to support their accusations and they decided to impeach him.

Warren Hastings' trial opened in Westminster Hall on 13 February 1788 and dragged on until 1795. Pitt behaved with considerable skill on this occasion. When the charges against Hastings were first aired, Pitt was expected to defend him. The government spokesman did indeed secure the rejection of the first charge. A fortnight later Pitt astonished the whole political world by voting in favour of the second charge and thereby making impeachment possible. As the impeachment dragged on year after year, discrediting the opposition leaders, Pitt's own position grew stronger. There was a tendency to credit him with far-sighted political skill when in fact he had been genuinely shocked by what Hastings had apparently done. The trial of Warren Hastings was the longest in history. It ended in a hollow victory for Hastings, for although he was acquitted the trial left him bankrupt and bitter.

Pitt's Imperial Policy

William Pitt tried to introduce efficient administration in the colonies. By the India Act, 1784, and the Canada Act, 1791, he made the government of both countries more efficient (see p.249 and p.257).

Pitt's Foreign Policy

William Pitt needed a period of peace to reconstruct England after the disastrous American War. When he became Prime Minister he inherited the problem of British isolation in the face of a hostile western Europe. His first piece of foreign policy helped to break down that isolation. In 1784 Joseph II of Austria caused unrest in Europe by trying to exchange his Belgian provinces (the Austrian Netherlands) for Bavaria. When this scheme failed he decided to redevelop the Belgian provinces, making the port of Antwerp as great as London or Rotterdam. To achieve this he had to force the Dutch to open the river Scheldt to give free passage to Antwerp. Holland (the United Provinces) refused to comply with Joseph's wishes and Austria attacked Holland in 1784. Russia took Austria's side in the dispute whilst France supported Holland. Eventually, Joseph abandoned his ambition to open the Scheldt. In 1785 France and Holland signed an alliance. This worried Pitt who was anxious that France should not gain undue influence in Holland for this could threaten Britain's safety. When trouble broke out in the Austrian Netherlands threatening the House of Orange Pitt's anxiety grew. Prussian troops suppressed the revolt. In 1788 the Triple Alliance of Britain, Prussia and the United Provinces was formed. The members agreed to maintain the status quo and to defend each other if necessary. Britain had thus emerged from 20 years of isolation and had secured two valuable allies.

In 1790 Britain came into conflict with Spain who claimed the whole western American coast from Cape Horn to Alaska. The Spaniards seized British ships and settlers on what is now Vancouver Island at Nootka Sound. Parliament voted £1,000,000 and prepared for war. Faced with the prospect of war, Spain gave way. It was agreed that the British had a right to peaceful exploitation of the Pacific provided that they did not come within 10 leagues of any Spanish settlements.

Another aspect of Pitt's foreign policy concerned Russia. When Catherine the Great of Russia seized the port and fortress of Oczakov from the Turks Pitt wanted to send a fleet to the Black Sea to make her return it. However, when Catherine refused to listen to a British ultimatum Pitt stopped short of war and the port remained in Russian hands.

3 The Impact of the French Revolution

Until 1789 France was ruled under the *ancien regime* in which the king, Louis XVI, had absolute power and the nobles and clergy were privileged whilst the bourgeoisie, or middle class, were dissatisfied and the peasants downtrodden. In that year the country was bankrupt after a succession of costly wars and the peasants were starving. Louis XVI was forced to convene the States General, or French Parliament, which had not met for 175 years. The States General met in May 1789. Louis XVI failed to dominate its meetings and it was soon transformed into the National Assembly, demanding reforms. When no reforms were forthcoming the starving mob became impatient and on 14 July 1789 attacked the Bastille, a prison in Paris which was regarded as a symbol of royal tyranny.

Violence and unrest spread throughout France. The National Assembly passed the Declaration of the Rights of Man which declared that all men were by nature equal and that the government must reflect the will of the people not the wishes of the king. In October 1789 the Paris mob marched to the magnificent palace of Versailles and brought the King and Queen back to the capital to share in their misery. The National Assembly went on to abolish the feudal privileges of the nobles and by the Civil Constitution of the Clergy church land was nationalized. In June 1791 the royal family fled from Paris to join their relations in Austria, but they were captured at Varennes and brought back to Paris as prisoners.

Britain's Reaction to the French Revolution

In Britain some people were pleased when they heard the news of the French Revolution, others were afraid. Pitt gave a cautious welcome to the news, believing that Louis XVI would be so burdened by the chaos in France that he would not be able to dominate the affairs of Europe. British Dissenters, or Nonconformists, also welcomed the news for they hoped that changes in France would lead to changes in England which would free them from various political restrictions. In 1789 Dr Richard Price (1723 – 91), a leading Dissenter, delivered a sermon entitled 'The Love of Our Country' in which he praised the French Revolution. Popular societies sprang up throughout the country and were joined by people who wished to follow the French example and make Britain more democratic.

As events in France passed into the hands of extremists enthusiasm for the revolution in Britain began to decline. In 1790 Edmund Burke published his *Reflections on the Revolution in France*, in which he analysed events in that country and prophesied that there would soon be great bloodshed and cruelty in France to be followed by the rise of a dictator and a long war. Burke's book had a large sale. In 1791 Tom Paine published a reply to Burke entitled *The Rights of Man*. In the following year he published a second volume of the book. In his books Paine supported the views of democrats and even advocated a republic as the best form of government. Differing opinions about the revolution were leading to unrest. In 1791 there were riots in Birmingham where supporters of the revolution had organized a dinner to commemorate the second anniversary of the fall of the Bastille. An anti-revolutionary mob took to the streets and burned down the chapels and houses of Dissenters.

In 1792 general opinion in Britain turned against the revolution.

In 1792 Louis XVI was forced to declare war on Austria. When France appeared to be losing the war the Jacobins (members of a political club who held extreme views and were becoming the dominant party in France) deposed Louis XVI and proclaimed France a republic. When Prussia joined Austria panic in France led to the September massacres in which over 2000 priests and nobles were killed by extremists. After these excesses few British people gave unqualified support to the French Revolution.

Summary
In 1792 Pitt had every reason to feel proud of his achievements both at home and abroad. Britain was no longer on the verge of bankruptcy. Her government was stable and her navy was strong. Revolutionary France did not seem to be too much of a menace. Pitt declared, 'there never was a time when a durable peace might more reasonably be expected than at the present moment'. No one seriously disputed this statement.

Exercises
1. Why does William Pitt deserve to be called a patriot rather than a party politician?
2. Give an account of Pitt's financial reforms and explain how Britain benefited from them.
3. What is free trade? Why did Pitt pursue a policy of free trade?
4. Describe William Pitt's dealings with France from 1783 to 1793.

7
William Pitt the Younger: the War Years, 1793 – 1806

In January 1793 the French King, Louis XVI, was executed. By this time the revolutionary armies had swept into Belgium and re-opened the river Scheldt. Not content with setting aside their monarchy, the French had set aside the victory Pitt had won over that monarchy five years before. Moreover, they announced that they intended to set aside all the treaties which that monarchy had made. These actions, together with the increasing violence in France, made Pitt realize that the French Revolution threatened British interests. On 2 February 1793 France declared war on Britain — a war which lasted, with one short break, for 22 years. William Pitt guided Britain's war effort until his death in 1806. He helped to inspire confidence in the British people in the difficult days when Britain stood without an ally in Europe, after the collapse of three European coalitions against France. Days of reforming zeal gave way to the grim struggle for victory so that there was a marked contrast between Pitt's peace-time ministry and his days as a war-time Prime Minister.

1 The Conduct of the War

In 1793 Pitt embarked on war with France with very limited aims, believing that the war would be short. Like his father he believed that Britain's interests lay outside Europe and at first his main interest, apart from driving French troops from the Austrian Netherlands, was to gain colonies at France's expense. As the war dragged on it became clear that Pitt would have to develop a European policy and work more closely with his allies. British troops began the war fighting for gains, they ended up fighting for survival. Throughout the war Pitt wore himself out working for victory. There appeared to be a marked contrast between the relaxed confidence of his early years as Prime Minister and the desperate sadness which marred the end of his life. The British public regarded Pitt as the man who gave his life in order to save Europe from the anarchy and tyranny which were the products of the French Revolution.

Pitt's Strategy

In the early stages of the war Pitt employed a three-pronged strategy against the enemy. Firstly, he used the bulk of Britain's forces to make conquests from France in the colonial sphere. Although thousands of troops died of fever in the West Indies this was the most successful aspect of Pitt's strategy. Secondly, he played the role of paymaster in Europe, subsidizing the allies to help them attack France. Over £2,000,000 was spent on subsidies in 1794 alone, but there was very little to show for it since the allies often used the money for their own purposes and fought amongst themselves rather than against France. Finally, Pitt sent an expeditionary fighting force to Europe. At first this consisted of three battalions of very poor quality, led by the Duke of York. This force failed miserably, giving rise to the nursery rhyme about 'the grand old Duke of York'.

The First Coalition, 1793

In 1793 Britain joined the first of four coalitions against France. The other member countries were Austria, Prussia, Holland and Spain. With such powerful forces Pitt expected a swift victory, but the allied armies were badly led and Austria and Prussia were more interested in partitioning Poland than defeating the French. After early defeats in which the French general, Dumouriez, deserted to the allies, the French army, directed by Carnot, was reformed. With the help of conscription the French directed hordes of half-trained men against the small, professional allied armies. Led by ruthless generals these ragged troops soon proved able to defeat the allies.

In August 1793 there was a royalist uprising in Toulon, a naval base in southern France, which enabled Admiral Hood (1724 – 1816) to set up an allied force there. However, his efforts were wasted for re-inforcements were slow to arrive in Toulon. At the end of December 1793 the republicans, with artillery commanded by Napoleon Bonaparte, regained control of the base. There was a similar lack of success in the Netherlands campaign. Initially coalition troops had driven the French from the Austrian Netherlands, but by 1795 French troops had recaptured the Netherlands and invaded Holland. The latter was transformed into the Batavian Republic. (See Fig. 4, French Expansion 1793 – 97.)

Britain met with more success in the West Indies than she had in Europe. During 1794 troops led by Sir John Jervis (1735 – 1823) captured Guadeloupe, St Lucia, Marie Galante and the Saints and established themselves at Haiti. French reinforcements were prevented from crossing the Atlantic by Lord Howe's naval victory off the Brittany coast on 'the Glorious First of June'. However, by 1796, 40,000 British troops had died in the West Indies and another 40,000 were unfit for service. Gaudeloupe was later regained by the enemy.

By 1795 the first coalition lay in ruins. In April 1795, to safeguard their interests in Poland, Prussia made peace with France; Holland followed suit in May and in July the Spaniards made friends with the French. When Holland changed sides Britain captured the Cape of Good Hope from her on the Indian route and went on to capture Pondicherry, Trincomalee, Ceylon, Malacca, Amboyna and Banda. Later in 1797 she captured Trinidad and Demerara from Spain. Britain was successful in the colonies but increasingly isolated in

Fig.4 French Expansion, 1793 – 97

Europe. Her isolation was complete when in 1797 Napoleon Bonaparte drove the Austrians out of Italy and compelled them to recognize French conquests by the Treaty of Campo-Formio, 1797.

1797: A Crisis Year

In 1797 Britain was forced onto the defensive and Pitt had to deal with one crisis after another. In October 1796 Spain declared war on Britain and hostilities broke out between the two countries in 1797. In February 1797 Sir John Jervis encountered a Spanish fleet off Cape St Vincent. The Spanish fleet was double the size of Britain's but Nelson (1758 – 1805) distinguished himself in the battle by sailing through the Spanish force to divide it. The result was a complete victory for Jervis which removed, for the time, any threat from the Spanish navy.

Another threat in 1797 came from Ireland. In December 1796 a French invasion fleet had sailed for Ireland and only bad weather and bad seamanship prevented its landing in Bantry Bay. Throughout the year the Irish became more rebellious and the Dutch were preparing an invasion of Ireland. At the same time Britain's position in India was threatened when the French encouraged Tipu Sahib to attack the British. To add to these worries the Bank of England was forced to suspend cash payments in February 1797 and Pitt had to concentrate his efforts on trying to solve the financial crisis.

A serious threat to Britain's security arose in April 1797 when the Channel fleet under Lord Bridport (1727 – 1814) mutinied at Spithead and refused to put to sea. The mutineers called for fair wages, sufficient food, better medical services and improvements in shore leave. They were well-organized and their demands were met within a week. No sooner had the Spithead fleet returned to duty then the sailors of the North Sea fleet at the Nore mutinied. They were led by Richard Parker (1767 – 97) and they demanded changes in the brutal rules of discipline and a fairer division of prize money. When their demands were not met they threatened to blockade the Thames, but instead began fighting amongst themselves. The mutiny was suppressed and Parker was hanged. In October 1797 the same fleet, commanded by Admiral Duncan (1731 – 1804) destroyed a Dutch invasion fleet at Camperdown.

By the end of 1797 Britain's position had improved. She was secure against invasion and was once more financially secure. However, this did not solve Pitt's problems for his idea of a limited war was unpopular especially with the King, who believed that the French Revolution had to be crushed before there could be peace. Just as Britain was isolated in Europe so Pitt felt politically isolated.

He comforted himself with the thought that if Britain had no allies she could not be betrayed by them and he set to work to rebuild Britain's strength.

The Second Coalition, 1798

In 1798 Britain feared a French invasion and this threat revived Pitt's popularity. However, when a direct attack upon England proved impossible the French government sent Napoleon Bonaparte to cut Britain's links with India by invading Egypt. On his way he captured Malta, and when he landed in Egypt he began to win startling victories and soon defeated the Turks at the battle of the Pyramids. At this stage, in August 1798, Admiral Nelson managed to destroy Bonaparte's fleet, which was anchored at the mouth of the Nile in Aboukir Bay. Since Napoleon could not now leave Egypt by sea he planned to capture Syria and march on through Asia Minor, Constantinople and the Balkans. His progress was halted at Acre by British forces and he turned back to suppress a revolt in Egypt.

These circumstances enabled Pitt to create a second coalition of European powers, including Austria, Russia, Naples and Turkey. For the first time since the outbreak of war he began to adopt a European stand-point. He continued to subsidize the allies who were victorious in 1799. Austrian and Russian forces drove the French out of Italy and Britain had a limited success in the Dutch republic. But by 1800 the coalition was on the verge of collapse, thanks to the staggering achievements of Napoleon Bonaparte who had, in November 1799, overthrown the French government and become First Consul. In 1800 Bonaparte recaptured Italy and forced the Austrians to sign the Treaty of Luneville. By this time Russia had already withdrawn from the coalition and once more Britain stood alone against France.

The Battle of Copenhagen, 1801

In 1800 Napoleon Bonaparte directed his attention to damaging Britain's trade and closed as many ports to British imports as he could. At the same time in the Baltic Denmark, Sweden, Russia and Prussia formed the 'Armed Neutrality', or Northern League, which laid an embargo on British ships and closed still more ports to British goods. When Prussia went on to invade Hanover and Denmark occupied Hamburg the time had come for Britain to retaliate. She despatched a fleet to Copenhagen under the command of Hyde Parker (1739–1807) with Lord Nelson as his second-in-command. Nelson sailed into Copenhagen harbour but when three of his ships ran aground Parker ordered him to abandon the action. Nelson believed that evacuation was unnecessary and there followed the famous incident in which he put his spy glass to his blind eye so that he could truthfully say that he could not see any signal to 'Abandon Action'. Nelson attacked the Danes until he had sunk, burnt or captured all 17 Danish ships cooped up in the harbour. The battle contained the worst carnage Nelson had ever witnessed. The result was an armistice and a convention which dissolved the 'Armed Neutrality'. Its armies withdrew from the areas they had occupied.

The Peace of Amiens, 1802

At the same time as Britain was emerging victorious from the ruins of the second coalition Pitt had resigned over the question of Catholic emancipation (see p.70). In February 1801 Addington (1757 – 1844) replaced Pitt. His views reflected the country's war-weariness and in March 1802 he was responsible for signing the Treaty of Amiens with France. By this treaty Britain was to give back all her conquests except Ceylon and Trinidad whilst France was to keep most of hers but was to withdraw from Rome, Naples and Egypt. It was agreed that Malta, which was now in British hands, should be returned to the Knights of St John. The peace was a recognition of the stalemate which existed in Europe. Britain was supreme at sea and France was supreme on land. Both countries needed a breathing space to recover from the devastation of years of war.

Neither side regarded the Peace of Amiens as conclusive and it only lasted 13 months. From the start French troops were active in Italy, Switzerland and the West Indies and French ports remained closed to British goods. Britain decided not to evacuate Malta and war between Britain and France was resumed in May 1803. Addington was criticized for the failure of the peace and Pitt came back to the Prime Minister's office in April 1804.

The Third Coalition, 1805

When he resumed office Pitt formed a third coalition to fight Napoleon, consisting of Britain, Austria and Russia. The coalition had scarcely been formed when Austria suffered a series of defeats, ending with her collapse at Ulm in 1805. A combined army of Austrian and Russian troops was defeated at the battle of Austerlitz in 1805. After this Napoleon began to create new states in what had been the Holy Roman Empire.

The Battle of Trafalgar, 1805

Ever since the renewal of the war in 1803 Britain had been threat-

Two inventions designed to carry Napoleon's troops across the Channel:
1   A balloon designed by Thilorière

ened by invasion. Napoleon had assembled an army of 100,000 men along the coast of France, Belgium and Holland and 1500 flat-bottomed barges were built to convey it across the Channel. Ingenious ideas were devised to carry the troops (see the pictures of the balloon and the floating fortress) but Britain's navy stood in the way of Napoleon's success. The French army waited for the arrival of

2. A floating fortress

Admiral Villeneuve with French and Spanish ships to escort it across
the Channel. However, the French and Spanish fleets were
imprisoned in the ports of Brest and Toulon, blockaded by British
ships, and further British ships guarded the Channel.

Napoleon devised a clever plan of campaign. He decided to break
the British blockade of French ports and send his ships across the
Atlantic on a false trail, acting as decoys to lure the British ships out
of the Channel. Then his ships would double back and enter the
Channel unopposed to escort his invasion fleet to Britain. According
to plan, in March 1805 Villeneuve slipped out of Toulon, picked up
a Spanish squadron at Cadiz and reached Martinique with Nelson,
after a false start, on his heels (see Fig. 5, The Trafalgar Campaign).
Villeneuve quickly left Martinique for Europe but he failed to link
up with the Brest squadron which was still blockaded in port. When
Nelson realized the French plan he sent a warning of Villeneuve's
approach and a British squadron under Sir Robert Calder
(1745 – 1818) was sent to intercept him. A battle took place off Cape
Finistere and at the end of it Villeneuve turned south for Spain and
put into Cadiz harbour.

Next Napoleon ordered Villeneuve to re-enter the Mediterranean
and intercept a British convoy. But by now Nelson was waiting for
him. It was while he was carrying out Napoleon's orders that on 21
October 1805 Nelson attacked Villeneuve off Cape Trafalgar. The
battle was marked by Nelson's famous signal 'England expects that
every man will do his duty', and by the destruction of two-thirds of

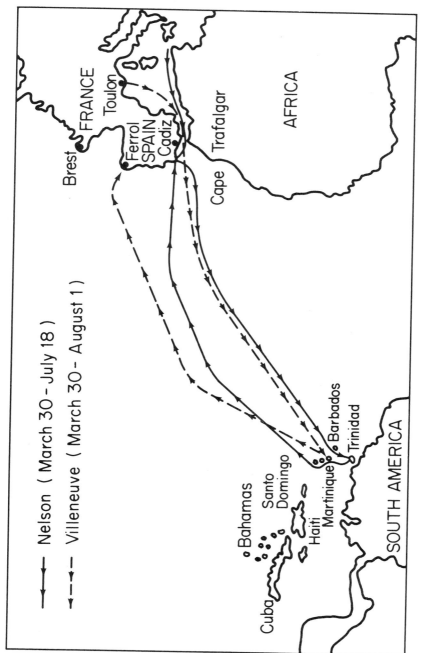

Fig. 5 The Trafalgar Campaign, 1805

the enemy's ships. It was Britain's greatest naval victory, marred only by the death of Nelson. As a result of Trafalgar Britain no longer feared invasion. It also became clear that to break the deadlock between an invincible naval power and an all-conquering land empire experiments would have to be made on both sides to fight opponents who could not directly be reached. From Trafalgar Britain learned that she might defeat France by sea if she could find a point on the Continent from which to fight, a point where the navy might act as a means of supply and defence.

After Trafalgar Pitt was honoured as the saviour of Britain. In a speech at the Lord Mayor's banquet in London he dismissed all praise, declaring, 'Europe is not to be saved by any single man. England has saved herself by her exertions and will, I trust, save Europe by her example'. Two months later, at the age of 46, Pitt was dead.

2 Domestic Policy

The French revolutionary war changed the character of Pitt's government. It became more conservative with its members and supporters constantly on the defensive. Ideas for reform were replaced by fears of radical upheaval. The war undid all Pitt's earlier achievements and by 1800 he spoke of 'evils and growing dangers of which I see no adequate remedy'. In the end the anxiety and tension of the war years broke his health and finally led to his death.

Repressive Measures

Fears that revolutionary ideas might spread from France to England led Pitt to act with a firmness that bordered on desperation. He set up a secret parliamentary committee to investigate various societies which were promoting reform in Britain by peaceful means. From 1793 onwards there was a succession of prosecutions in the courts against editors, authors, preachers and the leaders of reform groups. In May 1794 the secret committee reported that several societies were preparing to distribute arms to their members. Pitt immediately reacted by suspending the *Habeas Corpus* Act which meant that suspects could be imprisoned without a trial.

One of the first organizations to come under attack from the government was the London Corresponding Society founded by the shoemaker, Thomas Hardy (1752 – 1832). The society called for manhood suffrage, annual Parliaments, an end to enclosures and a simpler legal system. It soon had links with Manchester, Stockport, Norwich and Cheshire. Inevitably, it looked to France for inspiration. Hardy and a group of leading reformers were arrested in 1794 and charged with high treason. Eventually he and the other English reformers were acquitted, but similar trials in Scotland resulted in savage sentences of transportation and death. Pitt upheld the actions of the Scottish judges because he feared 'an enormous torrent of insurrection which would sweep away all the barriers of government, law and religion'. In 1799 the Corresponding Society and other organizations with linked branches, oaths or secret offices were suppressed.

The bad harvest of 1794 led to high food prices and considerable discontent. There were mass demonstrations in favour of peace during which a stone was thrown at the King. In 1795 Parliament passed two Acts to restore order. The Seditious Meetings Act prohibited meetings of more than 50 people, except where a licence was obtained from the local magistrate. The Treasonable Practices Act redefined the law of treason. Anyone who devised evil against the King, plotted to help invaders or sought to co-erce Parliament was guilty of treason. Anyone who attacked the constitution was liable to seven years' transportation.

At the end of this period of popular agitation Charles Grey (1764 – 1845), one of Fox's disciples, introduced a motion in the Commons for parliamentary reform. Pitt was opposed to the idea and, after a vote of 256 to 91 rejecting Grey's proposals, the Foxites decided to stay away from Parliament for some months.

In 1798 there was industrial unrest in Britain for the war was having a damaging effect on Britain's economy. The government responded by passing the Newspaper Publication Act which put publishers under the supervision of magistrates. In 1799 and 1800 trade unions came under attack from the Anti-Combinations Acts which stated that all combinations of workmen to persuade their employers to shorten hours or increase wages were to be punished. These Acts had little to do with the struggle against France or the fear of radical ideas. They were, according to J.Steven Watson, 'the first signs of a rising class struggle, of a new age of conflict which marked the nineteenth century'.

Financial Measures

The crises of 1797 led to a financial panic in Britain. There was a run on the banks which forced the government to suspend payments in gold and introduce a paper currency. Another innovation introduced by the government was income tax. Pitt had always wanted to avoid running the war on the basis of debt. However, by 1797 he faced a deficit of £19,000,000. He decided to introduce a tax on income from land, property, trade, professions, pensions and employment. Anyone earning more than £60 a year was liable to pay tax, which was graduated on incomes of between £60 and £200 a year. People who earned more than £200 a year had to pay a tax of 10 per cent on their incomes. Although the tax was criticized it was accepted as the price of war and yielded £5,000,000 a year.

How did the French Revolution Affect Pitt's Domestic Policies?
The French Revolution wrecked Pitt's health and it is also said to have wrecked his idealism. However, it is a mistake to see the young Pitt as a reformer and the middle-aged Pitt, battling against revolutionary France, as a reactionary. To him the law on *Habeas Corpus* was always of less interest than the cause of efficient administration. Come war or peace, Pitt was determined to improve the system of government and make it more efficient. Yet there is no doubt that the government over-reacted when introducing repressive legislation. One indication that the government was unnecessarily alarmed was that all its repressive measures were calmly accepted by a docile population. Most people were disillusioned by events across the Channel and had no intention of starting a revolution in Britain.

3 Ireland and Pitt's Resignation

The war with France intensified the Irish problem. Problems in Ireland had troubled England for many years but during Pitt's ministry they reached new heights. Pitt prevented Ireland from becoming a springboard for revolution in England and in 1800 he passed the Act of Union which united the Irish and British Parliaments. However, it was not a complete success for Pitt was unable to obtain Catholic emancipation, a proposal which he had promised the Irish; and so he felt obliged to resign in 1801.

The Irish Problem
Three areas of life in Ireland were unsatisfactory for the majority of its inhabitants. Irish peasants had the lowest standard of living in Europe. There was no agricultural revolution and no industrial development in Ireland. General economic problems were aggravated by the specific problem of land tenure. Most landlords rented their land to tenants at will, giving the tenants no security of tenure. In addition the official church in Ireland was not the one to which most people belonged. Four-fifths of the Irish population was Catholic and they resented paying tithes to the Protestant Church of

Ireland which already had generous endowments. Finally, no Catholic was allowed to stand for Parliament or become an MP. Even the Protestants who controlled the Irish government wanted to change this and to achieve a far greater degree of self-government than the English seemed prepared to concede. The Irish problem may be summed up as a combination of economic, religious and political factors.

Henry Grattan (1746 – 1820)

During the American War of Independence Henry Grattan, a Protestant Irishman, had organized the United Volunteers to protect Ireland from French invasion. In return he had secured concessions from the British government. In 1778 Roman Catholics were allowed to inherit property and hold long leases and in 1779 Irish ships were allowed to sail as British. In 1782 the Irish Parliament was given complete legislative independence. These measures had helped to alleviate the Irish problem but they had not solved it. After Pitt's failure to give Ireland free trade in 1785 resentment against the English was renewed. The outbreak of war in Europe made Pitt anxious to keep the two countries in harmony so that they would be better able to face a hostile world.

Theobald Wolfe Tone (1763 – 98)

When war in Europe threatened England several Irishmen believed that this was an ideal time to sever all links with that country. Britain was weak and the French had promised to help all peoples who were struggling to overthrow their kings. In 1791 Theobald Wolfe Tone, a Belfast lawyer, founded the Society of United Irishmen whose aim initially was to free Ireland from English control and establish religious equality. Gradually the society became a predominantly Roman Catholic organization whose aim was to overthrow English rule with the help of the French.

In 1795 Wolfe Tone set sail for America and then in 1796 he went to Paris to promote a French expedition against Ireland. He took part in Hoche's expedition which was dispersed in Bantry Bay. Repressive measures followed and the United Irishmen realized that if they did not immediately strike for freedom all would be lost. This meant that they could not synchronize their movements with the French. In 1798 their rebellion was easily crushed at Vinegar Hill near Wexford. Wolfe Tone, together with French troops, arrived too late. The small French squadron was captured in Lough Swilly. Wolfe Tone was condemned for treason by a court martial and cut his throat in prison. After this the Irish rebellion was at an end, but the Irish problem was still pressing.

The Act of Union, 1800

Pitt realized that a solution to the Irish problem was essential for success in war. He decided that to prevent Ireland from acting as a constant thorn in England's side the two countries must be united. He saw that unity alone would not necessarily stop unrest and declared, 'until the Catholics are admitted into a general participation of rights there will be no peace or safety in Ireland'. However, since there was such strong opposition to Catholic emancipation in the Protestant-dominated Irish Parliament and government Pitt decided not to include Catholic emancipation in the Act of Union but to grant it afterwards. In spite of this the Irish Parliament rejected the Bill in 1799. Pitt, Cornwallis and Castlereagh persuaded the Irish Parliament to agree to its own abolition in 1800.

George III signed the Act of Union on 1 August 1800 and it came into force in the following year. The Act stated that Ireland was to be joined with Great Britain into a single kingdom. The Dublin Parliament was to be abolished and Ireland was to be represented at Westminster by 100 Irish MPs and by 28 Irish peers and four bishops in the House of Lords. The Anglican church was to be the official church of Ireland. There was to be free trade between England and Ireland. Ireland was to keep a separate Exchequer and to be responsible for two-seventeenths of the expenses of the United Kingdom.

Pitt's Resignation

Once the Act of Union was passed Pitt felt compelled to keep his promise to the Irish of Catholic emancipation. Without this promise Irish Catholics would not have supported the union. On 28 January 1801 George III condemned Catholic emancipation as 'the most Jacobinical thing I have ever heard'. He declared that he would consider 'any man my personal enemy who proposes any such measure'. The King would never consent to Catholic emancipation, since he believed that to do so would be to violate his coronation oath in which he had sworn to uphold the privileges of the Church of England. In the end Pitt was forced to abandon Catholic emancipation and resign. He promised George III that he would never raise the subject again.

Summary

From 1793 to 1806, with a break of only a short time, Pitt led Britain in the fight against France. He helped to create three European coalitions but saw each of them collapse in the face of French troops. In spite of his many failures in Europe Pitt justly deserves Canning's description of him as 'the pilot that weathered the storm'. He is accorded with less praise for his domestic and Irish policies where his earlier regard for reform was cast aside to be replaced by repressive measures. Nevertheless, there is little doubt that Britain's youngest Prime Minister was also one of her greatest Prime Ministers.

Exercises

1. Account for the outbreak of war between Britain and France in 1793.
2. Describe any three naval engagements in which the British took part between 1793 and 1806. Explain the results of the engagements.
3. In what ways do you consider that Pitt's conduct of the war was unwise?
4. Show why Pitt felt compelled to resort to policies of repression after 1793.
5. Why did Pitt feel compelled to resign in 1801?

8
The Fight Against France, 1806 – 15

On the death of William Pitt Britain was governed by a 'Ministry of All the Talents' which included Fox, Addington and Grenville. They proposed to end the war with France but in September 1806 Fox died and the ministry collapsed. Grenville succeeded Fox as head of the government whilst the followers of Pitt, led by George Canning (1770 – 1827) who referred to this group as Tories, went into opposition. Grenville was dismissed in 1807 because his ministry supported Catholic emancipation and the Duke of Portland (1738 – 1809), a Tory, formed a government which lasted until 1809. He was succeeded by Spencer Percival (1762 – 1812) who was assassinated in May 1812. Lord Liverpool (1770 – 1828) then became

Prime Minister and, together with his Foreign Secretary, Lord Castlereagh (1769 – 1821) who was also the leader of the House of Commons, he governed Britain in the closing stages of the war with France.

The Collapse of the Third Coalition, 1807

By 1806 the third coalition was in danger of collapse. Austria had been defeated at Austerlitz and withdrawn from the coalition. In 1806 Prussia entered the coalition only to be defeated almost immediately by Napoleon at Jena. In 1807 the Russians were defeated at the battle of Friedland and retired from the coalition, leaving Britain once more alone. By the end of June 1807 Napoleon and Alexander of Russia had met on a raft at Niemen at Tilsit where they made peace and formed a pact to ruin England. Russia promised to close her ports to British ships and to force Denmark, Sweden and Portugal to join in the economic warfare against Britain. In return for her support in Europe Russia would be allowed to influence Dalmatia and govern Turkey.

When the Portland government heard about Tilsit they had to act quickly to prevent Denmark from being taken over by France. The government feared that if Denmark fell into French hands the French would not only gain a large fleet but an additional stretch of coastline which would further isolate Britain and renew the danger of invasion. A British fleet under Admiral Gambier (1756 – 1833) captured the Danish fleet and thereby prevented it from falling into French hands.

Economic Warfare

When the third coalition collapsed there was a repetition of the situation of stalemate in which Britain was supreme at sea whilst France was supreme on land. Since Napoleon could not defeat Britain directly he turned his attention to economic warfare and devised the continental system. Ever since 1797 the French had been trying to damage Britain's commerce to reduce her wealth and strength so that Napoleon's plans were by no means original. What was new after 1806 was Napoleon's immense power and the extent to which he dominated Europe. On 21 November 1806 he issued the Berlin Decree which placed the British Isles in a state of blockade and stated that no vessel coming directly from Britain or her colonies could be received in the ports under his control. In this way Napoleon hoped to damage British industry and cause a currency crisis in Britain for she would have to pay for her imports in gold instead of with exports.

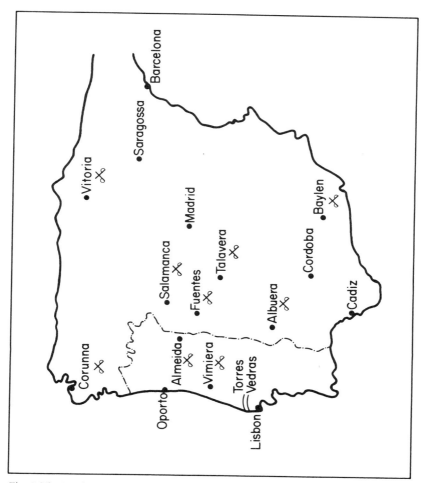

Fig.6 The Peninsular War, 1808–14

In 1807 Britain retaliated with orders in council which declared
that she would prevent ships of any other country entering ports

from which British ships were excluded. Napoleon answered in his turn on 23 November 1807 when he issued the Milan Decree. He replaced the prohibition of goods 'coming directly' from England by a provision which stated that all ships entering European ports which had touched down in England were to be confiscated and goods were deemed to be English unless it could be proved otherwise.

The continental system seriously damaged Britain's trade. 1811 was the worst year for Britain economically. In that year British exports to northern Europe fell to only 20 per cent of their 1810 level. The trade crisis was accompanied by monetary troubles. Firms went bankrupt and there were bad harvests in 1809 and 1810. By May 1811 Lancashire was working a three-day week and the workers' remedy for unemployment was machine breaking (see p.86). Napoleon failed to take advantage of Britain's partial collapse and he even had to break his own rules by ordering British supplies for his troops. Britain survived by trading with countries outside Europe and she was pleased to see that the orders in council which deprived Europe of manufactured goods was leading to increased resentment of France.

War Between Britain and the USA, 1812 – 14

Neutral countries suffered as a result of the economic warfare in Europe. Their trading vessels risked detention by the British navy or confiscation in Napoleon's ports. The United States had their vessels searched from 1808 onwards by Britain and this led to tension between the two countries. Britain finally agreed to exempt the United States from the orders in council but this concession came too late to prevent war between Britain and the United States. The war lasted from 1812 to 1814. It was marked by an unsuccessful American attempt to invade Canada, a number of naval encounters and the burning of public buildings in Washington by a British force. The war ended in December 1814 with the Treaty of Ghent with both sides reverting to their position before the war. Throughout the war Britain had always regarded its events as a side-show, an inconvenient distraction from the conflict with France. Once the war ended Britain gave her undivided attention to the defeat of France.

The Peninsular War, 1808 – 13

If the continental system was to succeed Napoleon would have to control the whole of western Europe including Spain and Portugal. As his ally, Spain could be counted on for support but Portugal was traditionally an ally of Britain and Britain used Portuguese ports to break the continental system. In 1807 the Spaniards agreed to allow Napoleon to send troops through Spain to attack Portugal. The French army arrived in Lisbon in November 1807 to see the Portuguese fleet sailing away. In the course of sending his army to Lisbon Napoleon had become involved in the politics of the Spanish court. In April 1808 Napoleon installed his brother Joseph as King of Spain declaring, 'Your nation is old: my mission is to restore its youth'. Spain reacted violently to this interference in her internal politics and began a campaign against the French. Sir Arthur Wellesley (1769 – 1852), leading 10,000 troops, was sent to help the Spaniards and Portuguese fight the Peninsular War against the French.

Sir Arthur Wellesley won battles at Rolica and Vimiero (see Fig. 6, The Peninsular War) in August 1808, but Britain immediately forfeited the gains won by the army due to petty personal squabbles. Wellesley was replaced by two uninspired senior officers who lacked the spirit of victory and on 30 August signed the Convention of Cintra with the French. By this convention French troops in Portugal gave up the fight but were allowed to return to France with all their arms and equipment. This provoked an outcry of indignation in Britain for the people, starved of military success, saw all their gains being thrown away by incompetent officers.

Whilst Britain held a post mortem on the Convention of Cintra Napoleon marched into Spain and on 5 November Madrid surrendered to him. The British army, led by Sir John Moore (1761 – 1809), was marching from Portugal to help the Spaniards when it heard of the fall of Madrid. Moore had reached Salamanca and prepared for a retreat into Portugal when he decided to turn north to cut Napoleon's lines of communication with France. His troop of 30,000 appeared at the rear of a quarter of a million of Napoleon's army. Napoleon detached half his force from Madrid and turned back to attack Moore, who retreated to Corunna and saw 24,000 of his 30,000 men embark on British ships before Napoleon could attack them. Moore was killed at Corunna but he had prevented France from subduing southern Spain. The French were unable to subdue the whole of Spain for events in Europe had taken a worrying turn for them, and on 22 January 1809 Napoleon left Spain to deal with the Austrians.

In April 1809 Sir Arthur Wellesley returned to resume command in Spain. In May 1809 he won a battle at Oporto and in July he was victorious at Talavera and was given the title of Viscount Wellington of Talavera. When France defeated Austria at Wagram troops were released for use in the Peninsular War and Napoleon appointed

Marshal Massena to command his army and speedily subdue Portugal. Wellington wanted to delay the enemy until the harvest was gathered and stores completed. On the frontiers Ciudad Rodrigo and Almeida were told to fight to the end. By these means Wellington prevented the French from making a push into Portugal until the late summer of 1810. Eventually Wellington was forced to retire to a position behind the lines of Torres Vedras, three ranges of defence which barred Massena from Lisbon. The French sat down beyond the lines and endured a winter of torment whilst British troops were amply supplied by the British navy from the sea. By March 1811, having lost 25,000 men, the French were forced to withdraw. Wellington followed hard on their heels and freed all of Portugal. In 1812 Wellington took Ciudad Rodrigo, Badajoz and Salamanca. He went on to occupy Valladolid and Madrid. In June 1813 Wellington won battles at Burgos, Vittoria, San Sebastian and Pamplona. He chased the French across the Pyrenees until not a single French soldier was left in Spain.

Napoleon referred to the Peninsular War as the 'Spanish ulcer' for it was a constant irritant to him. The Spaniards adopted guerilla tactics for which the French troops were unprepared. In addition France found it difficult to supply her troops overland whilst Britain supplied her army quite easily from the sea. Napoleon's efforts in Spain were hampered by the fact that he was forced to withdraw troops to fight against first Austria and then Russia. His generals quarreled amongst themselves whereas Britain was fortunate in having Wellington as her commander. He transformed British troops into an efficient fighting force and deserves credit for Britain's success in the Peninsular War.

Napoleon at the Height of His Career, 1810
The height of Napoleon Bonaparte's career seemed to correspond with the height of the Peninsular War. Even though all was not going smoothly for Napoleon in Spain and Portugal, elsewhere in Europe his position seemed secure. In 1809 a British expedition to seize the island of Walcheren in the river Scheldt, as a preliminary to closing the river and capturing Antwerp, ended in disaster. Also in 1809, Austria was defeated at Wagram and forced to sign a humiliating peace. In 1810 France dominated Europe (see Fig. 7, Napoleonic Europe, 1810). However, it was not long before France was on the defensive with Napoleon struggling to maintain his supremacy.

The Moscow Campaign, 1812
The agreement drawn up between France and Russia at Tilsit had

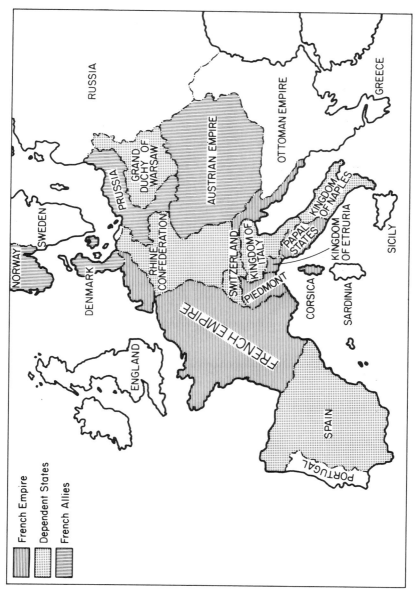

Fig.7 Napoleonic Europe, 1810

never worked. Neither side could watch the other making gains without fearing for its security. Russia demanded that France be less aggressive in Europe and cease to dominate Poland, Prussia and Sweden. For her part France did not wish to see Russia gain control of Constantinople. Napoleon was furious when in 1810 the Czar allowed English goods in neutral ships into Russian ports. In 1812 he decided to teach the Russians a lesson. He was confident that once Russia was defeated he would then be able to defeat England.

Napoleon created a grand army of 700,000 men and invaded Russia. Instead of fighting, the Russians retreated and he was unopposed as far as Smolensk. As the Russians simply retreated into the interior they adopted a 'scorched earth' policy, destroying crops, animals and buildings as they went. This made it difficult for Napoleon's army to obtain enough supplies. After a victory at Smolensk and an indecisive battle at Borodino Napoleon occupied Moscow on 14 September 1812. By refusing to talk or to fight Alexander forced Napoleon into his nightmare retreat from Moscow, in which his troops encountered the horrors of the Russian winter which added to the problems created by inadequate supplies. Napoleon arrived in Paris on 5 December. His grand army had ceased to exist for he had lost 400,000 men dead or wounded and 100,000 prisoners. Undaunted by this he planned to create another army, but his first task was to kill the French officers in Paris who had plotted against him in his absence.

The Fourth Coalition and the Battle of Leipzig, 1813

Napoleon's defeat in the Moscow campaign encouraged Britain, Austria, Prussia, Russia and Sweden to form the fourth coalition in 1813. Whilst the coalition was being formed Napoleon had created a new army. Even though it consisted of poorly trained men the allies found it difficult to defeat him. However, on 16, 17 and 18 October at the 'battle of the nations' in Leipzig the allies defeated France and proved that Napoleon was no longer invincible in Europe. By 1814 troops had invaded France from the east and Wellington had invaded from the south. On 31 March 1814 Paris fell into allied hands. Napoleon was banished to the island of Elba in the Mediterranean and the Bourbon King Louis XVIII was installed in Paris as a constitutional monarch. The allies turned their attention to working out the details of a peace treaty.

The Hundred Days and the Battle of Waterloo, 1815

Napoleon spent little more than 10 months in exile before escaping from Elba and returning to France. He landed in France on 1 March

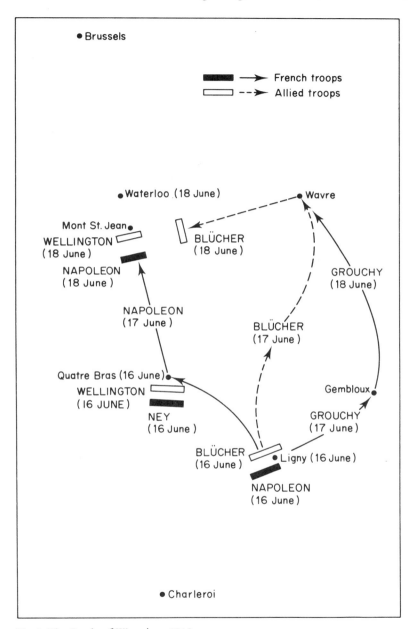

Fig.8 The Battle of Waterloo, 1815

1815 and there followed the Hundred Days in which he once more struck fear into the hearts of the allies. Within three weeks of his return to France Louis XVIII had fled and Napoleon had created an army. Castlereagh quickly reconstructed the fourth coalition. Napoleon did not want to be attacked and so he took the initiative and went on the offensive before Britain, Russia, Austria and Prussia could co-ordinate their armies.

Napoleon left Paris on 12 June 1815, intending to drive a wedge between the British and Prussian forces, capture Belgium and then defeat Austria and Russia. He attacked Prussian troops on the Sambre on 15 June and on 16 June part of Prussia's forces, led by Blücher, was defeated at Ligny. Wellington had gathered his forces at Quatre Bras to aid Blücher, but he was himself attacked on 16 June by Marshal Ney. Blücher fell back to Wavre during the night of the 16 and 17 June and Wellington followed suit, establishing himself at Waterloo, (see Fig. 8, Battle of Waterloo). Napoleon aimed to defeat Wellington before Blücher could join forces with him. On 18 June Napoleon attacked Wellington's army which withstood repeated charges of cavalry and infantry. By the afternoon Blücher had managed to evade the French troops which were preventing him from coming to Britain's aid. The French army was defeated in a battle which Wellington described as 'the nearest run thing you ever saw in your life'. Napoleon fled to Paris. He surrendered to Britain and was imprisoned on St Helena in the south Atlantic where he died in 1821.

Summary

In 1806 Britain's fortunes in Europe took a downward turn. Her government wanted peace with France but Napoleon would settle for nothing short of British surrender. Britain was faced with desperate economic warfare which brought her to the verge of collapse and led to war with the United States. When all seemed to be lost the Duke of Wellington gave Britain a much needed victory and boost to morale in the Peninsular War. From 1810 onwards Napoleon's power declined as he turned desperately from one theatre of war to another in search of victory. After his defeat in Russia the allies genuinely acted in concert for the first time and this led to victory at Waterloo in 1815.

Exercises
1. What was the continental system? What were its effects on Britain?

2. Describe the contribution made by Wellington to the struggle against Napoleon.
3. Why was Britain successful in the Peninsular War?
4. What were the origins of the Moscow campaign?
5. Why did Wellington describe Waterloo as 'the nearest run thing you ever saw in your life'?

9
Social Unrest and Government Repression, 1815 – 21

For five years after 1815 Britain was in a state of crisis. Rapid industrialization and population growth created a strain which was intensified first by war and then by the uncertainties of peace. Throughout this period the Tory government adopted a negative attitude to all forms of popular discontent, viewing unrest as a threat of revolution. Discontent began to decline in 1820, not because repression had succeeded, but because there was an upturn in trade and employment. Once distress ended popular agitation declined.

The Tory Government
There were few changes of personnel in the Tory government which remained in office from 1812 to 1822. Lord Liverpool was Prime Minister from 1812 to 1827. He was interested in the country's economic progress but, believing in *laissez-faire*, he did little to aid progress by government action. Viscount Sidmouth was Home Secretary from 1812 to 1822 and the man directly responsible for the repressive measures taken during this period. As Lord Chancellor from 1807 to 1827 Lord Eldon (1751 – 1838) was responsible for drafting the repressive legislation from 1817 to 1819. Viscount Castlereagh was Foreign Secretary and Leader of the House of Commons from 1812 until his death in 1822. Although he was mainly concerned with foreign policy, as the government spokes-

man in the Commons, he was closely identified with the repressive measures of the period.

1 The Radicals

In the nineteenth century there were a number of people who opposed the government and wished to reform the social and political system. They were known as radicals, but they were neither an organized party nor a united group of men.

Major John Cartwright (1740 – 1824)

Throughout his life Major John Cartwright carried out a ceaseless campaign for universal suffrage, annual Parliaments, and the secret ballot. With Sir Francis Burdett (1770 – 1844) he founded the Hampden Club in 1811. The club's aim was to build up support for a new electoral system. Cartwright travelled the country, speaking to working-class audiences in the industrial towns, and after each meeting petitions in favour of universal suffrage were sent to Westminster.

Thomas Spence (1750 – 1814)

Thomas Spence believed that the cure for all ills was a programme of land reform together with the imposition of a single tax to replace all other forms of taxation. His ideas were published in a book *The Restorer of Society to its Natural State* which resulted in a 12 months' prison sentence for him. Although Spence had only a handful of followers they were very well organized and were responsible for most of the big working-class demonstrations in London from 1816 to 1820.

William Cobbett (1763 – 1835)

Perhaps the most famous of all the radicals of this period was William Cobbett. Born in Surrey, he became a solicitor's clerk and then a soldier. After a stay in America in which he criticized the views of Tom Paine he returned to England in 1802 and founded a newspaper called *The Weekly Political Register*. At first his sympathies lay with the Tories. He criticized the bleak new towns and longed for a return to pre-industrial days. However, by 1805 he had become a committed radical.

Cobbett pioneered the popular press. In his newspaper he called for parliamentary reform and criticized the poor law, the factory system, the Corn Law and Lord Liverpool's government. However, at one shilling per copy *The Political Register* was too expensive for most working-class readers. Cobbett decided to evade the stamp duty and published a cheap edition of *The Political Register* in the form of a commentary for twopence. In 1819 the law was changed to include commentaries in the stamped press. *The Political Register* went underground; it was published secretly and unstamped and continued to sell over 60,000 copies.

The Radical Press
The Political Register was not the only publication of the unstamped press. Many writers followed Cobbett's example and defied the law since a stamp would make their papers too expensive for their working-class readership. T.J. Wooler (1786 – 1853) issued *The Black Dwarf* which carried contributions from Cartwright and Henry Hunt (1773 – 1835). Those who contributed to or published radical newspapers were frequently fined or imprisoned. They played an important part in maintaining working-class morale throughout the years of government repression.

Francis Place (1771 – 1854)
Francis Place was a central figure in the radical movement. His childhood was spent in great poverty and he was first employed as a leather breeches maker. Later, he became quite prosperous as a tailor and employed several journeymen. In his tailor's shop near Charing Cross he converted a back room into a working men's library and radical meeting place. From this room Place played an important part in the repeal of the Anti-Combination Laws and in the campaigns for parliamentary reform and the People's Charter.

Henry Hunt
Henry Hunt was the most prominent radical orator. He advocated parliamentary reform, believing that from a reformed Parliament would come social and economic reforms.

Radical MPs
The number of radical MPs was always very small. After 1815 the most active radicals in Parliament were Hume, Romilly, Burdett and Bennet. Joseph Hume (1777 – 1855) was active in the campaign to repeal the Anti-Combination Laws and he was an expert on government finance, helping to reduce taxes. Sir Samuel Romilly (1757 – 1818) specialized in penal reform. Sir Francis Burdett gained a reputation for his defence of free speech and his criticism of the suspension of *Habeas Corpus* in 1817. Henry Grey Bennet (1777 – 1836) worked to improve the lot of child chimney sweeps

and prisoners. He was also highly critical of the government's use of informers.

2 The Causes of Unrest

Many factors were responsible for the state of unrest which existed in Britain in 1815. The prolonged war against revolutionary France led to distress and the end of the war, far from bringing relief, created new hardships. In addition the scale and pace of economic change caused problems. The stresses and strains of life in the new towns were complicated by fluctuations in trade which led to unemployment and poverty for thousands of people. Finally, many people blamed the government for adopting unimaginative policies which did little or nothing to help the situation.

Rapid Economic Change

One source of discontent amongst the labouring classes arose from the rapid economic change which Britain experienced in the eighteenth century, the effects of which continued to be felt after 1815. At the time of the agricultural revolution enclosures had reduced the smaller peasant farmers to the status of landless labourers. The poor who remained in the countryside suffered from a decline in domestic textile work and the loss of common rights. The Speenhamland System, begun in 1795 to help the rural poor, led only to further hardships and humiliation (see p.124). Meanwhile, in the new industrial towns, men, women and children worked long hours in the factories in appalling conditions and returned exhausted to their insanitary, overcrowded homes. Wages were low in spite of the long hours and many people blamed the new machinery both for low wages and unemployment.

The Post-war Slump

After the Napoleonic Wars British industry and agriculture entered a period of economic depression. When the war ended government contracts for arms, clothing and other supplies came to an end. By the end of 1815 government spending was dramatically reduced and this created unemployment in the industries which had supplied the government's war needs. It was not easy for the 300,000 demobilized soldiers and sailors to find work in an already overcrowded labour market. Most European countries were devastated by the French wars and were not in a position to import goods from Britain, nor could most British people afford to buy manufactured goods. Agriculture was also hard hit by the ending of the war. In 1815 many farmers were burdened by debts and heavy poor rates and there were frequent bankruptcies. Stagnation in industry and agriculture led to great hardship for many people in post-war Britain.

The Corn Law, 1815

Although Lord Liverpool believed in *laissez faire* he was prepared to intervene in the economy to help Britain's farmers. In 1815 he passed the Corn Law in an attempt to prevent a fall in the price of corn from its wartime levels to a price which would endanger farmers' profits. The landed interest dominated Parliament and this accounts for the ease with which the Corn Law was passed. The law forbade the import of foreign grain, which was often cheaper than British grain, until the domestic price rose above 80 shillings a quarter. However, the law never worked as intended and prices fluctuated wildly. At the start of 1816 the price stood at 48 shillings, but later in the same year after a poor harvest it had risen to 103 shillings. To the many people who could no longer afford bread the Corn Law demonstrated the corruptness of the Tory government. High bread prices and near starvation were a continuing source of unrest from 1815 to 1821.

Financial Measures

Lord Liverpool's financial measures aroused resentment and hostility towards his government. His action on income tax was seen as selfish and callous. Income tax had been introduced in 1797 to meet the heavy costs of the French Wars (see p.67). During the war the national debt rose from £247,000,000 in 1792 to £902,000,000 in 1816 and the annual interest to be paid to debt holders rose correspondingly from £9,000,000 to over £31,000,000. In 1815 income tax yielded £15,000,000 or about one quarter of the government's revenue and the Tories were in no hurry to remove it. However, in 1816 Liverpool came under pressure from a flood of petitions and an attack on behalf of the wealthy was launched against him by Henry Brougham (1778 – 1868). The Prime Minister decided to remove the tax and replace it with indirect taxes which fell heaviest on the poor. The radicals criticized the abolition of income tax and also attacked the government's return to the gold standard in 1819, arguing that it produced a fall in prices and increased the burden of the national debt.

3 Demonstrations and Outbreaks of Unrest

From 1815 to 1820 the Tory government was faced with a number of outbreaks of disorder. The first sign of unrest occurred in the eastern counties where labourers protested against falling wages and rising food prices. They used violent tactics in an attempt to secure relief. Violent demonstrations spread to a number of industrial centres from south Wales to Scotland. London did not escape the unrest. In the capital demonstrations were well-organized on a massive scale by radicals who wished to make London the centre of a nation wide agitation for reform.

The Luddite Movement, 1811

The Luddite movement, named after Nedd Ludd, began in Nottingham in 1811. The Luddites' aim was to destroy the new machines which were replacing skilled workers in the hosiery business. Handloom weavers in Lancashire and Cheshire adopted the same tactics and smashed the new power looms which threatened their livelihood. After 1815 outbreaks of machine smashing spread to the countryside, notably to Littleport in the Isle of Ely.

Spa Fields, 1816

1816 was a year of great distress and unemployment. In that year a group known as the Spencean Philanthropists, followers of Thomas Spence, decided to bring pressure to bear on the government to introduce reforms. The Spenceans planned a mass meeting at Spa Fields, Islington, and invited the radical orator Henry Hunt to address it. He, however, did not believe in land reform and wanted to speak in favour of lower taxes and parliamentary reform. After some confusion two mass meetings were held on 2 December 1816. Fired by the propaganda from the platform, a large mob marched through the streets of London. Some wore French revolutionary 'caps of liberty' and carried the tricolour. They broke into a gunsmith's shop, wounded a bystander and marched towards the City where they were dispersed by a force collected by the Lord Mayor.

The Hampden Clubs, 1817

Radical leaders in Westminster planned a more moderate kind of demonstration from the one which had taken place at Spa Fields. They arranged a meeting in London to which the Hampden Clubs throughout the country should send delegates, bearing petitions for the reform of Parliament. After a meeting of all the delegates a petition would be presented to the House of Commons. The meeting was held in January 1817 and was addressed by Cobbett, Hunt and Cartwright. After considerable dispute amongst the leaders about tactics a petition, demanding universal suffrage, was eventually delivered to Westminster. Many delegates returned home disillusioned by the dissension amongst their leaders. They began to feel that peaceful persuasion was not the best line of approach to a government bent on repression.

The March of the Blanketeers, 1817

In 1817 the industrial population continued to suffer from low wages, the high cost of living and unemployment. In Manchester, where many people were on the verge of starvation, a march to London to present a petition for reform to the Prince Regent was organized in the spring of 1817. The men carried blankets for their night shelter and became known as the blanketeers. Magistrates arrested the leaders before the march was under way and most of the rank and file, who were not held up at Stockport, abandoned the scheme at Macclesfield. Wild rumours circulated about the marchers' intentions, but all they wanted was higher wages, lower prices and parliamentary reform.

The Pentrich Rising, 1817

In 1817 Jeremiah Brandreth (d. 1817), an unemployed knitter, planned to stir up the people of Derbyshire to seize Nottingham and then march on London. Brandreth and his followers were caught with weapons in their hands, thanks to the work of Oliver, the government spy. Nineteen men were sentenced to death and four were executed.

The Parliamentary Convention, 1819

In 1817 there was a good harvest and a revival of trade which brought a lull to social unrest. With 1819 came another trade depression coupled with unemployment and falling wages. Reform of Parliament seemed to be a basic pre-condition for much needed economic and social reform. In July 1819 the radicals of Birmingham put forward a new idea — since most people were unrepresented in Parliament, they should elect their own representatives and send them to London to a Parliamentary Convention where they could introduce reforms. Sir Charles Wolseley (1769 – 1846) was chosen as Birmingham's representative. Leeds and Manchester would have taken similar steps if the proceedings had not been declared illegal.

St Peter's Fields, 1819

Since 1815 Manchester had witnessed a good deal of unrest and the renewed economic depression produced still more discontent. Local radicals sought to end distress and to extend political rights. They invited Henry Hunt to address a meeting at St Peter's Fields on 16 August 1819. Men were drilled so that they might march without confusion to the Fields and there were to be no weapons. Opponents of the radicals argued that the men were drilled to prepare for armed resistance. On 16 August approximately 60,000 people assembled to hear Hunt's speech. They carried banners with revolutionary inscriptions but there was no disorder. Soon after the start of the meeting the magistrates, who had brought special constables and detachments of the Lancashire and Cheshire yeomanry, ordered Hunt's arrest. The soldiers who tried to reach the platform used their sabres to clear a way through the crowd. A troop of hussars was ordered in and in the confusion which followed 11 people were killed, including two women, and 400 people were wounded. This incident quickly became known as the Peterloo Massacre.

The Cato Street Conspiracy, 1820

In 1820 an outrageous conspiracy was detected in London which the government used as an example to justify the repressive measures it had taken after Peterloo. The conspiracy centred around Arthur Thistlewood (1770 – 1820) who had been imprisoned after the Spa Fields riot and was released in the autumn of 1819. He hatched a plot to murder the cabinet. This was to be followed by an insurrection and the seizure of London. The plot was discovered and the conspirators were arrested in Cato Street in London. Thistlewood and the other leaders of the conspiracy were executed. Thistlewood was the last person in England to be beheaded.

The Bonnymuir Riot, 1820

In April 1820 discontent led to violence in Scotland. During a strike amongst workers in Glasgow a number of them at Bonnymuir attacked a small group of soldiers who quickly retaliated. The riot was followed by trials and executions.

The Queen Caroline Riots, 1820

In 1820 London was in a state of unrest over the affair of Queen Caroline. It began in 1795 when, nearly 10 years after his illegal marriage to Mrs Fitzherbert (1756 – 1837), the Prince Regent married Princess Caroline of Brunswick (1768 – 1821). The marriage was not a success and in 1806 the Regent persuaded the government to conduct an inquiry into Caroline's conduct in the hope of divorcing her. Although her reputation was damaged, the charges against her were not proved. An important consideration was that the Prince Regent had no heir and wished to remarry to remedy the situation. The Prince Regent's desire to divorce Caroline became an urgent wish in 1820 when he succeeded to the throne and Caroline seemed ready to assert her rights as Queen.

An attempt to buy off Caroline and keep her out of the country failed. She arrived in England in June 1820 and became the centre of popular demonstrations which kept London in a state of uproar for months. The people identified with Caroline, seeing her as an underdog. They used her cause as an excuse to show their hatred for the new King and his government. A Bill of Pains and Penalties, based on the Queen's misdeeds, which included a divorce clause, was introduced in the House of Lords but eventually dropped by the government. Although there was no divorce Caroline was persuaded to abandon her claim to full royal status. She was refused entry to the coronation at Westminster Abbey and when she gave up the attempt the crowd turned against her. She died in the following month. The Queen Caroline affair was soon forgotten, but it had seriously weakened the reputation of the Tory government and the monarch.

4 Government Repression

After 1815 the Tory government seemed determined that the lower orders should be kept in their place. They refused to listen seriously to demands for parliamentary reform, took little interest in the sufferings of the destitute and made no attempt to deal with general economic problems, except where they concerned the landed interest. The government believed that Britain was nearer to revolution during this period than at any time since the seventeenth century (see the cartoon of Radical Reform attacking Britannia). If they could not appeal to reason, the Tories were quite prepared to resort to repression.

The Use of Capital Punishment

The reaction of the government to the activities of the Luddites was to make machine-breaking a capital offence. No doubt this deterred some would-be offenders. However, machine-breaking continued to be a problem for the government.

This Cruikshank cartoon was published in 1819 when social unrest was at its height. Its inscription reads, 'Death or Liberty! or Britannia and the Virtues of the Constitution in danger of Violation from the great Political Libertine, Radical Reform'.

The Use of Informers

The Tories used informers or spies to keep them in touch with radical agitation. Today these men would probably be called detectives. However, many of them acted as *agents provocatuers*, inciting rebellion in men who would otherwise have been quite peaceful. The government used informers to bring revolutionary leaders into the open for two reasons: firstly, to convince moderates of the dangers of revolution; and secondly, to justify its repressive measures. The most notorious informer was William Oliver. Shortly after the Pentrich rising *The Leeds Mercury* revealed the extent to which he had been responsible for the uprising. The government was discredited and thereafter it made less use of informers.

The Use of Troops

Since there was no professional police force in Britain in 1815 the government depended on magistrates to maintain public order. Magistrates had the power to call out the county yeomanry to deal with major disturbances. However, if rioting was extensive the army was called out. Troops were used to deal with machine-breaking in the riots of 1811 – 12. They were called out again from February 1817 to January 1818 and from August 1819 to the spring of 1820.

The Suspension of Habeas Corpus, 1817

The Tories were already alarmed by the Spa Fields meeting when in January 1817 someone threw a stone at the Prince Regent's carriage and broke a window. At the same time alarming evidence, produced by Sidmouth's spies, of a plot to seize the Bank of England and the Tower of London, was reported to Parliament. The government's response was the introduction of an Act to suspend *Habeas Corpus*, enabling people to be imprisoned without trial. The measure passed through both Houses of Parliament within a week and remained in force for 11 months.

The Seditious Meetings Act, 1817

This Act introduced measures against the holding of seditious meetings or attempts to weaken the loyalty of the troops.

Press Censorship, 1817

In 1817 Sidmouth secured a commission of inquiry which was followed by government measures against authors and printers of seditious and blasphemous pamphlets. Castlereagh believed that the unrest of 1816 and 1817 was caused by 'poisonous propaganda disseminated by men of culture and ability among the ignorant and suffering'. It was believed that press censorship would help to reduce unrest.

The Six Acts, 1819

The Peterloo Massacre caused great indignation throughout the country. The public was highly critical of the violence and deaths which had occurred in Manchester. The government took no notice of all the protests and made it clear that it supported the magistrates' decision to break up the meeting at St Peter's Fields. The Tories' response to the Peterloo Massacre was to add 10,000 men to the army and to summon a special session of Parliament to pass the Six Acts. The first of the Acts forbade assembly for carrying out drill or any other military exercises. The second made it illegal to possess or carry arms. The third imposed restrictions on the right of public meeting by limiting attendance at a meeting to the residents of the parish where it was held. The fourth Act imposed penalties for the publication of blasphemous or seditious libel. The fifth extended the stamp duty to pamphlets and other forms of political comment. The final Act put an end to legal delays which might work to the advantage of an accused person.

Summary

The years 1815 to 1821 were characterized by poverty and suffering amongst the working classes and increasing government repression in response to social unrest. Few people wanted a revolution. The leading radicals all favoured reform and had no wish to subvert the constitution. The radicals were weakened by divisions amongst themselves. Once there was an improvement in employment and trade after 1820 the radical cause declined in popularity. The Tory government has been accused of adopting a completely negative attitude to the problems of the day. Outbreaks of disorder were dealt with by unimaginative panic measures. Lord Liverpool, it is suggested, was far more interested in foreign policy and the Corn Law than in personal liberty. Certainly, his government lacked the knowledge and the administrative machinery necessary to alleviate distress, but it also lacked the will.

Exercises
1. What is a radical? Describe the influence of one radical leader in this period.
2. Identify and describe two causes of social discontent in Britain in 1815.

3. Give an account of two major incidents which indicate the existence of unrest in post-war Britain.
4. Describe the legislation introduced by Lord Liverpool to suppress protest.

10
The 'Liberal Tories', 1822–30

In 1822 Lord Liverpool's government appeared to change direction. The years of repression gave way to the dawn of reform. Historians look upon the 1820s as the era of the 'liberal tories'. Three issues dominated the politics of the decade — 'cash, corn and Catholics'. The Tories worked to advance commercial prosperity and to establish law and order. They were also responsible for Catholic emancipation. However, the Tory party was divided on many issues and by 1830 its position was seriously weakened.

Government Personnel
Early in 1822 Lord Liverpool moved Sidmouth from the Home Office and appointed Sir Robert Peel (1788–1850) Home Secretary. When Castlereagh committed suicide in August 1822 Canning became Foreign Secretary. In 1823 Frederick Robinson (1782–1859) was appointed to the Treasury and William Huskisson (1770–1830) to the Board of Trade. Seven former cabinet ministers remained at their posts, but this did not prevent the new men from making their mark on government policy. Unlike their aristocratic colleagues, they had more in common with the middle class. They understood the importance of industry and trade. Their policies were both a response to the country's growing prosperity and a cause of more profitable economic activity.

1 Tory Reforms

William Huskisson at the Board of Trade
William Huskisson entered Parliament in 1796 and later became MP for Liverpool where he was in close touch with commercial interests.

His policies, based on his belief in freer trade, marked a change in direction for the Tories. Huskisson argued that since Britain was more advanced than any other manufacturing country trade regulations were no longer needed.

One of Huskisson's first tasks was to repeal the Navigation Acts. Introduced in the seventeenth century against the Dutch, the object of these Acts was to prevent British cargoes being carried in any but British ships. The Navigation Acts led to retaliation from other countries and Britain benefited from their repeal. British shipping lines flourished under competitive conditions, largely because Britain took the lead in building iron steam ships (see p.276).

Huskisson also attacked many of the duties and prohibitions which regulated trade. By the Reciprocity Act, 1823, the government could conclude treaties with foreign states whereby duties on goods and shipping entering British ports would be reduced in return for similar concessions granted by the other country. Reciprocity agreements were signed with most European countries. They worked to Britain's advantage since her industrial output exceeded that of any rival.

Huskisson helped to free trade by reducing duties on many articles such as silk, cotton and paper. The general duty on manufactured goods was reduced from 50 to 20 per cent. Procedure was simplified for a single tariff replaced over 1000 customs Acts previously in force.

Huskisson believed that the British empire provided a valuable market for British goods as well as being a source of raw materials. He introduced a system of preferential duties for the colonies. Every colony benefited from the system of imperial preference and Britain gained since her goods were admitted to the colonies at a lower rate of duty than those of other countries. Huskisson's work at the Board of Trade was immensely important for British commerce. The benefits of his reforms continued to be felt throughout the nineteenth century.

Frederick Robinson at the Exchequer

Frederick Robinson's cheerfulness contributed to the general air of optimism felt in business circles in the 1820s and earned him the nickname 'Prosperity' Robinson. His first budget of 1823 reduced the 'assessed' taxes on items such as carriages, which helped the rich. This was followed in 1824 by measures to help the poor when taxes on commodities such as wool and coal were removed. In 1825 the house and window taxes on smaller houses were removed. All classes of society received some benefit from the Chancellor's measures.

Sir Robert Peel at the Home Office

As Secretary of State for Home Affairs from 1822 to 1827 and from 1828 to 1830 Sir Robert Peel was responsible for introducing important reforms. He reduced the number of crimes which carried the death penalty. He improved prison conditions and simplified criminal law. Most important of all, Peel was responsible for the creation of an efficient police force.

In the years before Peel's appointment as Home Secretary there had been a dramatic rise in crime. Since few criminals were caught savage punishments were inflicted on those who were convicted to act as a deterrent. The death penalty applied to about 200 crimes. However, since a relatively minor offence like shop lifting was punishable by hanging, shopkeepers often failed to prosecute. Only one in 20 of those condemned to death was executed. Since the offender had a good chance of escaping he was not deterred. If the death penalty was to be an effective deterrent the number of capital offences must be reduced. Sir Samuel Romilly and Sir James Mackintosh (1765 – 1832) led the way in calling for the abolition of the death penalty for minor offences. In 1823 Sir Robert Peel abolished the death penalty for over 100 offences.

Since imprisonment was to replace hanging Peel's next task was to reform prison conditions. Prisons were squalid, overcrowded places where lunatics and the sick mixed with children aged nine and upwards and hardened criminals. Wealthy prisoners purchased privileges from the prison keeper; for them prison was not much of a deterrent. Peel swept away the most glaring abuses. The Gaols Act, 1823, established a prison in every county and in most large towns. Prisons, funded by the rates, were to be administered by local magistrates and inspected three times a quarter by justices of the peace who were to send an annual report to the home office. Prison regulations were drawn up. Prisoners were separated into different categories, medical care was provided and there was some educational provision.

Peel helped to simplify criminal law. He reduced to a single enactment the 92 statutes which had dealt with theft. He improved procedure in the criminal courts and consolidated into one statute 85 Acts on the subject of the empanelling of juries.

Sir Robert Peel is remembered as the creator of the modern police force. Before 1829 400 policemen worked in London which had a population of one and a half million. They concentrated on detection rather than on the prevention of crime. The Metropolitan Police Act, 1829, created a new London police force of 1000 men. At first the force operated in a 10-mile radius under the authority of the

Home Secretary and two commissioners who were responsible for recruitment, training and discipline. The police were trained to prevent crime and they soon established a good relationship with the public. Such was the success of the Metropolitan Police that over the next 30 years similar forces were established in many parts of the country.

Trade Unions

Lord Liverpool's government legalized trade unions almost by accident. The Anti-Combination Acts (see p.67) were attacked by many for the same reasons as they attacked restrictions on trade. In spite of the prevailing belief in *laissez faire* it required a skilful campaign to achieve the repeal of the Anti-Combination Acts. Francis Place had been at work since 1814, collecting evidence and preparing working men to testify before a House of Commons committee. In 1824 the committee members were carefully selected by Joseph Hume, a radical MP, to prepare a Bill allowing skilled workers to emigrate. Inserted in the Bill was a clause repealing the Anti-Combination Acts and also preventing prosecution for conspiracy. The working men witnesses impressed the parliamentary committee with their education and moderation and the Bill was passed. Many Tories were annoyed to discover that they had repealed the Anti-Combination Acts. Widespread strikes followed. In 1825 the government passed an enabling Act which allowed trade unions to operate openly but which prohibited 'intimidation', 'obstruction' and 'molestation'. Since the Act effectively prevented picketing, trade unions found it difficult to enforce a strike. Thus the concessions granted in 1824 were virtually removed in 1825.

Banking

In 1825 there was a financial crisis. Several small banks failed and many businessmen found themselves in difficulty. The government decided to strengthen the banking system. Private banks were forbidden to print notes valued less than five pounds. The Bank Act, 1826, allowed new joint stock banks to be founded within a 65-mile radius of London. The Bank of England was allowed to open branches in the provinces. As a result of these measures English banks were more stable and commerce benefited.

The Corn Laws

The Corn Law of 1815 (see p.85) failed to produce the desired stability in prices or to guarantee prosperity for landowners. In 1822 imports of corn were allowed when the home price was 70 shillings on payment of a duty of 12 shillings; the duty fell to 5 shillings when the price of corn exceeded 80 shillings and to one shilling when the price rose above 85 shillings.

In 1826 trade slumped, unemployment rose and so did the price of bread. The government was flooded with petitions asking for cheap bread. As rioting broke out in many parts of the country Parliament was forced to take action. Stocks of corn in the ports of Liverpool and Hull were released after only a small duty had been paid. For a short period the import of foreign corn was allowed. The government had to rely on the Whigs for the passage of these measures since many of its supporters blamed Huskisson's measures for the trade recession and they did not want to see any further reduction of tariff barriers.

Opposition to the Corn Law continued. In 1828, although complete abolition was felt to be too revolutionary, a sliding scale, known as Wellington's scale, was introduced. As the price of English wheat increased so the duty on foreign wheat lessened, until at 73 shillings a quarter entry was free of duty. This did not free the corn trade as Huskisson had wished and divisions within the Tory party grew. The sliding scale did not bring stability. Dealers produced an artificial scarcity by keeping wheat off the market so that prices would rise and a lower rate of duty would operate.

2 The Divided Tories and Catholic Emancipation

Much to the surprise of the rank and file of the party, the Tories were responsible for Catholic emancipation in 1829. This reform was passed at a time of great confusion amongst the political parties. The Tories were already divided on economic problems, especially on the subject of the Corn Laws, when Lord Liverpool suffered a stroke in February 1827. He had been an able administrator, successfully holding the Tory party together. On his retirement divisions within the party became more pronounced.

Canning's Ministry

Canning succeeded Lord Liverpool as Prime Minister. Through the conduct of his foreign policy he had a liberal reputation. He was known to favour Catholic emancipation which separated him from Peel and the anti-Catholic Tories. Upon Canning's appointment six ministers resigned. They included Peel, who was opposed to Catholic emancipation, and Wellington, who disliked Canning. Canning turned to the Whigs for support. The Whigs held differing views about him. Some, including Grey (1764–1845), would not support Canning; others, like Brougham and Russell (1792 – 1878), decided to give him their vote. The Whigs were given three ministries and the distinctions between the political parties became blurred. The one achievement of Canning's ministry was the Treaty of London, 1827, which helped to settle the question of Greek independence (see p.114). In August 1827, after only six months in office, Canning died, leaving the problem of Catholic emancipation, which he had hoped to solve, to his successors.

Goderich's Ministry
When Canning died 'Prosperity' Robinson, now Lord 'Goody' Goderich, became Prime Minister. He did not have Canning's strength and was unable to settle cabinet disputes or to deal with the King. He resigned in January 1828.

Wellington's Ministry
By 1828 both the Tories and the Whigs were so divided that no party leader would take office. George IV sent for Wellington who accepted office, believing that it was his duty to carry on the King's government. The Whigs refused to serve under him, but the Canningite group of 'liberal Tories' remained and Peel returned to the Home Office.

The Question of Catholic Emancipation
British Catholics had been placed in a subordinate position by the Revolution Settlement of 1688. Over the years most politicians had accepted this situation. King George III was adamant that he would not grant Catholics equality with Protestants. His stance at the time of the Act of Union had caused Pitt's resignation in 1801 (see p.70). George IV held the same view as his father. Many Tories had no wish to impose Catholic emancipation on the King and country; others supported Catholic emancipation. They were so divided on the issue that it was recognized that if the question of emancipation was raised it would break the party and end Tory rule. Consequently, throughout the 1820s the Tories proclaimed that they had an open mind on the subject which allowed many of them to dismiss it from their thoughts.

Daniel O'Connell (1775 – 1847)
Whilst the British administration appeared unable to make up its mind on the question of Catholic emancipation there was an Irishman who was determined to gain emancipation peacefully. His name was Daniel O'Connell and he was a Catholic barrister.

O'Connell's aim was to repeal the Act of Union and he realized that Catholic emancipation was the first step towards repeal.

In 1823 O'Connell helped to found the Catholic Association, an organization which worked for emancipation. In the following year the association appealed to the poorer Catholics in Ireland, asking them to contribute one penny per month to help the cause of emancipation. By 1825 the 'Catholic rent', as this fund was called, was bringing in £1000 per week. The Irish authorities feared that the Catholic Association threatened public order and it was dissolved in 1825. O'Connell evaded the law by founding new associations, each one with a different name, and he continued to collect the 'rent'.

In 1825 the question of Catholic emancipation came before Parliament, accompanied by a scheme for disfranchizing the 40-shilling freeholders and endowing the Catholic clergy. When the Bill was defeated O'Connell decided to adopt new tactics. For years the votes of the 40-shilling freeholders in Ireland had been controlled by Protestant landowners. (In the counties every man who owned the freehold of land worth 40 shilling a year had the right to vote.) O'Connell set out to break this custom. In 1826 Catholics contested the county of Waterford where the ruling family, the Beresfords, lost the election. A similar result followed in county Louth. O'Connell had found a way to threaten rebellion without embarking on open hostility.

Repeal of the Test and Corporation Acts, 1828

Before O'Connell's campaign finally brought matters to a head a minor reform was introduced which indirectly helped the Catholics' cause. The Test and Corporation Acts dated from the reign of Charles II and were designed to prevent anyone who was not a communicant member of the Church of England from holding offices of state or positions on local corporations. In fact, Protestant Dissenters were not affected by the Acts for an annual Amending Act of Indemnity enabled them to hold such offices. Lord John Russell, a young Whig, secured the abolition of the Test and Corporation Acts in 1828. Their repeal made it difficult to ignore the question of Catholic emancipation.

Cabinet Re-shuffle, 1828

Early in 1828 a dispute arose in the cabinet over the fate of two boroughs, Penryn and East Retford, found guilty of corruption. Huskisson and the 'liberal' or Canningite Tories wished to transfer the seats to unenfranchised towns. The high Tories wanted to place them in the adjoining county constituencies. Finally it was decided that the representation of Penryn should be transferred to Manchester whilst East Retford was to be absorbed into the adjoining constituencies. When the House of Lords refused to create a new seat for Manchester Huskisson tendered his resignation and Wellington accepted it. When other Canningites left the cabinet Wellington had to make several new appointments and unwittingly played into O'Connell's hands.

The County Clare Election, 1828

Wellington appointed an Irish MP who represented county Clare, Vesey Fitzgerald (1783 – 1843), to succeed a Canningite at the Board of Trade. According to the law Fitzgerald had to stand for re-election and O'Connell decided to stand against him even though as a Catholic he could not be elected. O'Connell won the election but was declared not to have been returned to Parliament. The government realized that what had happened in county Clare would be repeated in most Irish constituencies at the next general election. Wellington knew that unless the law was changed Irish representation at Westminster would break down and civil war would follow. Peel was prepared to resign rather than accept Catholic emancipation but was persuaded to stay on the grounds that his support was essential to the Tory government. It is ironic that only a few months prior to this Wellington had rid his cabinet of all who supported Catholic emancipation.

The Catholic Relief Act, 1829

In April 1829 a Catholic Emancipation Bill passed both Houses at Westminster, allowing Roman Catholics to sit in Parliament and occupy most offices of state. Peel introduced the Bill in a four-hour speech and guided it through the Commons with help from the Whigs whilst Wellington forced its acceptance on the Lords and George IV. A reluctant reformer, Wellington tried to salvage something by disfranchizing the Irish 40-shilling freeholders and raising the property qualification for voting in Ireland to £10 a year. In addition he refused to allow O'Connell to take his seat at Westminster until he had re-submitted himself for election on the grounds that his first election to county Clare was illegal.

The End of Tory Rule

By the time Catholic emancipation was achieved the Tory party lay in ruins. It consisted of three groups — the Canningites who had left the ministry in 1828, the high Tories who had voted against emancipation, and the group of Tories who had followed Wellington and Peel. The Whigs were still divided between those who had opposed and those who had supported Canning. In the confusion Wellington seemed prepared to carry on, unaware of the fact that opponents in his own party were waiting for an opportunity to pay him back for what they regarded as political treachery on the question of Catholic emancipation.

In 1830 there were outbreaks of unrest in the south of England and the threat of revolution in the north. A revolution in France excited interest in reform in this country and in November 1830 Lord Grey, the Whig leader, gave way to pressures from his radical supporters and came out in favour of parliamentary reform. Wellington made it clear that he was opposed to reform. He believed that the existing parliamentary system was perfect. His opposition to reform sealed the fate of his ministry. He had lost the confidence of the Commons and when the high Tories turned against him and he suffered defeat on a motion concerning the civil list, he resigned. The long period of Tory rule was at an end.

Summary

The 'liberal Tories' were responsible for many reforms in the 1820s and for injecting new life into the country's economy. They created the modern police force and brought stability to the banking system. A belief in *laissez faire* led to a reduction of tariff barriers but not to the abolition of the Corn Laws. The Tories helped to end discrimination against Roman Catholics. However, Catholic emancipation divided the Tory party and led to its defeat in 1830.

Exercises

1. What do you understand by the phrase the 'liberal Tories'?
2. How did Sir Robert Peel help to raise standards of law and order?
3. What does the phrase Catholic emancipation mean?
4. Describe the role which Daniel O'Connell played in gaining Catholic emancipation.
5. How do you explain the collapse of the Tories in 1830?

11
Castlereagh and Canning: Foreign Policy, 1815 – 30

In 1815 Napoleon was finally defeated and war which had plagued Europe since 1792 came to an end. A period of international co-operation followed. At the Congress of Vienna, 1815, the great powers of Europe gathered to secure and maintain peace. Later, their representatives continued to meet at a number of further congresses. However, as the memories of Napoleon faded so the new found co-operation, always frail, began to disappear. Two men dominated British foreign policy in the 15 years after 1815 — Castlereagh and Canning. Since they adopted completely different styles in their conduct of foreign relations it has been suggested that Canning's foreign policy was very different from Castlereagh's.

1 Viscount Castlereagh

Robert Stewart, Viscount Castlereagh, was born in 1769 into a family of Ulster-Scottish descent. He was educated in Ireland and then at Cambridge and entered the Irish Parliament in 1790. He played a crucial role as Chief Secretary in securing the passage of the Act of Union with England and was soon in office after taking his seat in the new Parliament in London in 1801. His first government post was President of the Board of Control for India. Castlereagh then became Secretary of State for War and the Colonies, a post he held until 1809 when he resigned at the time of his duel with Canning. In 1812 he returned to office as Foreign Secretary and Leader of the House of Commons; he held both posts until his suicide in 1822.

Today Castlereagh is regarded as one of Britain's greatest Foreign Secretaries. This view was not shared by his contemporaries who considered that he was distant and cold. They regarded him as a politician who constantly opposed progress. Unlike Canning, Castlereagh seemed unable to explain his policies and win support for them. He believed that if his policies were just and beneficial to Britain everyone would recognize this without being told. Castlereagh must be blamed for this lack of communication which made his contemporaries suspicious of him and caused them to criticize him for views he did not hold.

The Congress of Vienna, 1815

In 1814 one of the most brilliant gatherings of monarchs and diplomats that Europe had ever seen took place in Vienna. France had been defeated and the allies were determined to return to the pre-revolutionary order. Proceedings were interrupted by Napoleon's escape from Elba and the Hundred Days (see p.78). However, once he was safely imprisoned on St Helena in 1815 the representatives could turn their attention to 'the real purpose of the congress' which according to Metternich's secretary, Gentz, was 'to divide among the conquerors the spoils taken from the vanquished'.

The Aims of the Congress

The Congress of Vienna was dominated by the representatives of the five major powers. Lord Castlereagh represented Britain, Prince Metternich represented Austria, Czar Alexander I represented Russia, King Frederick William III represented Prussia and Talleyrand represented France. In addition to seeking 'spoils' the representatives had two other aims — they wished to prevent any future French aggression and they sought to establish a balance of power in Europe.

The Division of the Spoils

At the Congress of Vienna Europe's frontiers were re-drawn in accordance with the requirements of the great powers. They were rewarded for having defeated Napoleon. Austria gained control of parts of northern Italy, including the republic of Venice. Prussia gained parts of Saxony and some Rhineland provinces. Russia gained Finland and control over the newly created Polish kingdom. Sweden, a member of the fourth coalition, lost Finland to Russia and was compensated with Norway which was taken from Denmark, one of Napoleon's supporters. Britain's naval supremacy enabled her to retain the Cape of Good Hope, Heligoland, Malta, Mauritius, St Lucia, Trinidad and Tobago; she also gained a protectorate over the Ionian Islands. (See Fig. 9, Europe in 1815.)

Areas of Dispute

Considerable argument occurred over the division of the spoils. There was serious disagreement over the fate of Poland and Saxony, both former allies of Napoleon. Czar Alexander demanded control

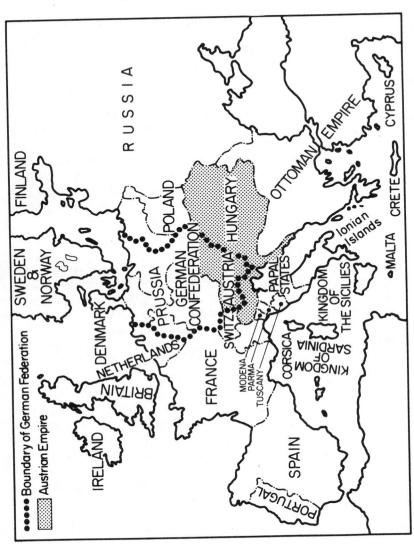

Fig.9 Europe in 1815

of the whole of the Grand Duchy of Warsaw. Prussia accepted these demands on condition that she obtain control of the whole of the kingdom of Saxony. Both 'Metternich and Castlereagh opposed these proposals. They joined forces with Talleyrand and compelled Alexander to reduce his demands to influence over a small Polish kingdom, whilst Prussian demands were also reduced to Danzig and Posen, western Pomerania and about two-fifths of the kingdom of Saxony. Another area of dispute concerned Alsace and Lorraine, two French provinces inhabited by German-speaking people. Prussia claimed these two provinces, but was eventually forced to abandon her claims when it was agreed that the loss of these areas would discredit the new French King and lead to discontent amongst his people.

The Prevention of Future French Aggression

After Napoleon's defeat Louis XVIII, a Bourbon, was placed on the French throne. He promised to rule as a constitutional monarch. France was dealt with leniently in the hope of discouraging further Bonapartist schemes. The French frontiers of 1792 were slightly reduced, an army of occupation was placed in France and she had to pay an indemnity. To prevent future French aggression the states on her borders were strengthened. The Austrian Netherlands were united with Holland to form a barrier state on the north-east frontier of France. The King of Sardinia was restored to power in northern Italy and given control of Nice and Savoy and the former republic of Genoa. In Germany the congress set up a new German Confederation of 39 states under the presidency of Austria. The great powers believed that the new German Confederation would stand up to France more effectively than the old Holy Roman Empire had done.

What was Castlereagh's Role at the Congress of Vienna?

The decisions taken at the Congress of Vienna have frequently been criticized. At the congress very little notice was taken of the spirit of nationalism and the wishes of smaller governments and resident populations. Castlereagh's part in the peace settlement was criticized by progressives throughout Europe. He was condemned for being a party to the overthrow of republics like Genoa and Venice and for neglecting constitutional and national principles. However, far from being criticized, Castlereagh should be praised for the moderating role he played at the congress. When dealing with France Castlereagh emphasized 'security and not revenge' for he believed that if France was humiliated she would only cause trouble in the future. Even after the Hundred Days his view triumphed over that of Prussia who wanted to punish France.

Castlereagh was less successful when he urged 'it is not our business to collect trophies'. However, he cannot be blamed for failing to create nation states in Italy or Germany. This was not feasible in 1815 and could only have been brought about by the use of force. Castlereagh did not believe that Britain should necessarily obtain constitutions for countries which had been handed back to their former rulers or protect small states such as Genoa. His aim was 'to bring the world back to peaceful habits' and this could not be done if a mass of small, weak states, which were open to aggression, were created.

Castlereagh always had 'the supremacy of English interests' in the forefront of his mind at the Congress of Vienna. He secured important gains for Britain overseas which greatly strengthened her position in the world. Castlereagh deserved praise for this and for the fact that there was peace in Europe for decades after 1815.

The Holy Alliance

In the autumn of 1815 Czar Alexander of Russia approached Austria and Prussia with the idea of a Holy Alliance. They signed the text of the alliance on 26 September 1815, agreeing that 'in accordance with the words of Holy Scripture, which command all men to regard one another as brothers, the three contracting monarchs will remain united by the bonds of a true and indissoluble brotherhood'. Alexander then invited all the Christian sovereigns of Europe to join the Holy Alliance. Castlereagh, distrusting the Czar's motives, referred to the alliance as 'a piece of sublime mysticism and nonsense'. It was not clear whether the Czar, by excluding Moslem Turkey from the alliance, was trying to isolate Russia's traditional enemy, or whether he was simply trying to maintain autocratic government in central and eastern Europe. Castlereagh refused to join the Holy Alliance, excusing Britain on the grounds that the Prince Regent was not allowed by the cabinet to sign a treaty. The Holy Alliance was never an effective force in international politics.

The Quadruple Alliance

On 20 November 1815 Britain, Prussia, Austria and Russia signed the Quadruple Alliance whereby they agreed to co-operate to prevent future unrest in Europe. Czar Alexander tried to widen the terms of the alliance to include not only a guarantee of all the existing European frontiers but also of governments so that any hint of revolution might be suppressed. Castlereagh refused to accept these proposals. He did not wish to commit Britain to a policy of supporting autocratic governments. In the end the only frontiers specifically guaranteed were those enclosing France. Castlereagh joined the Quadruple Alliance for he believed that British interests could be secured by working with the other powers to repel danger in Europe, particularly from France.

The Congress System

The Congress System sprang from Article VI of the Quadruple Alliance. This article stated:

> to facilitate and to secure the execution of the present treaty . . . the High Contracting Parties have agreed to renew their meetings at fixed periods for the purpose of consulting upon their common interests . . . and for the maintainance of peace in Europe.

Castlereagh was the author of Article VI and as such he is regarded as the architect of the Congress System. The idea of periodic meetings was a new departure in European diplomacy and the Congress System has been regarded as the fore-runner of the League of Nations. More recently, this interpretation has been rejected. The Congress System had no permanent organization or officials and the frequency of its meetings was not fixed. There were four congresses. Castlereagh attended the first but refused to be present at the second and third; he committed suicide before the final congress met.

The Congress of Aix-la-Chapelle, 1818

The first congress met at Aix-la-Chapelle in 1818 and was mainly concerned with France. She was now clear of her indemnity and the great powers decided to remove the army of occupation which had been placed in France in 1815. The question of Swedish debts to Denmark was settled and the treatment of Napoleon on St Helena was discussed. Trouble arose when Czar Alexander proposed that a general league of powers, including France, should be set up to guarantee the frontiers and thrones of all the sovereigns. This *Alliance Solidaire* was simply a wider form of his earlier proposals in November 1815 which Castlereagh had rejected. Castlereagh acted cautiously. He feared that a second rejection might encourage Russia to deal directly with France and thereby destroy the Quadruple Alliance. Eventually a compromise was reached. France was allowed to take part in future congresses and the Czar accepted a secret renewal of the Quadruple Alliance and abandoned the idea of an *Alliance Solidaire*.

The Congress of Aix-la-Chapelle appeared to end on an amicable note. Castlereagh had successfully challenged Russia's idea of an *Alliance Solidaire* but the British public failed to recognize his success. They regarded the Quadruple Alliance as an instrument to control France. In their view, by allowing France to join the Quadruple Alliance, Castlereagh had undermined it.

The Congresses of Troppau, 1820, and Laibach, 1821

The years 1820 and 1821 were marked by unrest in Europe. Revolts broke out in Naples, Portugal and Spain where revolutionaries wished to impose a liberal constitution on the rulers who had returned in 1815. At the same time the South American colonies of Spain and Portugal took advantage of the mounting chaos and declared themselves independent. These disturbances prompted the great powers to call a meeting. The Congress of Troppau was held in October 1820 and continued at Laibach in January 1821. Both meetings were concerned to find ways to suppress the revolts in Spain and Italy (see Fig. 10, The Congress System). Castlereagh refused to attend these congresses but sent his half-brother Lord Stewart as an observer.

The revolts produced a complex situation in Europe. Austria had a special interest in Italian affairs since its empire included most of northern Italy. The Austrians had a treaty with the king of Naples by which they would help him to suppress any revolution. In the House of Commons Castlereagh recognized Austrian rights under the treaty and declared that he had no objection to Austria's suppressing the Neapolitan uprising but refused to accept that this was a problem for the Quadruple Alliance. In spite of this speech, when Metternich dispatched an Austrian army to Naples to restore King Ferdinand, British radicals held Castlereagh responsible for the crushing of Neapolitan liberties.

Whilst Castlereagh recognized Austria's right to intervene in Naples he wanted to prevent Russia or France from intervening in Spain. He wished to protect British interests in Gibraltar and the western Mediterranean and to preserve Britain's newly acquired trade with the former Spanish colonies. By gaining Austrian and Prussian support he prevented Russia and France from taking action in Spain and South America.

The Troppau Protocol

At the Congress of Troppau Metternich persuaded the representatives of Russia, Prussia and France to accept a declaration known as the Troppau Protocol. This document declared that states which had undergone revolutions and threatened other countries because of

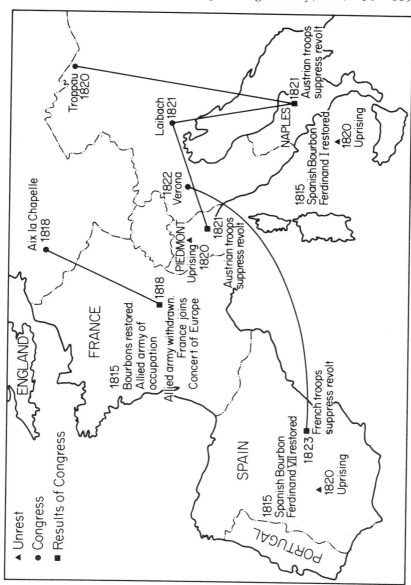

Fig. 10 The Congress System

their instability would cease to belong to the European alliance. The great powers would take steps to crush the revolts and bring the countries back into the fold. Castlereagh was angry when Lord Stewart seemed to be more closely connected with the Troppau Protocol than the Foreign Secretary wished. He therefore issued a circular to all British representatives in foreign courts criticizing the Troppau Protocol and questioning its validity. This resistance prevented further attempts to bring the South American colonies under the control of Spain and Portugal.

Castlereagh's Death
In spite of these differences of opinion Castlereagh did not abandon the Congress System. He was still trying to work with the great powers over the question of the Greek revolt against Turkey which broke out in 1821. A fourth congress was proposed for 1822 but Castlereagh was dead before it met. For years he had been appallingly over-worked and in the summer of 1822 he became seriously unbalanced. On 12 August, after his pistols and razors had been removed, he found a knife that had been overlooked by his attendants and slit his throat.

Was Castlereagh a Cautious Conservative?
After his death and for most of the nineteenth century Castlereagh was dismissed as an unsuccessful conservative, constantly fighting against progress. He has been seen as the man who secured the union between England and Ireland, thereby murdering Irish liberties. In the difficult years after the Napoleonic Wars when Castlereagh had his hands full with European diplomacy he also had the task of guiding the government's repressive domestic legislation through the House of Commons. He was taunted by the romantic poets. In *The Mask of Anarchy* Shelley wrote:
I met murder on the way —
He had a mask like Castlereagh
This criticism affected men's opinions of his foreign policy. Castlereagh was considered to be just as reactionary abroad as he was at home. For this he was partly to blame. If only he had been prepared to include 'the liberal catchwords of the day' in his speeches then in the estimation of Lord Salisbury there would have been far less criticism of his foreign policy.

2 George Canning

George Canning had an unconventional boyhood. His father was a barrister and when he died his mother, a great beauty, became an itinerant actress. Canning was brought up by his uncle and was educated at Eton and at Christ Church, Oxford. He was a brilliant scholar and soon attracted notice. He was horrified by the French Revolution and attached himself to William Pitt, becoming an MP at the age of 23. In 1796 he held junior office and by 1800 was a Privy Councillor. In 1801 he resigned from office with Pitt over the question of Catholic emancipation. He joined the cabinet in 1807 as Foreign Secretary, a post he held for two years until his duel with Castlereagh. In 1814 he became ambassador to Lisbon and in 1816 entered the government as President of the Board of Control. He resigned in 1820 over the Queen Caroline affair. When Castlereagh died in 1822 Canning became Foreign Secretary in Lord Liverpool's administration. On Lord Liverpool's death in 1827 he became Prime Minister, a post he held for a few months before his death in August of that year.

Was Canning a Contrast to Castlereagh?

In contrast to Castlereagh Canning was a brilliant speaker who constantly explained to the nation what he was doing as Foreign Secretary from 1822 to 1827. There was certainly a difference between the two men in the styles they adopted when conducting foreign policy. However, a difference in style does not necessarily amount to a change of policy.

A difference between the two men can be detected with regard to the Congress System. Canning regarded the Congress System as a 'new and very questionable policy'. He criticized it on the following grounds:

'it will necessarily involve us deeply in all the politics of the continent, whereas our true policy has always been not to interfere except in great emergencies, and then with commanding force.'

Canning did not trust the close relationships which Castlereagh had built up with foreign statesmen and he was not prepared to maintain them.

Another area of difference was that Canning stressed the national interest in his foreign policy speeches far more than Castlereagh had done. Castlereagh's policies were coloured by his war-time experiences; he was concerned to work with other European rulers to banish all further threats of war. Canning was much more directly concerned with the interests of Britain. He stated, 'in the conduct of political affairs, the grand object of my contemplation is the interest of England'. This stress on the 'Englishness' of his policies, together with his inability to work with

Metternich, has led many writers to declare that his foreign policy was very different from Castlereagh's.

The Congress of Verona, 1822

Canning sent the Duke of Wellington to represent Britain at the Congress of Verona. The first problem to be tackled there concerned Spain. Revolution in Spain had been followed by the introduction of a constitutional regime which had proved ineffective. King Ferdinand VII sought foreign help to overthrow the constitution. Czar Alexander wished to send troops to Spain to restore Ferdinand to autocratic power but Canning, Metternich and the French would not accept this. At the Congress of Verona Wellington refused to join in any common policy against Spain. However, he failed to prevent the French from invading Spain, crushing the constitutional government and restoring Ferdinand's powers. The presence of French troops in Spain shocked the British public who feared for the safety of Portugal and the independence of the Spanish South American colonies.

Portugal

Before French troops crossed the Pyrenees into Spain Canning made it clear that he would not tolerate any interference in Portugal. He also warned the Portuguese not to cause trouble. He maintained a tough approach even going so far as to dispatch British troops to Portugal in 1826 to maintain order. He explained this action in the House of Commons saying, 'We go to Portugal . . . to defend and preserve the independence of an ally'. After the invasion of Spain Canning believed that it was necessary to adopt a tough policy to restore Britain's prestige. His policy was successful for it prevented foreign interference in Portugal.

The Spanish South American Colonies

Since Spain's colonies in South America had rebelled Britain had built up strong trading links with them. Canning did not want to see the colonies revert to Spanish control once the revolt in Spain had been suppressed and the Spaniards had time to assert their former powers in South America. Canning warned France that any attempt to recover the colonies for Spain would lead to war with Britain. At the end of 1823 Canning was helped by President Monroe of the United States. In his message to the American Congress, known as the Monroe Doctrine, the President laid down the principle of non-interference by European powers in the independent states of the Americas. Since this announcement applied to Britain as well as to other European states it was not altogether acceptable to Canning. However, he welcomed the Monroe Doctrine and in 1825 the British cabinet recognized the independence of Buenos Aires, Mexico and Columbia. British commercial interests were safe since neither France nor Russia now contemplated intervention.

The Greek War of Independence, 1821

In 1821 the Greeks revolted against their Turkish overlords and Canning came face to face with the Eastern Question. Czar Alexander I felt inclined to support the Greek Christians as this would enable him to acquire influence in the Balkans. Both Canning and Metternich opposed this and persuaded Alexander to remain neutral.

British Public Opinion and the Greeks

Traditionally the British government had supported Turkey whenever she was threatened from within by rebellion or from without by Russia. Britain was unwilling to see Russia advance at Turkey's expense towards Constantinople and the Mediterranean where British trading interests might be threatened. However, Canning was not able to follow this line during the Greek War of Independence. The Greeks attracted support to their cause amongst the British people. The British upper classes had received a classical education which enabled Shelley to write, 'We are all Greeks'. Subscriptions were collected to help the Greeks and volunteers left for Greece to join in the struggle. Amongst the volunteers was Lord Byron; his death at Missolonghi in 1824 only served to make the Greek cause more popular. Canning did not wish to flout public opinion by opposing the Greeks and he worked instead to separate the Greek revolt from the quarrel between Russia and Turkey.

Canning's Diplomacy

The situation changed in 1825 when Alexander I died and was succeeded by Czar Nicholas I. Nicholas was determined to help the Greeks and his determination grew when the Sultan of Turkey secured the help of Mehemet Ali, the Pasha of Egypt, and his son Ibrahim. Europe was scandalized by the severity of their attacks on the Greeks who sent a deputation to London, begging for Britain's help.

Canning was anxious to come to terms with Nicholas I and sent the Duke of Wellington to St Petersburg. As a result of the Duke's discussions Britain and Russia signed a protocol in April 1826. This provided for an end to the conflict between Greece and Turkey on the basis of a virtually independent Greece which would pay tribute to the Sultan. After further successful diplomacy Britain, France and Russia signed the Treaty of London in July 1827. This treaty contained the same terms as the Anglo-Russian protocol but called for an immediate armistice. Austria and Prussia refused to sign the treaty; they resented the support given to the Greek rebels and were opposed to foreign influence in the Turkish empire.

Navarino Bay, 1827

Neither the Greeks nor the Turks were pleased with the Treaty of London. Turkey refused to accept the armistice and before the treaty could be put to the test Canning died in August 1827. Shortly after this the Turkish and Egyptian fleets were destroyed by a joint British, Russian and French naval force in Navarino Bay. The battle of Navarino Bay meant that independent Greece could not now be reconquered by the Turks.

The Duke of Wellington

Canning was succeeded by Wellington who did not approve of the Treaty of London nor of the battle of Navarino Bay. King George IV spoke of Navarino as 'an untoward event' and referred to the Turks as 'an ancient ally'. After this change in the situation Russia declared war on Turkey in 1828 and forced the Turks to sign the Treaty of Adrianople in 1829.

An Independent Greece

In 1832 Prince Otto of Bavaria became the ruler of a completely independent Greece. All the great powers recognized Greek independence but the outcome would not have pleased Canning. Although Russia had made no territorial gains during the Greeks' struggle for independence she had increased her influence in the Balkans and was to continue to be a threat to the Turkish empire.

Was Canning a Liberal Foreign Secretary?

Canning's biographer R.J.V. Rolo describes him as 'among the few who have successfully applied genius to politics'. In the conduct of his foreign policy Canning earned the reputation of a liberal. H.A.L. Fisher believed that he carried out a 'new type of popular and liberal diplomacy'. Often, in private, he showed little but contempt for some of the people and causes he openly supported. What made Canning appear progressive was the style of his foreign policy and his efforts to make it popular. The British public was pleased when he refused to take orders from European statesmen; they were not sorry to see the end of the Congress System.

Summary
In 1815 Britain made striking gains at the Congress of Vienna which reflected the part she had played in defeating Napoleon and which benefited her trade. In the following years Castlereagh took part in the Congress System and was criticized, in many cases wrongly, for the repressive measures taken by the great powers in post-war Europe. In 1822 he was succeeded by Canning who did not have Castlereagh's personal links with the statesmen of Europe and did not wish to work closely with them. He safeguarded Britain's interests in Portugal and South America and he aided Greek independence — a policy which went against Britain's traditional role of maintaining the Turkish empire. He is credited with the collapse of the Congress System. The difference between Castlereagh and Canning was one of style not substance.

Exercises
1. Describe Castlereagh's work at the Congress of Vienna.
2. What part did Castlereagh play in the Congress System?
3. Was Castlereagh a 'good European'?
4. What was Canning's attitude towards a) the Spanish South American colonies, b) Greek independence?
5. Why is Canning regarded as a more liberal foreign secretary than Castlereagh?
6. Why is Canning regarded as the man who wrecked the Congress System?

12
The Whig Reforms, 1830 – 41

In 1830 the new King, William IV, asked Lord Grey to form a government. Grey's cabinet of 13 members consisted of 11 peers. Several Canningite Tories who had broken with Wellington were chosen for office, among them was Lord Palmerston (1784 – 1865) who became Foreign Secretary. The Whig leader in the Commons was Lord Althorp (1782 – 1845). Once the Whigs were in office the gateway to parliamentary and social reform was at last open.

1 Parliamentary Reform

The Old System
Before 1832 the British electoral system was based on the medieval pattern of representation. Changes in the distribution of population had gradually made the system out of date. In the early nineteenth century there were two types of constituency which an MP might represent — a county or a borough. Large new towns which had grown up at the time of the industrial revolution were not represented in Parliament. In addition, the right to vote varied widely from place to place and there was widespread bribery and corruption during elections.

Before 1832 only three adult males in every 100 had the right to vote. In general they were people who owned property; it could be said that the British Parliament represented property rather than people. Every man who owned property valued at 40 shillings a year in a county constituency had the vote. In the parliamentary boroughs there was no standard qualification and the right to vote was based on customs and traditions that had grown up over the years and varied from place to place.

The distribution of seats was very uneven. Before 1832 70 per cent of the members of the House of Commons were returned from the south of England. All counties returned two members, regardless of their size; Rutland had 609 voters and Yorkshire had 17,000 voters — they both had two MPs. Wales was inadequately represented with only 12 county and 12 borough seats. Scotland returned only 45 MPs. By contrast, Ireland sent 100 MPs to Westminster. Five counties in south-west England — Cornwall, Devon, Somerset, Dorset and Wiltshire — elected one quarter of the House of Commons. Parliament reflected the structure of society before industrialization changed it.

Cities like Birmingham and Manchester had no MPs in 1831. On the other hand there were rotten boroughs which, although they often had few inhabitants, had full parliamentary representation. Part of Dunwich no longer existed because of coastal erosion but it still returned two members. Perhaps the most notorious rotten borough was Old Sarum in Wiltshire where two members were elected by the owner of a hill which had no buildings on it. Old

Sarum also falls into the category of pocket boroughs for it was controlled by the Pitt family. Pocket boroughs were another abuse whereby a wealthy patron had the power to nominate his own candidates as borough representatives. (See Fig. 11, The Old System.)

Very often the owner of an estate, not the voters, decided who MPs were going to be. A wealthy nobleman could threaten to throw tenants out of his houses unless they voted as he told them. As well as intimidating electors he could also buy votes. Although bribery of voters was illegal it was widespread. Robert Southey (1774–1843), writing in 1807, estimated that the price of a vote varied, according to the number of electors, from as low as 40 shillings to as much as £30. Candidates who spent a lot of money during their election campaign hoped to make up their losses once they were MPs by obtaining a government pension or sinecure.

The unreformed House of Commons had two redeeming features. However corrupt the rotten and pocket boroughs were, they acted as 'the nurseries of statesmen', giving young men the opportunity to prove themselves in the House of Commons. Secondly, the House of Commons had mirrored society. As the structure of society changed the political system came under attack, perhaps because it reflected all too accurately a social order which was passing away.

Early Reform Movements

In the last 30 years of the eighteenth century demands for a reformed Parliament increasingly occurred. One reason for this was that many people felt sympathy for the struggle of the American colonists to be independent of Britain. Groups were formed to discuss political liberty such as the Society for Constitutional Information, founded in April 1780 by Major John Cartwright. These societies made virtually no headway. It is true that in 1785 William Pitt introduced a measure which would have disfranchized 36 rotten boroughs, but it was easily defeated.

The outbreak of the French Revolution inspired many Englishmen and strengthened their determination for change. Many reform societies were founded to find out what was happening in France and to press for reform in Britain. The brilliant writer Tom Paine, inspired by the revolution, called for reform in his book *The Rights of Man*. However, the violence of the French Revolution and the Napoleonic Wars brought tougher government to Britain. This put an end to reform movements until the late 1820s, by which time the government was less afraid of Britain falling into chaos.

It is possible to exaggerate the extent to which a tradition of

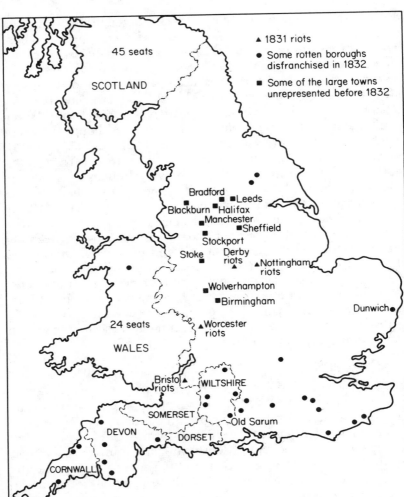

Fig. 11 The Old System

continuous reform agitation was kept alive in the early years of the nineteenth century. It is also doubtful whether the passing of the 1832 Reform Act can be explained simply by the pressures imposed on the government by popular demonstrations in favour of reform. However, it would be unwise to dismiss this early reform agitation as totally insignificant.

Support for Reform After 1815

In the years between the battle of Waterloo and the Great Reform Bill the movement for parliamentary reform had three 'wings'. There were the radicals who included Henry Hunt, William Cobbett and Major Cartwright. They were eager to achieve manhood suffrage, an ambitious scheme of redistribution and annual Parliaments. Then there were the Benthamites, an influential minority, supporting reform on the basis of utility and distrusting aristocratic governments as ineffective and corrupt. Jeremy Bentham (1748–1832) argued that good government was based on an identity between the government and the governed, and that this could only be accomplished if the members of the House of Commons were elected by an extended franchise based on household suffrage. Finally, there were the Whigs, full of distaste for the new world which was coming into existence, but prepared to make concessions if this would lead to stability. Concessions were urgently needed after the 1830 riots amongst labourers in the south of England, if revolution was to be avoided.

In 1829, following a campaign by the Irish leader Daniel O'Connell, Roman Catholics were allowed to sit in Parliament (see p.100). O'Connell had been helped by English reformers who linked the Irish struggle to the need for reform in England. The English reform groups were well-organized; the most influential was the Birmingham Political Union, founded by Thomas Attwood (1783–1856) in 1830. In 1830 events abroad helped the reform movement. A revolution in France, together with revolts in Poland, Belgium and Italy, encouraged the reformers and brought concessions from the government.

Passage of the Reform Bill, 1832

On 1 March 1831 Lord John Russell introduced the first version of the Reform Bill in the Commons. Opponents of the Bill spent so long debating it that it had only passed the second reading in the Commons (and then only by a majority of one — 301 to 302 votes) by the end of the session.

After the defeat of the Bill, Grey went to the country to test popular support for his proposals in an election. With a bigger majority, the Whigs introduced a second version of the Bill. It passed through the Commons on 21 September 1831 but was defeated at the second reading in the House of Lords on 8 October.

After a second defeat the Whigs at first seemed unwilling to press on. Agitation for reform passed to working-class organizations, notably the National Political Union, founded on 8 October 1831. There were riots throughout the country. Demonstrations were held in Bristol, London and Birmingham. Thomas Attwood claimed he had 200,000 supporters for his programme of 'the Bill, the whole Bill and nothing but the Bill'. In the north the riots were violent and several people prepared for an armed struggle. Amidst this agitation a third Bill, slightly amended, was introduced and reached the House of Lords on 26 March 1832. After Lord Grey had persuaded King William IV to create over 100 new peers if necessary to gain a majority for the Bill in the Upper House, the Lords gave way. The Bill became law on 7 June 1832.

The Terms of the 1832 Reform Act

The Great Reform Bill reflected a traditional rather than a radical approach to Parliament. It disfranchized 56 boroughs with less than 2000 people. Another 31 boroughs with between 2000 and 4000 people lost one member each. Sixty-five of these seats were redistributed among the counties. Seventy-eight seats were allocated to boroughs which had been unrepresented such as Greenwich, and to some of the new industrial towns such as Leeds, Birmingham and Manchester.

In the counties the franchise was widened to include £10 copyholders, £10 long leaseholders, £50 short leaseholders and tenants-at-will paying an annual rent of £50. In the towns the old franchises gradually died out along with their holders, the £10 householder franchise being substituted as the basic qualification. By these means the electorate was enlarged by about 50 per cent to a total of about 650,000.

What was the Significance of the 1832 Reform Act?

With the passing of the 1832 Reform Act there was no sensational break with the past, no sudden lurch towards democracy. The House of Commons was still not subject to the people, for annual Parliaments and the secret ballot were still shunned by the Whigs. The redistribution of seats had been cautious. The landed interest remained predominant in the new Parliament; the lower middle classes and artisans were still voteless. The north of England was still under-represented as compared with the south. Some rotten and pocket boroughs continued to exist. The old election practices continued. Men were still bribed and impersonated and the registration of electors provided an additional means to corruption.

Political Party Organization
With the passing of the Great Reform Act came the gradual acceptance of the necessity for and the value of party organization. The provisions of the Act for the registration of voters aided the creation of an effective party organization in the constituencies. Registration societies were formed to ensure that voters of a particular political outlook were registered. At Westminster the parties tried to integrate their electoral activities. The Tories founded the Carlton Club and the radicals founded the Reform Club to link their fortunes in the Commons with the registration of supporters in the country. The Reform Act compelled politicians to consider ways in which the new electorate could be disciplined and cajoled into supporting one or other of the political parties.

Summary
Lord John Russell believed that the 1832 Reform Act was a final measure for it endowed the representative system with perfection. This was not so since the new Parliament was not very different from the old, apart from the fact that a number of borough members now came from the northern towns. Of the 658 MPs in 1833, 500 were still connected with the landed interest. Nevertheless, the Reform Act was a break with the eighteenth-century mode of politics. The Act fell short of the radicals' demands and produced further demands for more far-reaching reforms. The changes meant that Parliament could no longer afford to ignore outside pressures and the Reform Act was followed by a dramatic spate of social reform.

2 Social Reform

The Whigs were returned to power with a majority of seats in 1833 and, except for one short break, remained in office until 1841. During this time they introduced a series of progressive measures touching many aspects of the lives of ordinary people. The Whigs responded to pressure from their radical supporters and their reforms were influenced by the views of the great nineteenth-century philanthropists and philosophers. Gradually, the government intervened more and more in social and economic affairs. Nevertheless, the punishment allotted to the 'Swing' rioters and later to the Dorset labourers from Tolpuddle indicates that the Whigs differed little from the Tories in their fear of the lower classes and their willingness to repress them (see p.130). However, the Whigs differed from the Tories for they had made a place in the constitution for the middle class and were willing to effect some social reform.

Philanthropists and Philosophers

The views of several philanthropists and philosophers influenced the Whigs' programme of social reform. One influential group was the Evangelicals (see p.290). Their influence was felt in the campaigns for factory reform and for the abolition of slavery.

The influence of Jeremy Bentham and his disciples, known as Utilitarians, can be detected in several of the reforms introduced in the 1820s and 30s. Bentham influenced the reform of the penal code and legal procedure and the reform of the poor law. However, he was not concerned with particular areas of reform but rather wanted his attitude to existing institutions to be adopted by the government. He believed in the utility principle, on which all progress depended, which prescribed 'the greatest good of the greatest number'. He wrote about the pleasure/pain principle in human affairs. Happiness consisted of the achievement of pleasure and the avoidance of pain. Bentham argued that all laws should be directed towards the attainment of these aims. The test he applied to every law and institution was 'what is the use of it?' If it had no use it should be swept aside. Bentham's ideas were spread by such men as James Mill (1773-1836), Samuel Romilly, Francis Place and Edwin Chadwick (1800-90).

Robert Owen (1771-1858) was an idealistic socialist whose influence was felt in the fields of factory reform and advances in education. In his cotton mills at New Lanark, Scotland, he pioneered improved factory conditions. He advocated that communities should live according to the co-operative principle and later set up a commune at New Harmony in the United States. Owen called on the government to regulate conditions of children working in factories. He wanted them to spend less time at work so that they could devote more time to learning and leisure activities.

The Abolition of Slavery in the British Empire, 1833

In 1807, after an energetic campaign led by William Wilberforce, the British government abolished the slave trade. Following this success Wilberforce concentrated his efforts on putting an end to slavery as an institution. His supporter in Parliament was Thomas

Foxwell Buxton (1786–1845), a brewer, and together they founded the Anti-Slavery Society in 1823. From then on the question was constantly raised in Parliament. In 1828 coloured people who were not slaves were given legal equality with white people in the British colonies. In 1833 news was brought to Wilberforce, then in his eighty-fourth year and on his death bed, that the government had passed an Act which abolished slavery throughout the British empire. As compensation £20,000,000 was allotted to the slave owners; this worked out at £27 per slave which was considered to be their market value. The Act brought dislocation to the West Indian sugar trade and ruined many planters. It was one of a number of factors which embittered the Boer farmers of Cape Colony against the British and they began their Great Trek to seek a life beyond British control.

The Factory Act, 1833

In 1833, following a strong campaign for factory reform in the industrial areas of the north of England, Grey's government passed Lord Althorp's Factory Act. This marked the end of a struggle which had begun at the start of the century. In 1802 Sir Robert Peel (1750–1830) had secured the passage of an Act to regulate the working conditions of pauper apprentices. The Act limited the hours they worked in the cotton factories to 12 a day. This was followed in 1819 by an Act to limit the hours worked by very young children in factories; this measure owed much to the work of Robert Owen and Sir Robert Peel. It extended the twelve hour day to all children under 16 years in cotton mills, and forbade the employment of children under nine years. However, neither of these measures was successful for they did not include any adequate means of enforcement. It was left to unpaid magistrates to see that the law was enforced and they rarely visited the factories. In addition, apart from cotton mills, the hours and conditions in all other factories remained unregulated.

Agitation for reform reached new heights in 1830 with the publication of a series of letters by Richard Oastler (1789–1861) in the *Leeds Mercury*. The Ten Hour movement grew up and was supported at Westminster by the Tory Evangelical, Michael Sadler (1780–1835). As a result of Sadler's efforts a Parliamentary Committee on Child Labour was set up in 1832. When Sadler lost his seat in the 1832 election Lord Ashley, later the Earl of Shaftesbury (1801–85), took up the leadership of the campaign. In 1833 a Royal Commission was set up, following pressure from opponents of reform, to re-examine the whole question.

As a result of the Commissions of 1832 and 1833 a Factory Act was passed in 1833 which applied to all textile factories except silk. It stated that children under nine years were not to be employed in textile factories; children aged nine to 13 years were not to work more than 12 hours a day or 48 hours a week; children aged 13 to 18 were not to work more than 12 hours a day or 69 a week; night work was prohibited for all workers under 18 years of age. For the first time paid factory Inspectors were appointed to see that the regulations were carried out. Since there were only four Inspectors for the whole country and it was difficult to prove a child's true age until the compulsory registration of births in 1836 the Factory Act was not very effective. Long hours for adults were left untouched and the Act only scratched the surface of many of the problems faced by employees in the factories of industrial Britain.

The Government Grant to Education, 1833
In 1833 the Whigs voted a sum of £20,000 for the erection of school houses to help increase the provision of elementary education (see p.280).

The Poor Law Amendment Act, 1834
The Elizabethen Poor Law, 1601, decreed that the able-bodied poor should be 'set on work' and that the old and infirm should be provided with the necessities of life or the money to buy them. It stated that the parish should be the unit of administration for the poor law and that a special rate should be levied to cover the cost of relief. This system of poor relief operated for many years. Over the years modifications occurred, e.g. in 1782 Gilbert's Act provided for parishes to combine into unions as this would make the building and management of a workhouse easier. In some areas a 'roundsman' system operated whereby ratepayers employed paupers in return for their contribution to the poor rate.

This system of poor relief was stretched to the limit by the strain of the French Wars and the depression which hit British agriculture at the end of the eighteenth century. In 1795 the JPs of Berkshire met at the Pelican Inn in the village of Speenhamland and devised an 'allowance' system of poor relief. To relieve acute distress an allowance of money was made to all poor families. It was calculated according to the number of children per family and the current price of bread.

The allowance system may have saved Britain from a revolt of the starving masses but by the 1830s it was widely criticized. The system, it was believed, had led to an increase in the numbers applying for relief, a reduction in labourers' wages together with a loss of self-respect, and an ever-increasing burden of poor rates on the ordinary householder. The cost of poor relief was £8,000,000 in 1818.

In 1832 the Whigs appointed a Royal Commission to examine the poor law. Its chairman was Bishop Blomfield (1786 – 1857). Among its members were Nassau Senior (1790 – 1864) and Edwin Chadwick who had been Bentham's secretary. The commissioners' proposals for reform were incorporated in the Poor Law Amendment Act, 1834. The Act restricted outdoor relief to the aged and the sick, declaring that in future the able-bodied who sought poor relief should enter a workhouse. Conditions in the workhouses were to be harsh in order to discourage applicants. Parishes were to group together to build workhouses and Boards of Guardians were to supervise the administration of poor relief. A central Poor Law Board was set up to administer the scheme on a national basis.

The Effects of the Poor Law Amendment Act

As a result of the Poor Law Amendment Act the numbers on relief dropped and there was a consequent drop in the poor rates. Slowly, the level of wages rose. It is argued that these improvements might have occurred anyway, especially as the expansion of railways began to provide an increasing number of jobs. However, if the long-term effects of the Act were good, the immediate effects in many parts of the country were bad. Conditions in the workhouses were needlessly harsh. Families were split up according to age and sex, food and bedding were in short supply and the inmates could neither go out of the workhouse nor receive visitors except in the presence of an official. The workhouses were hated and referred to as 'Bastilles'. Such was the opposition to them in the north of the country, where slumps often placed men out of work for a few weeks at a time, that the Boards of Guardians were unable to build them. They continued to distribute outdoor relief to the able-bodied and the Act was modified long before they were forced to apply it.

The Municipal Corporations Reform Act, 1835

In 1833 the Whigs appointed a commission to examine local government in England. Its report indicated that local government was inefficient, confused and often corrupt. It reported that 246 towns were incorporated, governed by a mayor and corporation. They included some of the smallest towns in the country. On the other hand, many towns were not incorporated, especially the ones which had grown up during the industrial revolution. Thus in 1833 cities like Manchester and Birmingham still remained in theory under the control of the Lord of the Manor.

The commission reported differences in the manner in which the boroughs were governed. In some towns 'freemen' elected their local government officials. In others officials were co-opted to fill vacancies as they arose by officials already on the corporation. These 'close' corporations were unrepresentative and offended many radicals. The commissioners highlighted a further area of confusion when they examined the provision of lighting, paving, refuse collection and sewage disposal in towns. These facilities were provided by Improvement Committees authorized by separate Acts of Parliament. The areas which these committees supervised did not always correspond to the town boundaries which led to over-lapping and, inevitably, to conflict.

The Municipal Corporations Reform Act of 1835 abolished 'close' corporations, declaring that all borough councils were to be elected. Male ratepayers were to elect councillors for a period of three years. The councillors elected their mayor and aldermen. The aldermen constituted one quarter of the council and held office for six years. The council's accounts were to be published annually to prevent corruption. The new councils were to take over the work of the Improvement Committees, if the latter agreed. Provision was made for non-corporate towns to become boroughs; Manchester sought incorporation in 1838 and Birmingham in 1839. This Act established the principle that councils were responsible to the ratepayers. It produced uniformity and order and gave the middle class control over the towns.

Other Reforms

In 1836 the Whigs introduced legislation for the Compulsory Registration of Births, Marriages and Deaths. This enabled the government to keep accurate statistics. It paved the way for future public health measures and enabled the Factory Acts to be enforced.

In 1836 the Tithe Commutation Act was passed and the Whigs redistributed clerical incomes more fairly (see p.289). Also in 1836 the stamp duty on newspapers was reduced from four pence to one penny per issue.

In 1840, thanks to the work of Rowland Hill (1772 – 1842), the penny post was introduced. Prior to 1840 payment for postage was made on delivery and at different rates for different distances. Hill highlighted the inefficiencies of the system. He insisted that charges were too high and that lower rates would lead to an expanding system. He proposed that postage should be prepaid by means of a stamp and that there should be a uniform series of charges by weight, beginning at one penny, regardless of distance. The penny post led to a massive increase in the number of letters and parcels carried annually by the Post Office. This reform brought benefits to Britain's industry and trade and helped to reduce the isolation of many rural districts.

The Whigs and Political Developments

Lord Grey gave up his office in July 1834 and was succeeded as Prime Minister by Lord Melbourne (1779–1848). During Melbourne's premiership the pace of reform slackened for he was not a reformer at heart. Within a few months of accepting office Melbourne resigned and William IV asked Sir Robert Peel to form a government. Helped by Wellington, Peel formed a Tory administration but since he did not have a majority he was defeated six times in six weeks. By April 1835 Melbourne and the Whigs had resumed office. The accession of Queen Victoria in 1837 had involved a general election but once more the Whigs were confirmed in office and Lord Melbourne instructed the young Queen in affairs of state. However, in 1839 he lost the support of the radicals and the Irish and resigned. Since Victoria had been raised in a Whig environment she dreaded working with the Tories but was forced to send for Peel.

Peel made it a condition of becoming Prime Minister that the Queen should dismiss her ladies-of-the-bedchamber, who were all Whigs, and appoint Tory ladies in their place. When the Queen refused the absurd 'bedchamber crisis' occurred. The Queen's stance encouraged Melbourne and the Whigs to resume office and, since Peel did not wish to lead another minority government, he agreed to stand down.

Ireland

Although Daniel O'Connell had achieved Catholic emancipation his real aim was to repeal the Act of Union. O'Connell was prepared to work in stages. He declared, 'I am always for taking an instalment when I cannot get the whole'. He was partly responsible for the downfall of Peel in 1835 and the return of the Whigs to office. He accepted the Lichfield House Compact which was an agreement between Russell and the Whigs and O'Connell and his followers. By the compact the Irish undertook to vote for the Whigs in the Commons in the hope that Ireland would benefit. When Melbourne became Prime Minister he passed a series of measures which pleased both the Non-conformists and the Irish (see p.289). In addition Catholics were enrolled in the Royal Irish Constabulary and chosen to serve on juries. In 1840 Irish corporations were reformed.

During Melbourne's second ministry the Whigs ruled Ireland using only the normal legal processes, they did not resort to the use of Coercion Acts. O'Connell continued to co-operate with the Whigs until it became clear that Melbourne was doing less than he could for Ireland. O'Connell began to agitate for repeal. This placed the Whigs in a difficult position and so they decided to strengthen their position by calling a general election which they hoped would make them less dependent upon the Irish in the Commons. The Whigs had miscalculated and they lost the 1841 general election.

Summary
Although the Whigs introduced a number of reforms in the 1830s this does not mean that things improved overnight. The Whigs had difficulty in applying the Factory Act and the new poor law never operated satisfactorily in the north of England. The Whigs had very little sympathy for working-class movements; they clashed with the trade unions and the Chartists and finally with the Irish. A series of slumps and outbreaks of cholera in the 1830s added to the Whigs' difficulties. Even when the Whigs were willing to introduce reforms they were often hampered by a lack of civil servants to implement them. During the last five years in office they were faced with deficits when they failed to balance income and expenditure. In spite of all these short-comings the Whig reforms helped the social and economic life of the nation and paved the way for the expansion of the collective state.

Exercises
1. In what respects could the pre-1832 parliamentary system be criticized?
2. How did the 1832 Reform Act affect a) the distribution of parliamentary seats, b) the right to vote?
3. How did the Whigs make local government more democratic?
4. Describe legislation introduced by the Whigs which a) benefited children, b) gave freedom to an under-privileged group of people.
5. How far did the Whigs improve working conditions?
6. Why were the Whigs unpopular by 1840?

13
Popular Movements, 1825 – 48

In the years 1825 – 48 working-class movements sprang up throughout the country. They developed outside Parliament, sometimes in opposition to Parliament or to the social and economic system of which Parliament was the guardian. Poor men without education found it difficult to press their cause. The leadership of popular movements therefore often fell into the hands of outcasts or adventurers or unsuccessful men with a grudge against the existing order. It is necessary to keep these facts in mind and to remember that working-class movements were never completely separate from the movements of other classes. Both the trade union movement and the Chartist movement had some middle-class support whilst the anti-Corn Law league, the first modern pressure group, was dominated by the middle class but had some working-class support.

1 Trade Unions

Since the Trade Union Act of 1825 (see p.96) was open to wide interpretation and left the unions in an unclear legal position the period which followed was one of experimentation. Various types of union developed and they began to adopt new policies. As this was a period of economic depression one of the unions' aims was to assist unemployed members. Another aim was to introduce some form of socialism, to re-organize industry in the interests of the workers.

In the period of economic depression following the repeal of the Anti-Combination Laws small local unions of working men had little chance of organizing a successful strike. The collapse of many of these smaller unions led to attempts at organization on a larger scale with greater resources and bargaining power. The cotton spinners of Lancashire favoured amalgamation and in 1829, led by John Doherty, they formed a Grand General Union of All the Operative Spinners of the United Kingdom. The union did not last long but, undaunted, Doherty suggested that a combination of all the workpeople in the country should be formed. In 1830 he founded the National Association for the Protection of Labour which trade societies from all over the country were invited to join. However, the funds of the association were never large and its members quarreled amongst themselves so that it collapsed in 1832. In 1830 a builders' union, known as the General Trades Union, was founded. It published a journal and held 'Parliaments' in which its members made speeches against their employers and capitalists in general.

The movement towards the creation of large unions culminated in the foundation of the Grand National Consolidated Trades Union in 1834 under the influence of Robert Owen. It was an important attempt to organize the power of the working class and was a direct answer to the 1832 Reform Act which had left five out of six working men without the vote. Its aims were to join all trade unions into a single national union, to overthrow the capitalist organization of industry, re-organizing it in the interests of the workers and to remodel local and central government on socialist lines. Within a few weeks the union had half a million members but within a year it had collapsed.

Several reasons account for the failure of the GNCTU. As soon as it was formed its members became involved in sectional and local strikes. This lack of co-ordination absorbed funds and weakened the union. In several areas employers presented their workers with the 'Document', forcing them to sign it and denounce the union. In a period of economic uncertainty many workers chose to retain their jobs rather than their trade union membership. The sentence of the Tolpuddle Martyrs diminished enthusiasm for trade union activities. In March 1834 six labourers from the village of Tolpuddle in Dorset were sentenced to seven years' transportation for administering an illegal oath when they became affiliated to the GNCTU. Public opinion was outraged at the harshness of the sentence and there followed the first monster petition to Parliament. Petitions were to become a central part of the tactics of working-class movements during the next 14 years.

After the GNCTU was dissolved in 1834 there was a turning away from trade unions. Workers turned to other means of bettering their conditions such as Chartism and the Co-operative movement. However, as early as 1841 there were signs of a trade union revival when the Miners' Association, a national union, was formed. But it did not survive the depression in the coal industry of 1847 and 48. In 1845 the National Association of United Trades for the Protection of Labour was founded, but it lasted little more than 10 years.

2 The Chartist Movement

The collapse of the GNCTU disappointed thousands of poorly paid workers. The failure of direct economic action led working-class leaders to see that they could not hope to carry important measures of social change until their supporters had the vote. They decided to apply pressure to the reformed Parliament and this was the origin of the Chartist movement. Chartism began in 1836 and remained a powerful movement until 1848. It marked a new era in the reform movement for it was organized on a nation-wide basis and had many working-class supporters.

Chartism had three 'roots'. The London Working Men's Association, led by William Lovett (1800 – 77) and Henry Hetherington (1792 – 1849), had been agitating for reform for some years. In 1837 it joined forces with the revived Birmingham Political Union which, under the leadership of Thomas Attwood, gave Chartism its middle-class support. The third strand of Chartism was centred in the north of England and tended to be more violent. Northern leaders like Feargus O'Connor (1794 – 1855) with his newspaper the *Northern Star* helped to make Chartism militant.

The original aim of the Chartists was to present a National Petition to Parliament in the hope that it would accept the terms of the People's Charter which was published in May 1838. The six points of the Charter were: annual Parliaments, universal male suffrage, equal electoral districts, the removal of the property quali-fication for MPs, a secret ballot and payment of MPs. For the poor who were suffering from the effects of a prolonged trade depression and the hardship of the new poor law the Charter became a battle cry.

By May 1839 the Petition had gathered 1,250,000 signatures from meetings held up and down the country and it was presented to Par-liament in June of that year. On 12 July Parliament rejected the Petition by 235 votes to 46. This rejection brought the divisions which existed within the Chartist movement to the surface. O'Connor suggested that force should be used to obtain the Chartists' demands whilst Lovett declared, 'the physical force agita-tion is harmful to the movement'. High prices and unemployment in 1839 helped those who advocated the use of physical force. On 21 July 1839 the National Chartist Convention, which had been meet-ing since February to decide policy, called for a 'Sacred Month', or general strike, on 12 August. The strike was a dismal failure. Few men were willing to risk their livelihood for the People's Charter. Apart from riots in Birmingham and an attempt to capture Newport on the part of local miners on the 3 November 1839 it seemed that the Chartist movement had run out of steam.

When the first National Petition failed the Chartist movement fragmented and its leaders worked individually to solve workers' difficulties. Lovett concentrated on a scheme for a national system of education whilst O'Connor worked on a land scheme to provide small-holdings for the poor. Nevertheless, the Charter continued to be brought before Parliament by the National Charter Association which was led by O'Connor. In May 1842 a second Petition was presented to Parliament. It was supported by only 51 MPs.

Following the rejection of the second Petition Chartist fervour once more collapsed. O'Connor concentrated on his land scheme but this too collapsed in 1847 due to lack of funds. In 1848 revolutions in Europe revived the Chartists in England who decided to make a third attempt to present their Petition to Parliament. Meetings were held to collect signatures and a mass demonstration on Kennington Common was planned for 10 April (see the picture of the demonstration). After a number of speeches, which were ended with a heavy downpour of rain, the Petition was taken in three cabs to Parliament. The Petition was found to contain a number of false signatures such as Sir Robert Peel, the Duke of Wellington and 'Mr Punch'. It was once more rejected.

The fiasco of 1848 marked the end of Chartism as a national movement. Its leaders had been divided by personal rivalries and by disagreements about tactics. It was never seriously considered by Parliament. However, the Chartist agitation compelled people to think about 'the condition of England' and to seek ways of distributing the country's resources more equally.

3 The Anti-Corn Law League

After the summer of 1836 there was a succession of bad harvests and an industrial depression. This led to a revival of the demand for the repeal of the Corn Laws. An anti-Corn Law association was formed in London in 1836 but a larger movement, the anti-Corn Law league, was formed in Manchester in 1838 and began operations in March 1839. Its main supporters were manufacturers and merchants from the north of England who had plenty of funds. They enlisted the support of the working class and carried out a campaign throughout the country, holding public meetings and printing pamphlets by the thousand which they were able to distribute cheaply by means of the penny post. In their campaign they tried to prove that when grain was cheap wages would be high. Several people, including Engels and many Chartists, considered that the league was dishonest

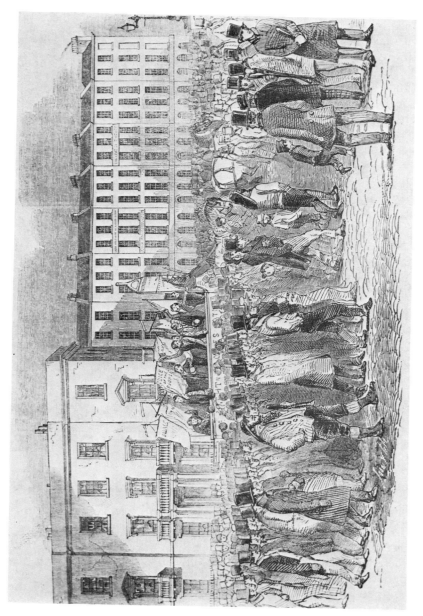

The Kennington Common procession, 10 April 1848

in adopting this argument, for they believed that its real object was to make bread cheaper so that manufacturers could keep wages down.

The leaders of the anti-Corn Law league were Richard Cobden (1804–65) and John Bright (1811–89). Both were MPs and fine speakers. Cobden was able to bring forward the most convincing arguments whilst Bright, a superb orator, was able to sway his audiences with beautiful Biblical English. They both took full advantage of parliamentary debates to produce numerous arguments in favour of the repeal of the Corn Law. They declared that the Corn Law had not prevented depression in agriculture. The Corn Law favoured one class, farmers, unfairly whilst it harmed the poor, industry and trade, the merchant navy and the entire British economy. They argued that Britain's population was growing so rapidly that the import of foreign corn was necessary to prevent starvation. Cobden and Bright also pointed out that the government claimed to follow a policy of *laissez faire* and yet continued to interfere in trade.

Enthusiasm for repeal declined after 1842. The harvests of 1842, 43 and 44 were good. Farmers and land owners formed their own league to oppose the anti-Corn Law league. They argued that the Corn Law encouraged self-sufficiency in food which was an important strategic consideration. The protectionists were never as well organized as the anti-Corn Law league. The purpose of the league was simple and easily understood. It appealed to the desire for equality for it attacked privilege and monopoly. It appealed to the middle and working classes because it offered cheaper food. For all these reasons the league was successful and the Corn Law was repealed on 25 June 1846 (see p.143). Following the repeal small duties were to be paid on imported corn until 1849 and thereafter a nominal duty of one shilling a quarter was paid until it was abolished in 1859.

Following the repeal of the Corn Law bread prices were not immediately reduced nor was British agriculture immediately ruined. In fact repeal acted as a stimulus to farmers and for the next 30 years there followed the golden age of English agriculture known as the period of 'High Farming'. British farmers did not face any large scale competition in the years following repeal because no part of the world was producing sufficient surplus with which to flood the British market.

Summary
In a period of economic depression such as existed from 1825 to 1848

the trade union movement had little chance of success. Government policy and public opinion were opposed to the unions. Trade union members were easily intimidated by their employers, and before 1840 communication between branches was often difficult and expensive. In a similar way the Chartist movement found that enthusiasm for its programme was not constant. Enthusiasm waned in years of good harvest and full employment; it took new force with the return of bad times. Its leaders were divided and it was diverted in its later stages from a political programme to a crude agricultural programme. Consequently it was never taken too seriously by the government. The anti-Corn Law league also experienced fluctuations in support. However, with two energetic leaders and the backing of the northern manufacturing towns it believed that success was only a matter of time. Unfortunately, repeal did not bring the cheap bread for which so many people yearned.

Exercises

1. Trace the development of the industrial and political activities of trade unions in the period 1825 – 33.
2. Show how the foundation of the GNCTU either assisted or hindered the development of trade unionism in Britain.
3. List the six points of the People's Charter and explain fully the meaning of each point.
4. Describe the tactics of the Chartists. Why in your opinion did the Chartist movement fail?
5. What arguments did the anti-Corn Law league put forward in favour of the repeal of the Corn Laws?
6. Why do you think that the anti-Corn Law league was successful?

14
Sir Robert Peel, 1841 – 6

Sir Robert Peel began his second ministry with a large majority in Parliament, estimated at between 76 and 91 MPs. A feeling of relief swept over political circles. Peel was trusted and respected and received a great deal of support. People were glad that the days of uncertainty associated with the last years of the Whigs were over. Peel appointed Lord Aberdeen (1784 – 1860) to the post of Foreign Secretary and Earl de Grey (1781 – 1859) became the Lord Lieutenant of Ireland. Although he had a Chancellor of the Exchequer Peel introduced two budgets himself. During his ministry Peel tackled the problem of the trade depression and he put the country's finances on a more secure footing. He was also concerned with social questions and helped to reform conditions in the mines and factories. He improved standards of public health at a time when the nation was suffering from the scourge of cholera. Like other Prime Ministers before him Peel was faced with trouble from Ireland and by affairs in China and the United States.

Early Life
Sir Robert Peel was born in 1788 and spent his childhood on the family's estate at Drayton near Tamworth. Unlike other leading Tories Peel came from the middle class and his family's wealth came from a successful cotton business not from land. He was educated at Harrow and Christ Church, Oxford, where he was the first person to obtain a double first. He became a Tory MP at the age of 21. His abilities were soon recognized by Lord Liverpool who appointed him Secretary for Ireland from 1812 to 1818 and then Home Secretary in 1822. As Home Secretary he introduced many reforms (see p.95). He left that post when Canning became Prime Minister but resumed his position in 1828 under Wellington's premiership. He helped Wellington to steer Catholic emancipation through the Commons and was at the heart of the disagreements which split the Tory party in 1830. In that year the Tories lost most of their progressive members to the Whigs. They were opposed to the movement for parliamentary reform and in the election of 1832 the party was reduced to a rump of 150 MPs.

The Conservative Party
In the years after 1832 Peel worked to remould the Tory party and he was responsible for the creation of a new Conservative party. As chief opposition spokesman in the Commons he constantly aired his views and tried to gain the support of moderate middle-class reformers. In the Tamworth Manifesto of 1835 which was addressed to his constituents he put forward his political philosophy. He accepted the changes made by the 1832 Reform Act; until then the Tory party had been bitterly opposed to them. He upheld strong government and the conservation of whatever was sound in the existing system, whilst at the same time calling for the reform of recognized abuses.

This philosophy had a wide appeal especially amongst the middle class. It revitalized the Tory party which was henceforth known as the Conservative party.

Foreign Policy

When Peel took over from the Whigs in 1841 Lord Aberdeen replaced Palmerston at the Foreign Office. A new era of foreign relations dawned in which the rights and feelings of other countries were recognized and Britain became a power to be respected and liked. Aberdeen was responsible for signing the Treaty of Nanking, 1842, with China which brought the Opium War to an end. By the treaty China was compelled to open five 'treaty' ports to foreign trade and Hong Kong became part of the British empire.

Aberdeen also dealt with two disputes about the border between Canada and the United States. One dispute related to the boundary between New Brunswick and Maine, the other to the division of the Oregon territory. For some time Oregon had been jointly administered by Britain and the United States but agitators in the United States now claimed the whole of the territory. Their slogan was 'Fifty-four forty or fight'; in other words they claimed that the United States should control the territory up to the line of latitude 54° 40′. The first dispute was settled by the Ashburton Treaty, 1842, and the second by the Oregon Treaty, 1846, which defined the boundary in the far west as the forty-ninth parallel. Palmerston denounced the settlement, declaring that Aberdeen had given away far too much to the Americans, but he had in fact given away far less than the Americans had demanded.

Social Reform

During Sir Robert Peel's administration the working conditions of miners and factory operatives were improved and foundations were laid for improvements in public health. Sir Robert Peel's father had played an important part in the promotion of the Factory Acts of 1802 and 1819 (see p.123) and Peel himself witnessed considerable reform during his second ministry. However, it must be said that reform occurred largely as a result of the efforts of individuals rather than from a concerted effort on the government's part.

In 1842 a commission established as a result of Lord Ashley's agitation published its report on female and child labour in the mines. Its findings shocked the nation. The commissioners reported that young children, some of them only five years old, were employed underground in coal mines (see the pictures of children employed in the mines). The smallest worked as trappers, operating

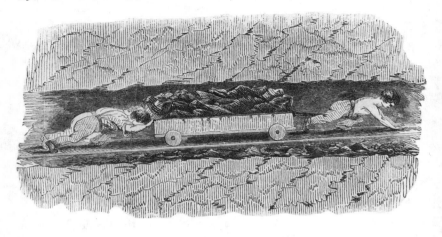

Children at work in the mines:
1. Pushing a cart of coal in cramped conditions
2. Being lowered into the pit

the trap doors which were essential for ventilation. They worked for 16 hours a day in dark, damp, solitary conditions. Women miners fared little better. They were usually employed in transporting the coal from the shaft to the surface. The Coal Mines Regulation Act, 1842, prohibited the employment of female labour and of boys under 10 in the mines. Inspectors were appointed to enforce the new law.

Supporters of the Ten Hour movement had never been satisfied with the 1833 Factory Act and they continued to agitate for reform. Some of their hopes were fulfilled when Sir James Graham (1792 – 1861), the Home Secretary, passed a Factory Act in 1844. The Act reduced the age at which children might be employed from nine to eight. Although this seemed to be a backward step it was now at least possible to check the age of an eight-year-old child accurately for the first babies registered under the compulsory registration of births, marriages and deaths would be eight years old in 1844. In other respects the Act was a considerable advance. It stated that children between the ages of eight and 13 could work a maximum of six and a half hours per day instead of nine; young persons between the ages of 13 and 18 and women had their hours of work restricted to 12 per day. The Act forbade those covered by its terms to clean moving machinery and in the interests of safety factory owners were required to fence machines.

Gradually, opinion was moving in favour of 10-hour day for women and young persons. Aware of this, Ashley introduced another Bill in 1846 but discussions were postponed because of the crisis over the Corn Law. At the end of that year Ashley lost his seat and leadership of the Ten Hour movement in the Commons passed to Fielden (1784 – 1849). In March 1847 an Act limiting the hours of women and young persons to 10 was passed. Supporters of the Ten Hour movement had hoped that this Act would force down the hours of work for men as well as women and children. However, employers worked women and children in relays and thus were able to employ men for longer than 10 hours a day. To overcome this difficulty Ashley, now returned to the Commons, introduced a Bill in 1850 to limit the hours during which a factory might open. He succeeded in this but only at the cost of increasing the hours of work for women and young persons to 10 ½ a day. Although the extra half hour lost him much support amongst the working class it established the principle of a 'normal day' with a Saturday half holiday.

During Sir Robert Peel's ministry there was increasing concern about public health and the man most responsible for improvements in that area was Edwin Chadwick. His *Report on the Sanitary*

Condition of the Labouring Population, 1842, presented an appalling picture of squalor and disease in Britain's towns. Chadwick was not a sentimentalist. He wanted to improve conditions because in their present state towns wasted resources. They created an environment in which filthy habits and dangerous ideas could develop. Chadwick dedicated himself to ending moral depravity and the threat of revolution. In 1843 there was a commission on the state of large towns and in 1845 there was an inquiry into water supply. No legislation followed the issuing of reports.

It was not until 1848 with an outbreak of cholera threatening that Lord Morpeth's (1802–64) Public Health Act was passed. The Act set up a central Board of Health in London. It permitted local Boards of Health to be set up where either 10 per cent of the ratepayers petitioned for one or the death rate in a town exceeded 23 per 1000 per annum and the government required a local board to be set up. Local boards had the power to enforce proper drainage, provide and maintain sewers, pave and cleanse streets, control offensive trades, inspect meat, control burial grounds and inspect common lodging houses. This legislation was permissive. Except in the case of an unusually high death rate there was no question of the government forcing local authorities to act for the public good. In spite of this the Bill aroused opposition. It was attacked by those who resented interference by the central government in local affairs.

Railways
In the 1840s railway companies prospered. They made their profits from carrying goods, not passengers. Peel extended passenger travel to the poor. By the Railway Act, 1844, he compelled railway companies to provide a passenger service and to charge not more than one penny per mile to third-class passengers.

Ireland
By 1840 Daniel O'Connell had decided that it was time to renew the agitation for the repeal of the union between England and Ireland. The Loyal National Repeal Association worked for this cause and in October 1842 the *Nation* newspaper was launched with strong editorials calling for repeal. In February 1843 O'Connell delivered a four-hour speech before the Dublin corporation in support of repeal. A series of mass meetings began in Ireland to agitate for repeal. O'Connell hoped that the tactics he had used in 1828 of threatening revolution would work again. Yet O'Connell still firmly believed in peaceful persuasion to obtain repeal and he was opposed to the use of force. Forty monster meetings were held and by the end

of June 1843 over £3000 a week 'repeal rent' was being collected from the people of Ireland.

O'Connell was at the head of a mass movement but Peel was determined not to be intimidated. He refused to countenance repeal even though he knew that such refusal might lead to civil war in Ireland. In October 1843 O'Connell unwittingly played into the government's hands. He planned to hold the last mass meeting of the year at Clontarf, outside Dublin. Before the meeting took place a poster, with military wording, was issued giving details of the meeting. Although it was speedily withdrawn the poster gave the government the right to ban the gathering. Earl de Grey was instructed to ban the meeting and to arrest the repeal leaders. When O'Connell heard that the Clontarf meeting had been banned he was faced with a terrible dilemma. He had either to accept the ban and lose his credibility with the mass of his supporters or to go ahead with the meeting and be responsible for the bloodshed which would inevitably follow. O'Connell cancelled the meeting and immediately lost all his influence. He was criticized by young radicals, the Young Irelanders, who were committed to the use of force if necessary to gain repeal, but who failed miserably in their efforts at an uprising in 1848.

Although Peel dealt strongly with O'Connell he was not against reform in Ireland. He instructed Earl de Grey to promote Irish Catholic laymen to official positions. He wanted to remove the inequalities in Ireland which were based on religion. He set up three Queen's Colleges, two of which were to be controlled by Catholics, where an unprejudiced sectarian education would be provided. He also increased the grant to the Catholic college of Maynooth where Irish priests were trained from £9,000 to £26,000. These reforms were not very popular in Ireland and they led to an outcry in England.

In 1845 a new crisis occurred in Ireland in the shape of a famine. In the early years of the nineteenth century Ireland's population increased dramatically, placing a great strain on the country's resources. Most Irish peasants lived in mud huts without windows or furniture. Many came close to starvation in the summer months of every year. In many areas of Ireland dependence upon the potato had become complete. A good year's crop provided just enough to feed a family with the small surplus being used for the next planting or being sold to buy essential supplies. By 1845 four million people were totally dependent upon the potato and it was not difficult to foresee disaster if the crop failed. This happened in 1845 when three-quarters of the Irish potato crop was destroyed by blight.

When the starving peasants could not pay their rents they were evicted and if they resisted the army was brought in to enforce the law. Peel responded to the famine by importing maize from the United States and by organizing relief works. He also decided that corn duties should be lowered and this led him on the path to the repeal of the Corn Law. The famine was a turning point in Irish history. The Irish began to emigrate to north America and the figure reached 200,000 in 1847. Henceforth an anti-English tradition amongst the Irish outside the United Kingdom provided another obstacle to the improvement of Anglo-Irish relations.

Trade and Finance
When Peel became Prime Minister the country was suffering from a trade depression which led not unnaturally to popular unrest. He was determined to curb the excesses of popular agitation whilst at the same time introducing legislation to cure the economic depression which bred discontent. His remedy for the country's slack trading position was to reduce tariffs. In 1840 the Board of Trade had produced evidence to show that tariffs on raw materials were counter-productive. They raised the price of British manufactured goods, making them less competitive abroad. The tariffs did little to increase the government's revenue because the cost of collection was very high. The Board also claimed that no industry, except for ship-building, silk weaving and agriculture, needed protection.

Given the evidence from the Board of Trade Peel introduced a budget in 1842 which extended free trade. Import duties were reduced to a maximum of five per cent on raw materials, 12 per cent on semi-manufactured goods and 20 per cent on manufactured goods. This budget has been seen as one of the greatest of the nineteenth century. Peel's second budget of 1845 went further along the path of freeing trade. By the end of his term of office in 1846 Peel had abolished two-thirds of the duties which existed in 1841. In his opinion free trade would lead to a greater demand for British goods and therefore to more consistent and better paid employment for the British work force. To a certain extent his opinion was sound for at the Great Exhibition of 1851 the strength of Britain's manufacturing position was confirmed.

Peel helped to restore the nation's finances from the sorry state in which the Whigs had left them. The Whigs had failed to balance their income and expenditure and in the financial year of 1841–2 there was a deficit of two and a quarter million pounds. Peel realized that by reducing tariffs he had reduced the government's revenue and he understood that drastic action was needed if the deficit was not to grow. In 1842 he re-introduced income tax at the rate of seven pence in the pound on incomes over £150 per annum. The tax yielded £5 million or 10 per cent of the government's needs. It reduced the burden of taxation on the working class for even skilled men did not qualify as income tax payers. Except for Peel's first year in office he managed to return surpluses every year and he substantially reduced the national debt.

Peel brought stability to Britain's banking system. There were hundreds of small country banks in England which were free to issue notes so long as they were able to exchange the notes for gold on demand. These banks often issued more notes than they had gold, leading to inflation and, in some cases, to the collapse of banks. To put an end to this situation and restore confidence in Britain's banks Peel passed the Bank Charter Act in 1844. It was designed to control the amount of paper money in circulation. By the Act the Bank of England was divided into two sections, one dealing with note issue the other with ordinary banking business. The issuing section was allowed to issue £14 million worth of notes without any gold backing, but apart from this 'fiduciary' issue every note had to be backed by gold. No new note issuing banks could be created and existing banks were limited in their note issue to the totals they had issued up to the passage of the Act. If a note issuing bank went bankrupt or amalgamated with another bank it lost the right to issue notes. This banking system remained in operation until well into the twentieth century and served Britain during her period of world economic domination.

The Repeal of the Corn Law
In the area of trade it is not necessarily for his budgets that Peel is best remembered but for his decision to repeal the Corn Law. In 1842 Peel's budget altered the corn duties by introducing a sliding scale but at that stage he still believed in agricultural protection. Agriculture needed protection he believed because of its heavy tax burden, its dependence on good weather and its vital role in the country's economy. However, within three years Peel had changed his mind and this put him in a very difficult position for he was the leader of the Conservative party — the party which had traditional links with the landed interest.

In the autumn of 1845 there was a poor wheat harvest and a failure of the Irish potato crop. Peel and the Home Secretary called for immediate action to avoid suffering and they were convinced that the duties on grain should be suspended so that stocks in the ports could be released to prevent starvation. On 31 October 1845 Peel asked the cabinet to agree to the opening of the ports and to a recall of Parliament so that a Bill to lower the sliding scale could be introduced. When some members of the cabinet refused to accept his proposals Peel resigned. Lord John Russell was asked to form a government but he could not and so Peel was asked to continue in office. He decided to press on with the repeal of the Corn Law, believing that his colleagues would prefer to support him and the national interest rather than destroy their party. He was wrong. Repeal took five months, during which time Peel was subjected to more criticism than he had ever known. He was attacked by a fellow Conservative, Benjamin Disraeli (1804 – 81), whom Peel had refused to admit to office in 1841, and by Lord George Bentinck (1802 – 48) who argued that Peel had betrayed not only his own principles but those of his party by calling for the repeal of the Corn Law. The Bill passed its third reading on 25 June 1846. Many Tories were incensed by Peel's action on the Corn Law. On 29 June he was forced to resign because on the previous day a number of his former supporters had joined with the Whigs to defeat the government over a Co-ercion Bill for Ireland. Once more the party to which Peel belonged was shattered.

Summary
The period 1841 – 6 when Sir Robert Peel was Prime Minister is seen as one of outstandingly good government. Peel founded the modern Conservative party with its stress on retaining what was good and reforming what was not. His policies appealed to the increasingly important middle class. He introduced reforms to help miners and factory workers and when he died in 1850 the poor wept at his funeral. He helped to free trade and stabilize banking and he reduced the burden of taxation on the working class. He dealt firmly but humanely with Ireland. Over the question of the repeal of the Corn Law he put his country before his party. This commendable course of action benefited the economy but led to a period of party political confusion.

Exercises
1. How did the Tamworth Manifesto reflect the changing attitudes of the Tory party?
2. Show how the domestic measures of Peel's second ministry benefited the working class.
3. How did Peel extend free trade?
4. Why did landowners feel that Peel threatened their prosperity?

15
Lord Palmerston: Foreign Policy, 1830 – 65

Lord Palmerston was one of the most successful of all British politicians. He became Secretary of War in 1809 at the age of 29 and held the post for 19 years. He was Foreign Secretary from 1830 to 1841. At first he was regarded as rather weak and was nicknamed 'Lord Cupid' because he seemed to be more interested in love affairs than in diplomacy. Before the end of his term of office, however, he had raised English prestige in Europe to new heights and the new nickname for this forceful diplomat was 'Lord Pumicestone'. Without any particular following in Parliament, he became the most popular statesman in the country because of his vigorous defence of England and the rights of Englishmen abroad.

Palmerston played a crucial role in the creation of Belgium, saved Portugal and Spain from chaos and tyranny, rescued Turkey from Russia and safeguarded the route to India from France. He became Foreign Secretary for a second time from 1846 to 1851 when he was dismissed by the Queen. It is said that he would probably have averted the Crimean War had he been Foreign Secretary at the time. In 1855 when he was in his seventieth year he became Prime Minister and was seen by the public as the only man who could win the war. With a break of 16 months he remained Prime Minister until he died in 1865.

Lord Palmerston's Principles of Foreign Policy

Palmerston's aim was always to protect and strengthen Britain's interests. He kept his ambassadors well informed and he went as far beyond Canning in instructing the public as Canning had gone beyond Castlereagh. Palmerston rejected the idea of a 'system' of foreign policy, believing that this had led to the failure of European statesmen like Metternich, but he was governed by certain principles. In 1832 he pledged Britain to uphold 'the independence of constitutional states'. He also believed that the British government should act upon the principle of 'non-interference by force of arms in the affairs of another country' but should rely instead on 'friendly counsel and advice'. When it came to conducting foreign policy Palmerston was not always governed by these principles, he was rather a master of improvization.

The Belgian Question

The first problem which Palmerston faced when he became Foreign Secretary related to Belgium. In 1815 at the Congress of Vienna Belgium and Holland had been united into the Kingdom of the United Netherlands. The union was dominated by the Dutch whose king, William I, showed favouritism to his own people and discriminated against the Belgians. A combination of economic, political and religious discontent led to an uprising in Brussels in 1830 when Dutch troops were expelled from the city. At this stage the great powers became anxious for the Vienna settlement seemed to be severely threatened.

The situation was complicated for there had been a revolution in France in 1830 in which the autocratic Charles X had been replaced by Louis Philippe, a member of the Orleanist branch of the French royal family. He was determined to rule as a constitutional monarch and he tried to assure the great powers that he had no intention of leading France on a second path of revolution throughout Europe. In spite of these reassurances there was growing concern that France might try to annex Belgium especially since the Belgians looked to France for help. The danger of general war grew. Prussia and Austria seemed prepared to support the Dutch whilst France seemed prepared to support the Belgians.

Palmerston did not support the Prussian and Austrian calls for an immediate end to the Belgian revolt, nor did he wish to see France gain control of Belgium. Palmerston and Talleyrand met in London and then persuaded the Dutch and Belgians to accept an armistice. Matters took an awkward turn when the Belgians chose Louis Philippe's second son, the Duke of Nemours, as their King. This was quite unacceptable to Palmerston who cajoled and then threatened Louis Philippe until he disowned the idea. The Belgians then chose someone who was acceptable to Palmerston — Prince Leopold of Saxe-Coburg, the uncle of the future husband of Queen Victoria — but their choice proved to be unacceptable to the Dutch who sent troops into Belgium. Palmerston permitted French troops to invade Belgium to oust the Dutch forces. He was then compelled to join with Austria and Prussia to pressurize a reluctant Louis Phillipe to evacuate Belgium. Louis Philippe was forced to accept Palmerston's wishes for the safety of his throne depended upon British support. A combined British and French force then drove the Dutch out of

Antwerp. In 1839 the great powers of Europe signed the Treaty of London which defined Belgium's frontiers and guaranteed her neutrality.

Palmerston's first foreign policy venture had been a success. He had secured a peaceful solution to a situation which could so easily have ended in war. Britain's interests had been safeguarded and her influence extended. Belgium was independent and no major European power could use that country as a base from which to threaten Britain. The creation of an independent Belgium is seen as one of Palmerston's greatest triumphs and it is even more remarkable when we realize just how inexperienced he was in matters of foreign policy.

Spain and Portugal

In the 1830s there was a struggle for succession in Portugal and Spain where in both cases girl heirs to the throne were challenged by their uncles. In 1828 Dom Miguel had seized the throne of Portugal from the young Queen Donna Maria, whilst in Spain Don Carlos opposed the accession of the young Queen Isabella to the throne. In both cases the Queens were identified with constitutional rule and their uncles with the forces of reaction. Opinion in Europe on the matter was divided but Palmerston felt that Britain should support the young Queens. He sent British forces to expel the uncles. In 1834 he made an alliance with Spain, Portugal and France which he described as 'a quadruple alliance among the constitutional states of the west, which will serve as a powerful counterpoise to the Holy Alliance of the east'. It led to the flight of the despotic uncles from Spain and Portugal.

The Slave Trade

After a long career Palmerston had many achievements to his credit. He regarded the suppression of the slave trade as 'the achievement to which I look back with the greatest and purest pleasure'. He kept a naval squadron off the west African coast to stop the trade and signed treaties with France in 1831 and Spain in 1835 which gave rights of search to suspected slave ships. He forced Portugal and Brazil to abandon the trade so that the slave trade was only carried on in ships from the United States until that too was stopped by a treaty in 1862.

The Eastern Question

Throughout the decade of the 1830s Palmerston was concerned with the Eastern Question, in particular with the struggle between the

Sultan of Turkey and his nominal vassal Mehemet Ali, the Pasha of Egypt. Mehemet Ali had helped the Sultan during the Greek War of Independence on the condition that when hostilities ceased he should be given the Morea and Crete. When the Greeks gained the Morea he demanded in its place the greater part of Syria. The Sultan, who had already lost Greece, refused to give any territory to Mehemet Ali.

In 1831 war broke out between Mehemet Ali and the Sultan and in 1832 the Pasha's son, Ibrahim, advanced into Asia Minor and conquered Syria. The Turkish army was defeated at Konieh. Britain was unprepared for this situation and whilst Turkey seemed to be on the verge of collapse the only country ready to help the Sultan was Russia. Russia sent troops to protect Constantinople and this saved Asia Minor from Mehemet Ali's clutches but the Sultan had to assign the government of Syria and Palestine to Mehemet Ali. Turkey and Russia signed the mutual defence agreement of Unkiar Skelessi in 1833 which had a secret clause excluding Turkey from her part of the agreement provided she kept the Straits closed to the warships of all nations, except Russia, whenever Russia demanded. Palmerston was shocked when he learned of the secret clause for he believed that it gave Russia too much influence in the Turkish empire. He was determined that in future Britain would not remain passive when the Turkish empire was threatened and he worked hard to reverse the terms of the secret clause. He instructed his ambassador Ponsonby (1770 – 1855) to build up influence with the Turks and the sultan Mahmud began a programme of modernization.

In 1839 in an attempt to regain Syria the Sultan sent an army to attack Mehemet Ali's forces but it was easily defeated. The Egyptian army had been reorganized by the French on the initiative of Thiers who hoped to extend French influence in the Middle East. He also hoped to gain a part of Syria in return for his help. During the conflict Mahmud died and was succeeded by a young weak ruler. Palmerston set to work to organize a conference in London, which he hoped would put an end to Mehemet Ali's schemings and bring stability to the Turkish empire. However, he had to accept a conference in Vienna instead which resulted in the Collective Note of July 1839. This called on the Sultan to trust the great powers to maintain his empire. Neither France nor Russia seemed happy with this outcome. Palmerston was determined to press on and in July 1840 he secured two conventions.

By the Convention of London, from which Palmerston had excluded France and which was signed by Britain, Austria, Russia and Prussia, Mehemet Ali was offered the southern half of Syria, was recognized as the hereditary ruler of Egypt and was ordered to make peace with the Sultan within ten days. When he refused to accept these terms an allied fleet captured Crete, a British squadron bombarded Alexandria and British troops captured Acre. Mehemet Ali was conquered by force and Louis Philippe was so frightened that he dismissed Thiers and took part in the second Convention of London. By the terms of this conference Mehemet Ali gave back Syria and Crete to the Sultan but his position as hereditary ruler of Egypt was confirmed. Palmerston had succeeded in strengthening Turkey, controlling Russia and dealing with French ambitions of expansion

In 1841 at the Straits Convention Palmerston reversed the situation created by the Treaty of Unkiar Skelessi. At the Straits Convention the Sultan agreed to close the Black Sea to the warships of all nations.

China and the Opium Wars

Britain fought two Chinese wars in Palmerston's time which resulted from a difference in outlook between the societies of the East and West. The rulers of China wished to keep out strangers so that their empire would not be contaminated whilst western traders wanted to take part in what they saw as a highly profitable trade. In 1833 the East India Company's trading monopoly was abolished and large numbers of British traders entered the markets of the Far East, taking part in the opium trade with China. In 1839 the Chinese government seized British cargoes of opium at Canton and put an embargo on trade with Britain. Palmerston demanded compensation for the losses suffered by British traders and when this was refused he bombarded Canton. By the Treaty of Nanking, 1842 most of Palmerston's demands were met (see p.137).

The trading concessions given to Britain in 1842 were also granted to other powers. The settlement could not last long for foreign merchants wanted more concessions whilst the Chinese government wanted to withdraw the concessions it had given. Further complications between Britain and China arose in 1856 when the Chinese seized a trading vessel, the *Arrow*, which was engaged in the opium trade and piracy. The vessel had an English registration but a Chinese owner who lived in Hong Kong and a Chinese crew. A joint British and French naval force seized Canton in 1857 and bombarded Tientsin in 1858. The Chinese signed the Treaty of Tientsin in 1858 and the opium trade was legalized. Several more ports were opened to British and French traders. When the Chinese refused to ratify the agreement a second expedition was sent to Peking in 1860 and the Chinese were forced to give way.

Palmerston was accused of high-handed action in his dealings with the Chinese. He was roundly criticized in the Commons. He put his case to the electorate in simple, patriotic terms and they gave him overwhelming support in the general election. He had protected Britain's trade and safeguarded Englishmen in China at a time when the Chinese had put a price on the head of every Englishman.

The Spanish Marriages

When he was Foreign Secretary Lord Aberdeen had worked with the French minister, Guizot, to find husbands for Queen Isabella of Spain and her sister the Infanta Louisa. They had agreed that Isabella should marry a Spanish Bourbon — either the Duke of Cadiz or the Duke of Seville. The former was believed to be incapable of having children whilst the latter was unacceptable to Isabella's mother. It had been decided that Louisa should marry one of Louis Philippe's sons when the Queen of Spain had married and had an heir.

When Palmerston became Foreign Secretary he supported the Duke of Seville. He made the mistake of allowing the French to copy a dispatch in which he criticized the Spanish government. The French promptly showed their copy to the Spaniards. Spain was so irritated that Isabella married the Duke of Cadiz whilst at the same time her sister married one of Louis Philippe's sons. Palmerston and Queen Victoria protested to Louis Philippe about his treachery. However, France did not benefit in the end and, more by luck than anything else, Britain's policy of preventing a union of the thrones of France and Spain was not defeated.

The 1848 Revolutions

In 1848 revolts broke out all over Europe. The press of liberalism and nationalism had been ignored at the Congress of Vienna. The desire for freedom and independence had smouldered in the hearts of many Europeans and it erupted in 1848 in the form of violent outbreaks of unrest. In France Louis Philippe was overthrown and a republic was established. In Austria Metternich was forced into flight and in the Austrian empire in Hungary, Bohemia, Croatia, Lombardy and Venetia the people demanded independence. In Italy there were revolts in several states where the rebels called for unity and constitutional governments. Revolts in Germany led most of the 39 states to grant constitutions. Before the revolutions broke out Palmerston had stressed the need to make concessions to the liberal movements so that violence could be averted. His advice went unheeded.

Palmerston's approach to the 1848 revolutions gives us an insight into his general approach to foreign affairs. He did not follow any particular principles and was prepared to deal with different rebels in different ways so long as British interests were protected. He allowed British arms to reach the rebels in Sicily and he recognized the new French republic once he was sure that it posed no threat to Britain. However, he ignored the appeals of the Hungarian rebels for help even when Russian troops marched against them. Palmerston spoke out against the brutal suppression of the Hungarian revolt but he took no action, for he wished to preserve the unity of the Austrian empire as a check to any future Russian expansion in the Balkans.

In 1850 General Haynau, who had carried out reprisals against the Hungarian rebels, came to Britain on an official visit. The British public nick-named him 'Hyena' and he was attacked by draymen at Barclay's brewery. Palmerston called him 'a great moral criminal' and gave only a mild apology to the Austrian government. He would not have apologised at all had not Queen Victoria insisted upon it. She disliked Palmerston's high-handed methods of dealing with foreign governments, especially as she was related to many of the royal families of Europe.

Don Pacifico

Palmerston's popularity prevented the Queen and Russell from dismissing him even though they would have liked to. His popularity reached new heights with the Don Pacifico incident. During anti-government riots in Athens in 1847 the home and stores of Don Pacifico, a merchant, were destroyed. He applied to the Greek government for £20,000 compensation, but got nowhere for the Greeks believed that his claim was excessive. Since he was a Gibraltarian-born Jew and claimed to be a British subject he applied to the British government for help. Palmerston sent a fleet to Athens which seized a number of Greek vessels as surety for compensation.

France and Russia, who had signed the Treaty of London which guaranteed Greek independence, were furious when they heard the news of Palmerston's action. The French ambassador was recalled from London and Palmerston was challenged by British liberals who attacked his bullying methods. The Don Pacifico affair led to one of the most famous debates in the Commons in the nineteenth century. Palmerston defended himself in his greatest speech which lasted for over four hours. In a survey of British foreign policy he declared,

> 'The Roman in days of old held himself free from indignity when he could say, "Civis Romanus sum", so also a British subject, in whatever land he may be, shall feel confident that the watchful eye and the strong arm of England will protect him against injustice and wrong.'

Palmerston defeated the motion of censure by 56 votes. He had protected Englishmen's rights throughout the world and received much popular support. Yet all he had really done was to gain a cheap triumph over the weak Greek state.

Palmerston's Dismissal

In 1848 the French overthrew Louis Philippe and elected Louis Napoleon as President of the Second Republic. In 1851 he staged a coup d'etat and became an absolute ruler. When he heard the news of the coup Palmerston privately congratulated the French ambassador in London. His anti-constitutional stance was not popular with the Queen and Prime Minister. Russell used his action to force Palmerston's resignation. However, Palmerston obtained his revenge in the following year for he persuaded a majority in the Commons to vote against Russell on the Militia Bill. Palmerston told his wife, 'I have had my tit for tat'. In 1855 Palmerston became Prime Minister. He was appointed to that post to win the Crimean War and he quickly brought matters to a successful conclusion (see p.161). He remained Prime Minister, except for one short break, until his death in 1865, and he continued to pursue his interest in foreign affairs.

The Italian Question

Until the 1860s there was no Italian kingdom; Italy consisted of 13 separate states with some of the northern ones dominated by Austria. Austria naturally opposed Italian unity. On the other hand Napoleon III tried to champion the cause of Italian unity, whilst at the same time upholding the Pope's position in the Papal States. As far as Palmerston was concerned, he did not mind seeing the Austrians driven out of Italy. He wanted to secure constitutions for the Italian states, but he also wanted to prevent France from gaining undue influence in Italy.

In 1858 an Italian patriot, Orsini, tried to assassinate Napoleon III, claiming that the emperor had not given enough support to the cause of Italian unity. Orsini sought refuge in Britain. Palmerston introduced a Conspiracy to Murder Bill so that Orsini could be sent back to France to face a trial. He was defeated on this issue and resigned. He returned to power in June 1859 when the Italian question threatened the peace of Europe.

In 1859 war broke out between Sardinia and Austria and Napoleon III came to the Italians' aid but he backed down and made peace with Austria, before he had fulfilled the agreement made with Sardinia at the Spa of Plombières in 1858. In spite of Napoleon III's betrayal Sardinia gained Lombardy and there were popular movements in Modena, Parma and Tuscany in favour of uniting with Sardinia. Palmerston declared that anyone who tried to defeat these popular movements in the three duchies would face opposition from Britain. This was a direct challenge to Austria, for Austrian dukes ruled the duchies, and it was effective. By 1860 most of northern Italy was united. Nice and Savoy were awarded to Napoleon III as promised in return for his help.

In 1860 a new phase of the Italian question occupied Europe. In May 1860 Garibaldi and his 1000 volunteers landed in Sicily and overthrew the Bourbon government. Palmerston had to act cautiously for, although he sympathized with the Italians, he distrusted Napoleon III and was very anxious to maintain peace in Europe. Popular opinion in England supported Garibaldi and subscriptions were raised to help his cause. At this stage Napoleon III tried to get British co-operation to stop Garibaldi from crossing the Straits of Messina and landing in Naples, on the grounds that he feared for the Pope's safety at the hands of Garibaldi. Palmerston and Russell opposed this idea and Garibaldi crossed over to the mainland. The Neapolitan kingdom collapsed and Cavour, the Prime Minister of the Kingdom of Sardinia, sent troops into the Papal States to forestall any action against Rome. On 15 October 1860 Garibaldi presented the two Sicilies to the King of Sardinia, Victor Emmanuel II, who became the constitutional King of Italy. The Italian revolution had succeeded. Palmerston had supported Italian unity, not because he strongly upheld the principles of nationalism, but because he was anxious at all times to maintain a balance of power in Europe. The creation of a new state, which bordered on the Mediterranean, and which was friendly towards Britain, would serve to check the growing power of France.

The American Civil War, 1861–5
In 1861 civil war broke out between the northern and southern states of America. Palmerston pursued a policy of neutrality for he wished 'to give no pretext to the Washingtonians to quarrel with us'. Two incidents disrupted this policy. The first occurred in 1861 when two

southern envoys were seized from the British ship the *Trent*. Palmerston protested strongly whilst Prince Albert helped to secure moderation in Britain's dealings with America. When the northern states refused to release the envoys Britain sent troops to Canada and prepared for war. At this stage President Lincoln apologized and released the two men.

The second incident related to a British vessel the *Alabama*. The southern states had ordered this ship to be built at Birkenhead and, even though it was an unarmed merchant ship, it was designed in such a way to make it readily convertible into a battle ship. Lincoln protested and Russell reluctantly ordered the shipyard not to deliver the *Alabama*. His orders arrived too late and the ship carried out a series of raids on the northern states. It was left to Gladstone to make amends for the North's losses (see p. 174).

The Schleswig Holstein Question
Palmerston's biggest failure came in 1864 over the question of the two duchies, Schleswig and Holstein. Holstein was inhabited by German-speaking people and was a member of the German Confederation, Schleswig was not. These two territories were ruled by the King of Denmark and in 1852 the great powers signed the Treaty of London, by which the duchies were to continue to be ruled by the King of Denmark but were to remain separate from Denmark.

In 1863, as part of his plan to unite Germany, Bismarck, the Prussian Chancellor, persuaded Austria to occupy Schleswig. In 1864, in spite of Palmerston's warnings, Prussia and Austria attacked Denmark. They dictated peace terms to the Danes and took over the duchies themselves. The British public disliked the way Bismarck had dealt with Denmark and they were disturbed when the two duchies, which were strategically important, passed into German hands. But there was no popular movement in favour of war against Prussia and, in spite of his threats, Palmerston never intended that Britain should fight to defend the Treaty of London. He should not have made threats to Prussia if he did not intend to carry them out as this weakened Britain's standing in Europe. This incident shows just how much the European situation had changed since Palmerston first became Foreign Secretary. Policies which had previously been successful now no longer worked. Palmerston the blusterer had finally had his bluff called.

Summary
Throughout the many years in which Palmerston directed Britain's foreign policy he declared that he had 'endeavoured to maintain the

dignity and to uphold the interests of the country abroad'. He secured Belgian independence and supported progressive movements in Spain and Italy. He handled the crisis which arose in the Turkish empire with great skill and safeguarded British interests when they were threatened by Russia. He gained a reputation as a progressive for his work against the traffic in slaves. However, he realized that peace in Europe best served Britain's interests and for this reason he failed to help the Hungarians in the 1848 revolutions for he did not want to see the Austrian empire wrecked. His aggressive defence of Englishmen's rights abroad can best be seen in the case of the opium wars with China and in the Don Pacifico affair. However, by 1864 threats of aggression no longer worked and Bismarck triumphed in Schleswig and Holstein. By this time Palmerston was a very old man and public opinion did not blame him too much for his failure.

Exercises
1. What principles guided Palmerston in his conduct of foreign affairs?
2. From Lord Palmerston's career describe an example of each of the following:
    a) an incident in which Britain bullied a lesser power,
    b) an episode in which Palmerston secured future European stability,
    c) an episode in which Palmerston was unwise and unsuccessful.

16
The Crimean War, 1854-6

In 1852 Lord Aberdeen became Prime Minister at the head of a Whig – Peelite coalition. In 1854 this government entered the only European war which Britain fought between 1815 and 1914 — the Crimean War. Britain 'drifted' into this war which took place almost by accident and she was not prepared for what faced her troops in the Crimea. Hostilities dragged on for almost two years and as reports of the sufferings of the troops were published British public opinion turned against the government and the army administration. In the end Britain and the allies claimed a great victory at the Peace of Paris, 1856. However, the fruits of victory did not last and the Eastern Question continued to plague British politicians.

1 The Causes of the War

Russian Ambitions

For many years Russia had sought to expand at Turkey's expense and in the 1840s Czar Nicholas I became increasingly aggressive. Britain was aware of the Czar's aims for, on a visit to London in 1844, Nicholas proposed that Britain and Russia should come to an agreement about Turkey. He argued that since the Turkish empire was about to collapse it ought to be partitioned and suggested that Britain take Egypt and Crete, allowing Russia to occupy Constantinople. In addition Nicholas suggested that Moldavia and Wallachia, Serbia and Bulgaria should become independent provinces 'protected' by Russia, but with their status guaranteed by the great powers (see Fig. 12, p.160). In 1853 Nicholas repeated these proposals to the British ambassador in Moscow. It could only be a matter of time before the Czar sought a way to achieve his ambitions.

The Holy Places, 1852

The dispute which led to war in 1854 arose over the Holy Places in Palestine. French monks had increasingly lost control of the right to guard the Holy Places to Greek Orthodox monks. In an attempt to pursue a forward policy and to win the support of French Catholics Napoleon III demanded restitution of the ancient rights to French Roman Catholic monks. In February 1852 the Sultan agreed to French guardianship of the Church at Bethlehem and of the Grotto of the Holy Manger. At about the same time the Sultan told the Greek monks that the status quo would be maintained. Russia protested against the privileges allowed to the French whilst France protested against the reassurance given to the Greeks.

The Invasion of Moldavia and Wallachia, 1853

The concessions awarded to the French monks at the expense of the Greeks angered the Czar. As the champion of the Orthodox monks he felt snubbed. Early in 1853 he sent Prince Menshikov to Constantinople to seek satisfaction from the Sultan. Menshikov demanded that the Greek monks should retain their privileges with regard to the Holy Places. He also demanded that the Czar should be recognized as the protector of all Orthodox Christians in the Turkish empire. This demand alarmed the great powers of Europe for it would have given Russia the right to interfere constantly in Turkish affairs. Turkey refused to accept the demands. In June 1853 the British fleet moved to Besika Bay outside the Dardanelles as a warning to the Russians not to press their claims too far. Russia seemed undeterred and decided to occupy the Danubian provinces — Moldavia and Wallachia — in pursuit of her demands. On 3 July 1853 Russian troops crossed into Moldavia. At this stage Napoleon III agreed to support Britain with a squadron of his Mediterranean fleet.

The Vienna Note, 1853

In the summer of 1853 efforts were made to prevent war. A conference of Austria, France, Prussia and Britain met in Vienna. The conference proposed that the Turks should observe the spirit of previous treaties with Russia and that they should not change the position of their Christian subjects without consulting Russia and France. The Czar accepted the Vienna Note containing these proposals but the Turks did not. War between Russia and Turkey seemed inevitable.

Sinope, 1853

In October 1853 Turkey declared war on Russia, attacking her troops in Moldavia. In November the Russian fleet destroyed a Turkish squadron at Sinope on the Black Sea. After this battle the British government agreed to co-operate with the French in blockading the Russian navy in Sebastopol and protecting Turkey in the Black Sea area. Finally, Britain and France issued an ultimatum demanding that Russia withdraw from the principalities. When Russia refused war was declared on 27 March 1854.

Who was Responsible for the Outbreak of the Crimean War?

Czar Nicholas I is held partly responsible for the outbreak of the Crimean War. He misread the feelings of the other great powers and was too proud to back down when Menshikov's demands were rejected. Napoleon III must bear some of the blame as he pursued an expansionist policy and refused to compromise as the quarrel developed. Austria did not seek a quarrel with Russia but disliked the Czar's policy towards Turkey. Prussia had no Near Eastern policy at all.

The British government cannot be held responsible for the

original crisis, but its failure to take a strong line made matters worse. Lord Aberdeen presided over a coalition government. The cabinet was divided between neutrality and involvement. It failed to give the British ambassador in Constantinople, Sir Stratford de Redcliffe (1786 – 1880), a clear lead. Several writers have argued that the ambassador bears some responsibility for the outbreak of the Crimean War. He is said to have persuaded Turkey to resist Menshikov's demands and the terms of the Vienna Note. Even those writers who do not accept this view of the ambassador's conduct agree that his presence in Turkey, where he took a strongly pro-Turkish line, seemed to confirm Britain's support for the Turks and gave them the confidence to face war. Whilst the cabinet could not make up its mind upon a course of action, British public opinion was in no doubt that the Russians should be resisted. After Sinope the people demanded war and the government found it difficult to resist their demands. Some years later when hostilities had ceased Lord Aberdeen declared that the Crimean War was a just war but he seemed to imply that it was quite unnecessary.

2 The Events of the War

Britain's War Aims
Since Britain had slipped into the war almost by accident her war aims were not clearly defined. The cabinet agreed that they wanted the army to keep the Russians out of Constantinople and to drive them from Moldavia and Wallachia. They also had some idea of an attack upon Sebastopol, the great Russian naval base on the Black Sea.

The Evacuation of Moldavia and Wallachia
The course of the Crimean War was dramatically altered almost at the outset when, under Austrian demands, the Russians withdrew from the Danubian principalities of Moldavia and Wallachia. The allied plans for an advance through the principalities became impossible. Instead it was decided that the allied troops should invade the Crimean peninsula with the aim of eliminating Russian power in the Black Sea.

The Allied Army
Lord Raglan (1788 – 1855), a man of 66 who had not seen active service for 40 years, was appointed commander-in-chief of the British forces. He was a brave and conscientious soldier but had little more than average ability. St Arnaud led the French troops. He was a

clever man, lacking in moral authority, who suffered from ill health. He died during the war and was succeeded by Canrobert who was irresolute and timid. The British force in the Crimea was about 26,000 strong with 66 guns, the French about 30,000 with 70 guns and there were about 5000 Turks. The allied troops never worked well together and this hampered their war effort.

The Battle of the Alma, 1854
The allied troops landed in the Bay of Eupatoria to the north of Sebastopol; on 19 September they moved forward over open country. Their first objective was to dislodge the Russian troops on the banks of the river Alma. British troops carried out this operation successfully but the French refused to follow up this success and the chance to bring the war to a swift conclusion was lost. The allied troops then moved inland to more protected positions south and south-west of the fortress of Sebastopol.

The Battle of Balaclava, 1854
Since the allied landings in the Crimea the Russians had not been idle. They had strengthened the defences of Sebastopol. They knew that unless they made a great effort to drive off the allies they could not save the fortress. Their best chance of success lay in a surprise attack. In October the Russian field army carried out a surprise attack on the British base at Balaclava.

The battle of Balaclava is remembered for its two famous cavalry charges. The first of these charges made by the heavy brigade of 900 men under General Scarlett (1799 – 1871), was uphill against 3000 Russian horsemen and it prevented the enemy from sweeping down onto British positions. The second of the charges was made by the light brigade. Raglan had ordered it to charge after the retreating Russians and recapture some guns that they were bearing off. Due to confusion in the orders the light brigade charged up a mile long valley which was dominated by Russian artillery. The brigade, led by Lord Cardigan (1797 – 1868), captured the wrong set of guns. When they realized their mistake they rode back again. Their retreat was greatly assisted by the French who had driven back enemy troops and guns on the northern slopes above the valley. Out of 673 horsemen in the light brigade 113 were killed and 134 were wounded; 475 horses were killed. The Russians withdrew and Raglan, still thinking in terms of an attack on Sebastopol, did not pursue them.

The Battle of Inkerman, 1854
In November 1854 the Russians attempted another surprise attack

on the British positions at Inkerman. They attacked at dawn under cover of a thick mist. The battle of Inkerman has been described as 'a soldiers' battle' because there were few large tactical moves and the issue was decided by hand-to-hand fighting of the fiercest kind. In the end the Russians were beaten off with severe losses.

The Sufferings of the Troops

After the battle of Inkerman there was no hope of capturing the fortress at Sebastopol until the spring of 1855 (see Fig. 12, The Crimean War). The allies had to face a Crimean winter in which the troops suffered terrible hardships. British troops spent the winter on open ground without adequate supplies of food, fuel or clothing. These privations led to outbreaks of cholera, dysentery and malarial fever. In January, 14,000 British troops lay in hospital. The hospitals were insanitary, badly managed and short of stores. Gradually Florence Nightingale (1820 – 1910) began to reform the hospitals at Scutari.

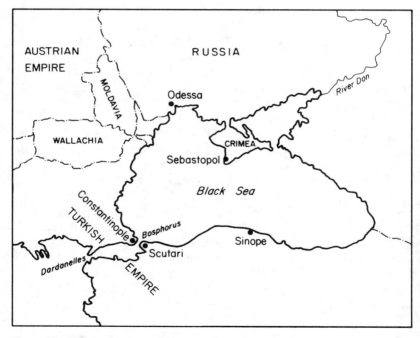

Fig.12 The Crimean War, 1854 – 56

Lord Aberdeen's Resignation, 1855

W.H. Russell, the special correspondent of *The Times*, reported on the chaotic administration of the war and highlighted the sufferings of the soldiers. Press censorship as we know it today did not exist in the 1850s. Amongst the British people there was a growing demand for an inquiry into the conduct of the war. When Parliament reassembled in January 1855 a motion to inquire into the conduct of the army and supply services was supported by a large majority. Aberdeen resigned and Palmerston became Prime Minister. The commission of inquiry was set up and commissioners went to the Crimea in March 1855. They praised the troops and blamed the cabinet for the breakdown of the supply services. The worst defects were quickly remedied.

The Capture of Sebastopol, 1855

In June 1855 the allies attacked Sebastopol but failed to capture the fortress. In August the French captured the Malakov redoubt which dominated the fortress. The Russians quickly abandoned their positions, leaving Sebastopol in allied hands.

The End of the War

Even after the fall of Sebastopol peace seemed little nearer. Czar Nicholas died and was succeeded by Alexander II but the war continued. Napoleon III demanded that the war be ended or widened with such aims as the reconstitution of Poland. Finally an Austrian ultimatum to Russia in December 1855 forced the Czar to accept the allied peace terms.

3 The Results of the War

The Treaty of Paris, 1856

On 25 February 1856 the peace congress opened in Paris and on 30 March the Treaty of Paris was signed between Britain, Russia, Turkey, France and Piedmont. The Treaty covered four main points. First, the Black Sea was to be neutralized. It was to be open to all trading ships and closed to all war ships and military or naval fortifications on its coastline were prohibited. This 'Black Sea Clause' dealt a humiliating blow to the Russians. Secondly, the Danubian principalities of Moldavia and Wallachia were given independence under nominal Turkish sovereignty which was guaranteed by the great powers. Thirdly, it was decided that the river Danube should come under international control. The fourth section of the treaty dealt with Turkey. Russia was made to abandon her claim to be the protector of the Christians in Turkey, whilst the Sultan promised better treatment of his Christian subjects. The great powers pledged themselves to support Turkish integrity.

The Domestic Effects of the War on Britain

The Crimean War affected British life in several ways. A parliamentary committee investigated army administration and called for changes. Reforms were introduced but more than a decade elapsed before the army was thoroughly overhauled (see p.175). The army medical service was investigated by a select committee and a more efficient hospital service resulted. In 1859 a medical school began the special study of gun-shot wounds and diseases of armies in the field. Model hospitals were built at Netley and Woolwich. Florence Nightingale continued to foster the development of a good nursing service in civilian hospitals. For a short time the British garrison in India was below strength for troops had been withdrawn to serve in the Crimea. Whilst this did not cause the Indian mutiny it had some bearing on the timing of it. Finally, Lord Palmerston gained great prestige from the Crimean War. He was praised as the man who had won the war and his reputation reached new heights.

What did Britain Gain From the Crimean War?

Although Britain was riding high on the crest of victory in 1856 it is necessary to consider how far the Treaty of Paris and its aftermath fulfilled the purposes for which Britain had fought the Crimean War. One of the reasons why Britain fought the war was to prevent the Turkish empire from being divided and to preserve its independence. However, although Turkey had been protected, the empire remained weak and unable to look after itself. The Sultan did not introduce the reforms he had promised and became increasingly unresponsive to pressures for change. Britain entered the war to defeat Russia and to prevent her gaining control of Turkey. Here too, she was only moderately successful. In 1870 Russia renounced the 'Black Sea Clause' and she renewed her attack upon Turkey in 1877, (see p.174 and p.186). These two events indicate that Britain had failed to deliver a decisive check to Russian aggression. The Crimean War and the Treaty of Paris did not provide a permanent settlement to the Eastern question.

Summary

In 1854 Britain entered the Crimean War almost by chance. She opposed Russian expansion at Turkey's expense, fearing that

Russian domination of Turkey would threaten her interests in the
Mediterranean. Britain's war aims were confused and the inefficient
conduct of the war led to great sufferings amongst the troops. The
war ended with the Treaty of Paris but the gains resulting from the
treaty proved to be insubstantial. It was not long before further
British Prime Ministers were faced with a new outbreak of Russian
aggression in the Turkish empire.

Exercises
1. Explain the reasons why the British government decided to go to
   war with Russia in 1854.
2. Why did the government decide to invade the Crimean
   peninsula?
3. Outline the main events of the war in the Crimea.
4. Show the importance of the work of Florence Nightingale.
5. What were the main terms of the Treaty of Paris?

17
Political Party Confusion, 1846 – 67

The division of the Conservative party over protection in 1846
marked the start of a confused period in party history. From July
1846 until the passing of the Reform Act in 1867 there were eight
administrations. Party discipline was still loose and it was impossible
after a general election to know the exact state of the parties until the
first division in the Commons. MPs grouped themselves around particular leaders in support of general ideas, but permanent loyalties
either to men or ideas were rare. Between 1846 and 1867 Britain's
politicians were concerned with many questions of foreign policy
and they were forced to consider parliamentary reform. There were
administrative reforms but many MPs took the same view as Palmerston on the question of social reform. Before the opening of Parliament in 1864 he was asked what reference should be made in the
Queen's speech to domestic affairs and legislation. He replied, 'Oh,

there is really nothing to be done. We cannot go on adding to the Statute Book ad infinitum'.

1 Party Confusion

Lord John Russell

At the general election held in 1847 the protectionists (Conservatives who were opposed to the repeal of the Corn Law) gained 226 seats against 105 gained by the Peelites (Conservatives who supported the repeal of the Corn Law). Whigs and radicals together numbered about 325 so no party had a clear majority; but the Peelites supported Lord John Russell and his Whig government lasted over five years. Factory reform and public health measures were passed (see p.139 and p.140) but the government was preoccupied with foreign affairs. At the end of 1851 Russell forced his Foreign Secretary, Lord Palmerston, to resign and three months later Palmerston was revenged by organizing a government defeat in the Commons. This occurred when Russell proposed to meet the danger of a possible French invasion by setting up a local militia. Palmerston insisted on the creation of a national militia and on 20 February 1852 Russell was beaten.

Lord Derby (1799–1869)

Lord Derby became Prime Minister in 1852 but the Conservatives were still divided on the issue of protection and his government was not very stable. By 1852 Disraeli had made it clear that he was now prepared to accept free trade but not all conservatives agreed with him. In the general election which followed in the summer of 1852 Lord Derby was not confirmed in office. He resigned at Christmas when a speech by William Gladstone (1809–98) persuaded the Commons to reject Disraeli's budget, which was designed to compensate farmers and the shipping and sugar interests.

Lord Aberdeen

After a period of muddle Lord Aberdeen formed a government and he was Prime Minister from 1852 to 1855. He was a Peelite and six members of the new cabinet of 13 came from that small group. A cabinet with Aberdeen as Prime Minister, Russell as Foreign Secretary, Palmerston as Home Secretary and Gladstone as Chancellor of the Exchequer included in Palmerston's words, 'almost all the men of talent and experience in the House of Commons except Disraeli'. The main domestic interest of the coalition government centred on Gladstone's budgets. In his first budget he abolished import duties on more than 200 items. Gladstone also wished to abolish income tax because he regarded it as inequitable and a temptation to fraud but he was unable to do so. The costs arising from the Crimean War and the Indian mutiny forced him to double the rate. Aberdeen's premiership did not survive the public anger over the mismanagement of the war and he resigned in January 1855. In 1861 Gladstone established the Post Office Savings Bank. In 1864 he was able to reduce income tax to four pence in the pound. In October 1865, just short of his eighty-first birthday, Palmerston died. Russell became Prime Minister and Gladstone was the Liberal leader in the House of Commons. For the next two years British politics was dominated by the question of parliamentary reform.

2 The 1867 Reform Act

Many people were not satisfied with the 1832 Reform Act. The Chartists called for further reforms and occasionally MPs raised the matter in Parliament. In 1837 Thomas Wakely, MP for Finsbury, introduced proposals for reform in the Commons. Lord John Russell opposed his scheme in a reply which gave him the nick-name 'Finality Jack' for, although he did not say that the 1832 Reform Act had been a final measure, he implied that he viewed it as such. His views were shared by nearly all of the governing class.

Gradually, changes in society made leading politicians realize that the system of representation required further reform. Ironically, it was 'Finality Jack' who made the first proposals in 1852 and again in 1854, but they had little support. Five years later Disraeli introduced another proposal for reform. In a speech he referred to 'the mechanic whose virtue, patience, prudence, intelligence and frugality, entitle him to enter the privileged pale of the constituent body'. His Bill of 1859 failed, as did a third attempt by Russell in 1860. However, the fact that Reform Bills were being introduced frequently meant that it was probably only a matter of time before reform was achieved.

In 1864 Gladstone told the Commons that every man 'who is not presumably incapacitated by some consideration of personal unfitness or of political danger, is morally entitled to come within the pale of the constitution.' The quest for parliamentary reform reached new heights with Gladstone's Bill of 1866. Gladstone proposed to reduce the property qualification for voting and to give the vote to lodgers paying £10 a year. He defended his proposals saying, 'You cannot fight against the future. Time is on our side'. A leading Liberal, Robert Lowe (1811 – 92) who had formed an unfavourable view of democracy whilst living in Australia, led a revolt against the Bill. The Russell government resigned in June 1866, and Derby became Prime Minister with Disraeli as Chancellor of the Exchequer and Leader of the Commons. The Conservatives introduced their own Reform Bill. Plans to allow double voting to the wealthy were considered but these 'fancy franchises' were discarded in the end because they were too complicated. Surprisingly enough Disraeli's Bill gave the vote to far more men than Gladstone's had planned to.

The Terms of the 1867 Reform Act

The 1867 Reform Act gave the vote in the boroughs to all male householders who had been resident for more than 12 months and to all lodgers who paid a rent of more than £10 a year. In the counties the franchise qualification was reduced to include the £12 householder and the £5 leaseholder. There was also a measure of redistribution. Forty-five seats were taken from the smaller towns and allocated to the counties and larger boroughs. The electorate increased by 88 per cent to a total of just under two million. The industrial towns accounted for most of the increase. In Birmingham the electorate reached three times its former size whilst in Leeds the figure was multiplied four times.

The Significance of the 1867 Reform Act

The 1867 Reform Act was the most dramatic of the nineteenth-century extensions in the franchise. But working-class householders in the counties were still without the vote, and the failure to introduce the secret ballot meant that landowners could influence their newly enfranchised tenants. The distribution of seats was still uneven. Seventy boroughs had less than 10,000 inhabitants; 40 boroughs had more than 200,000 inhabitants; both types of constituency had only two MPs.

The Development of Party

The 1867 Act marked a turning point in the development of political parties. The new urban electorate had to be marshalled and disciplined. In 1867 the National Union of Conservative and Constitutional Associations was formed. In 1877 the National Federation of Liberal Associations was founded. Henceforth, elections were fought by national parties, with a national leader and national policies.

Summary

The years of party confusion between 1846 and 1867 were

dominated by foreign policy. Britain fought the Crimean War and there was a considerable change in the map of Europe as Italy and Germany were united. At home some social reforms were introduced and Gladstone's budgets brought the country closer to free trade. Throughout these years of party confusion the question of parliamentary reform was often raised. Reform came in 1867 thanks both to Gladstone and Disraeli. Some contemporaries viewed the second Reform Act with great anxiety, calling it a 'leap in the dark', but the newly enfranchised voters looked to the future with optimism.

Exercises
1. Describe and show the importance of Gladstone's financial measures.
2. Trace the campaign for parliamentary reform from 1848 to 1867.
3. Explain the importance of the 1867 Reform Act for the development of democracy in Britain.
4. What further progress remained to be made in the development of democracy after 1867?

18
W.E. Gladstone, 1868 – 74

In 1868 at the general election the Liberals secured 1,500,000 votes to the Conservatives' 1,000,000. This produced the first clear-cut majority in the House of Commons since 1841. With Gladstone as Prime Minister the country had a leader whose all-round parliamentary ability, according to Ensor, has never been equalled. He was his own Leader of the Commons and rarely missed a sitting of the House. He kept himself informed about each department of state and submitted every important matter to his 15 cabinet colleagues. From 1868 to 1874 his attention was divided among vital problems — the question of the Irish church and system of land tenure, European affairs and a settlement with the United States and the reduction of class privilege in Britain.

Early Life

William Ewart Gladstone was born in 1809 into a family of Scottish descent. He was educated at Eton and Christ Church, Oxford, where he obtained a double first degree. When he died in 1899 he was recognized as the greatest Liberal of the nineteenth century. Yet, for the first 27 years of his political career he had been a Conservative. He entered Parliament when he was 23 years old and he was a minister in a Conservative cabinet by the age of 34. When the Conservative party split in 1846 he remained loyal to Sir Robert Peel and he was a member of the coalition which governed Britain during the Crimean War. It was not until 1859 that he became a Liberal in any party sense, when he joined Palmerston's government and remained in it until the Prime Minister died in 1865. From then onwards Gladstone became the leader of the Liberals.

1 Ireland

In 1868 when Gladstone heard that he was to become Prime Minister he declared, 'My mission is to pacify Ireland'. Unrest had reached new levels in that country but that was not the only reason for Gladstone's interest in Ireland. He wanted to restore to the Irish certain basic rights which had been withheld from them by the English. Gladstone was determined to atone for past injustices whilst at the same time regenerating Ireland.

The Irish Problem

Gladstone understood the Irish problem with its combination of economic, religious and nationalist factors but he was unable to solve it. In 1868 one quarter of the Irish people were still helpless paupers. General economic problems were aggravated by the specific problem of land tenure. Most landlords rented their land to tenants-at-will, giving the tenants no security of tenure. The religious aspect of the Irish problem related to the fact that four-fifths of the Irish population was Catholic and yet the Established Church of their country was the Protestant Church of Ireland. This Anglican Church received large tithe payments from the Irish people in addition to its generous endowments. The religious problem was linked to their economic problems in the minds of the Irish since it was the Protestant landowners who caused great hardship to their Catholic tenants. The final dimension of the Irish problem was political. The Lord Lieutenant of Ireland, with the help of a Chief Secretary, supervised the government of that country and saw to it that English law was enforced. From the Viceregal Lodge in Dublin he controlled the Royal Irish Constabulary and the English army, based at the Curragh. The Irish wanted greater self-government and their demands for independence, and later for Home Rule, grew.

The Fenian Brotherhood

The Irish Republican Brotherhood, later known as the Fenian Brotherhood, was founded in 1858 and based amongst Irish immigrants in the United States. Its aim was to establish an independent Irish republic, by force if necessary. The American Civil War interrupted the Brotherhood's development but after 1865 its influence in Ireland spread rapidly. The British government introduced Coercion Bills and suspended *Hebeas Corpus* in Ireland in response to Fenian acts of terror in that country.

Most Fenian acts of violence were followed by arrests (see the picture of the pursuit of Fenians). When several members of the Brotherhood were imprisoned in England terrorist activities transferred from Ireland to the mainland. In Manchester a prison van containing two Fenians was attacked; a policeman was shot in the course of their release. Three of the rescuers were later hanged and the Fenians dubbed them 'the Manchester Martyrs'. Later, the Fenians tried to rescue a number of their members from Clerkenwell prison by blasting through a prison wall. Twelve people were killed and 100 were injured in this incident.

In spite of these activities and the publicity which ensued, the Fenians never gained the whole-hearted support of the Irish peasantry. Yet Gladstone understood that if nothing was done to remedy Irish grievances the Fenians would eventually achieve their aims. As soon as he became Prime Minister Gladstone began to tackle the problem of the church and the problem of land tenure in Ireland. He considered that if these two problems were solved there would be peace in Ireland and talk of independence would cease.

The Disestablishment Act, 1869

Within two months of taking office Gladstone passed the Disestablishment Act which deprived the Anglican Church of its established position in Ireland and confiscated most of its property. This Act removed a long standing grievance and resentment towards the Church was no longer a source of trouble. However, resentment of landlords continued and Gladstone soon turned all his attention to the question of land.

The Irish Land Act, 1870

The Irish Land Act, 1870, limited the landlords' powers of arbitrary

Pursuit of the Fenians in Tipperary, 1867

eviction and enforced compensation for improvements carried out by tenants, even in cases of eviction for non-payment of rent. It also allowed loans of public money to tenants for the purchase of their holdings. The custom of tenant right in Ulster, together with similar customs elsewhere, was recognized in law. A scale of damages, which varied according to the size of the tenant's holding, was established for eviction, though there was no payment for disturbance in cases of eviction due to the tenant's failure to pay rent.

What Were the Strengths and Weaknesses of the Land Act?

Although the Land Act is usually seen as a modest reform, it was an immense step forward. Writing about the Irish agricultural problem, Pomfret describes the Act as an instrument which ended the two ideas which had dominated British policy in Ireland. The first was that *laissez faire* was a virtue and the second was that the landlord had an absolute right of property. Gladstone's Land Act gave protection to the Irish peasants whereas all previous legislation had destroyed their rights and given power to the landlords.

Nevertheless, the Act did not please the Irish tenants. Their aim was to secure the 'Three Fs' demanded by the Irish Tenant Right Party — fair rent, fixity of tenure and free sale of the tenant's interest in the property. Although the Act offered protection to tenants, landlords found it easy to evade the spirit, if not the letter, of the law. The Act provided courts which had the power to protect the tenant by revising 'exorbitant' rents. However, since it was difficult to define exactly what an exorbitant rent was the courts usually dismissed tenants' appeals and upheld the high rents. One indication that the Land Act was not a complete success was that it had to be followed in 1871 by a Co-ercion Bill to stamp out agricultural crime in Ireland.

Other Schemes for Ireland

Gladstone had two other plans for Ireland; one was concerned with its government, the other with the education of its people. Gladstone wanted to make the government of Ireland more sympathetic to the Irish people and less distant from them. He wanted to abolish the Lord Lieutenancy and institute a viceroy. He wanted to establish a royal residence in Ireland and he proposed to make the office of Viceroy purely ceremonial. He wanted the Prince of Wales to fill this post and he also wanted to give Ireland a minister who would be a Secretary of State. The queen refused to accept these plans. She hated the idea of giving the Prince of Wales any important duties and she disliked the idea that she might have to visit Ireland more frequently.

In 1873 Gladstone introduced a Bill in which he proposed to reform the Irish universities. He proposed that Trinity College, Dublin, Maynooth, and the colleges of Cork and Belfast should be combined in a single university. He excluded theology, history and moral philosophy from the curriculum in the hope of reconciling Anglicans and Roman Catholics. The Bill was defeated by three votes and education continued on sectarian lines. This defeat caused Gladstone to resign but Disraeli did not seem anxious to fight a general election. After a short crisis Gladstone's cabinet continued to carry out its duties.

Home Rule for Ireland
In 1870 the Home Rule League was founded in Dublin. Its leader was Isaac Butt (1813 – 79), a Protestant lawyer. The league wished to set up an Irish Parliament to govern internal affairs but it was not opposed to the Act of Union. Supporters of Home Rule won some 59 seats in the 1874 general election and it did not take long for Gladstone to change from a policy of pacification in Ireland to one of Home Rule for Ireland.

2 Foreign Policy

The foreign policy which Gladstone pursued in his first ministry brought him discredit because it wounded British pride. In matters of foreign policy Gladstone was guided by his sense of justice and his sense of the possible. He took a keen interest in the work of the foreign service, working closely with Clarendon (1800 – 70) and, when he died from overwork, with the new Foreign Secretary, Granville (1815 – 91).

Gladstone's Principles of Foreign Policy
In the conduct of his foreign policy Gladstone stressed the need for the rule of law. He appeared to champion the rights of subject nations. However, as the British empire expanded it was bound to come into conflict with aspiring nationalist movements. Gladstone was torn between a duty to Britain's interests and sympathy towards the nationalists. It is not surprising therefore, that his foreign policy often seemed hesitant and ineffective. Gladstone did not hold such exalted ideas of what was demanded by Britain's national honour as Disraeli. It was this apparent lack of concern which brought Liberal policies under attack. Many people could not bear to see their great

industrial nation relegated to a back seat in the councils of Europe.

The Prime Minister set out his principles of foreign policy in a letter to the Queen's secretary on 17 April 1869. He declared that it was dangerous for England

'to assume alone an advanced, and therefore an isolated position in regard to European controversies; that come what may it is better for her to promise too little than too much; that she should not encourage the weak by giving expectations of aid, to resist the strong, but should rather seek to deter the strong, by firm but moderate language, from aggression on the weak; that she should seek to develop and mature the action of a common European opinion, as the best standing bulwark against wrong . . .'

Belgian Neutrality, 1870

One of Gladstone's first tasks in foreign policy was to defend Belgian neutrality which seemed threatened by the amalgamation of two Belgian railways with a French one. Gladstone indicated to the French that he was determined to defend Belgian independence. Belgian neutrality seemed threatened again when a draft Franco – Prussian treaty of uncertain date was published in *The Times* on 25 July 1870. In the treaty Prussia recognized French ambitions to increase her influence in Belgium. Gladstone acted quickly and drew up a new treaty which he persuaded France and Prussia to sign in August 1870. Britain also signed the document and it supplemented the guarantee of Belgian neutrality drawn up in 1839 (see p.147).

The Franco – Prussian War, 1870

When war broke out between France and Prussia in 1870 Britain adopted a policy of neutrality. Critics suggested that more energetic action by Gladstone could have averted the outbreak of war. There may have been some truth in their suggestions, but Britain could only have prevented war by intervening on one side or the other and public opinion was opposed to this. After the French defeat at the battle of Sedan in 1870 Bismarck was sure of victory. On 22 September 1870 he had a note delivered in London proclaiming his intention to secure Germany's western frontier by annexing Alsace and Lorraine, without consulting the one and a quarter million inhabitants of the region. Gladstone declared that this proposal was 'repulsive to the sense of modern civilization'. However, the cabinet was not prepared to support him and he was forced to witness the annexation which he was powerless to prevent.

The Black Sea Clauses, 1870–71

In October 1870 Russia, acting in secret concert with Prussia, denounced the clause in the Treaty of Paris, 1856, which forbade her to keep a fleet on the Black Sea. Both Britain and Turkey were affected by this decision and Gladstone's handling of the issue brought him much criticism. A conference was held in London to discuss the matter and the Treaty of London, 1871, resulted. The conference declared that no treaty could be denounced without the consent of all the signatories. The Treaty of London left the Straits closed but removed all restrictions on Russia in the Black Sea. Gladstone regarded the conference as a success. To him what mattered was that the rule of law in international affairs had been upheld. To the British public what mattered was that Russia had got her way and British interests in the Mediterranean continued to be severely threatened. Gladstone had let the country down and henceforth, his leadership in foreign affairs was distrusted.

The Alabama Claims, 1871–2

Gladstone and Granville became even more unpopular when the issue of the *Alabama* claims was reopened in 1871. The Americans claimed compensation for the damage caused by such British built ships as the *Alabama* in the Civil War. In May 1871 Britain and America agreed to submit the dispute to arbitration. Eventually, in September 1872 five arbitrators announced that Britain should pay £3,250,000 in damages to the United States. The money was promptly paid. There was an immediate outcry in Britain. It was felt that the country had paid far too much. Some people felt betrayed; they longed for the aggressive style of foreign policy associated with Palmerston. Others felt that Gladstone stuck too rigidly to his belief in the rule of law and this made him unfit to handle foreign affairs.

The Ashanti War, 1873–4

The Ashanti campaign, described as a 'little war', arose out of Britain's embargo on the slave trade and the Ashanti leader Kofi's claim to Elmina, a British protected area. Fighting began in Elmina in June 1873. In September on the request of Lord Kimberley, the Colonial Secretary, Sir Garnet Wolseley (1833–1913) set out for Cape Coast. British troops forced the Ashanti warriors to retreat and Kofi soon came to terms. He renounced all claims to British and former Dutch spheres of influence, promised free trade and an end to human sacrifices. He also agreed to pay 50,000 ounces of gold as a war indemnity. Britain's success in this campaign enabled her to retain her Gold Coast colony.

3 Domestic Policy

In 1868 there began a period of rapid reform which was to have profound effects on all sections of the community. In some respects the
situation was like that of 1832. The 1860s had been a stagnant
decade and the new Parliament found, like the first reformed Parliament, that a number of urgent problems had to be tackled. Gladstone's ministry was devoted to the treatment of those problems. It
modernized institutions, created new machinery, removed abuses
and helped to introduce equality of opportunity. In some areas the
government was so successful in abolishing class privileges and
unlocking the doors of political, economic and cultural opportunity
that Ensor believes that it was the greatest administration of
Victoria's reign. In other areas it failed, with grave consequences for
the fortunes of the Liberals.

Education

In the second session of Gladstone's ministry W.E. Forster
(1818 – 86), Vice-president of the Privy Council Committee for
Education, secured the passage of the Education Act, 1870, which
set up board schools in areas where no schools existed (see p.281).
This Education Act attacked privilege and the right of the church to
control education. However, it was full of compromises and failed to
please anyone. It offended the Nonconformists who had hoped for
secular education, for it continued to give grants to church schools.
It also offended churchmen who believed that their schools would
suffer from competition from the board schools where religious
teaching was non-denominational. Despite the shortcomings of the
Act it provided a most important advance in educating the nation's
youth. In 1871 the University Tests Act was passed which opened all
teaching posts at Oxford and Cambridge to men of any religious
creed.

Army Reforms, 1868 – 74

By the time Gladstone became Prime Minister in 1868 the British
public was seriously worried about the weak state of the army. The
Crimean War and the Indian mutiny had highlighted deficiencies in
the army. The public was made still more anxious by the overwhelming defeat inflicted on France in 1870 by the efficient
Prussian army. Gladstone entrusted reform of the army to Edward
Cardwell (1813 – 86) at the War Office. His was a difficult task for the
commander-in-chief, the Duke of Cambridge, opposed all change.
The Conservatives had a vested interest in existing army practices,

whilst many Liberals took the view that as little money as possible should be allocated to military purposes.

Cardwell began in 1868 by abolishing flogging in the army in peace time. Once flogging was abolished, a better type of recruit was attracted to the army. Consequently, two years later Cardwell was able to abolish 'bounty money' for recruits and to discharge known bad characters. In 1869 Cardwell started to withdraw troops from the self-governing colonies. In 1870 and 1871 20,000 men were restored to the home establishment and the colonies were encouraged to raise their own local forces. He also introduced the Martini-Henry rifle into the infantry; this was the first successful breech-loading rifle to be supplied to the army.

Next Cardwell dealt with the problem of enlistment. From 1815 to 1847 men enlisted for 21 years' service with the colours. The period was reduced in 1847 to 12 years; but it was still too long. After 12 years, with some time spent in India or the tropics, the men were unfit for service. In 1870 Parliament passed the Army Enlistment (short service) Act. This altered the period of service to six years with the colours and six years in the reserve. As a result recruiting improved and service in the army became popular. Later in 1870, on 28 June, the Queen signed an order in council subordinating the commander-in-chief of the army to the Secretary of State.

In 1871 Cardwell introduced the Army Regulation Bill. This Bill proposed far-reaching changes and was most unpopular in privileged circles. The section of the Bill which aroused most opposition was the proposal to abolish purchase — the practice by which officers bought and sold their commissions. The Bill contained less controversial elements. It proposed to reorganize the regiments, placing all infantry on a territorial basis. New county areas were to contain two battalions of the old regulars and these linked battalions took it in turn to serve overseas. The War Department was to be divided into three sections, with greatly increased powers being given to the commander-in-chief. The Bill introduced a measure of staff reform and transferred the right of appointing officers from the Lords-Lieutenant of the counties to the War Office. There was great opposition to the Bill. In the House of Lords a motion was passed which shelved the Bill and in effect defeated it. However, Gladstone was so determined to reform the army that he persuaded the Queen to secure the abolition of purchase by royal warrant. When it became clear that the warrant did not include compensation for officers who had purchased commissions, the Lords decided to pass the Army Regulation Bill without further opposition, for it had provided generous compensation. Thus all Cardwell's reforms became law.

The constant opposition to Cardwell's reforms left him worn out. In 1874 he retired. He had failed to reorganize the cavalry regiments and he retired in the knowledge that his work was partly responsible for Gladstone's defeat in 1874. Yet the significance of his reforms continued to be felt long after his retirement. The British army performed well in the colonial campaigns of the next 40 years, gaining several successes as in the Egyptian campaign of 1882 (see p.197). There was no shortage of recruits for the army. The army's strength was increased by 25 battalions, 156 field guns and abundant stores. All this was accomplished efficiently and cheaply and Cardwell left the army estimates lower than he found them.

Civil Service Reform, 1870–71
Until the 1850s posts in the British civil service were obtained by family connections or on the recommendation of an influential friend. Jobbery, patronage and nepotism were the order of the day. With increasing legislation and the growth of new government departments the work of the central administration was increasing and becoming more complex. The country could no longer afford to leave such important work in the hands of amateurs. At the same time there was a need for a great increase in the number of civil servants.

Reform began in 1853 when Macaulay's suggestion that posts in the Indian civil service should be open to all by means of a competitive examination was accepted. Then, on 4 June 1870, an order in council opened to competitive examination the entry to nearly all branches of the civil service except the Foreign Office. This decision was embodied in an Act of 1871 which also established three grades within the civil service — clerical, executive and administrative. Morely has summed up the importance of the Act by stating that it 'placed the whole educated intellect of the country at the service and disposal of the state.'

Trade Union Legislation, 1871
As a result of several judicial decisions, the legal position of trade unions was confused when Gladstone became Prime Minister. Union members wished to clarify the position of their right to strike, their right to hold corporate property and their ability to enforce agreements by suing in court. Trade union legislation introduced by Home Secretary Bruce (1815–95) in 1871 both pleased and infuriated trade union members (see p.220). When they objected to certain parts of his legislation Gladstone paid no attention to their protests.

Public Health, 1871 – 2
The Royal Sanitary Commission, appointed by Disraeli in 1868, reported in 1871 and the Liberals acted upon its findings. The commission recommended that 'the present fragmentary and confused sanitary legislation should be consolidated, and the administration of sanitary law should be made uniform throughout the kingdom'. The Local Government Act, 1871, placed the administration of public health in the hands of a minister at the newly created Local Government Board. In the following year a Sanitary Act divided the country into sanitary areas each of which had to appoint a medical officer of health and an inspector of nuisances.

The 1871 Budget
Robert Lowe was Chancellor of the Exchequer in Gladstone's government from 1868 to 1873. At first his term of office was uneventful but trouble began in 1871 when the government needed money to finance the army increases. Lowe decided to raise £1 million by placing a tax on matches. Manufacturers protested and match girls demonstrated at Westminster. Eventually, Lowe was forced to withdraw his tax and increase income tax instead. Although this was a storm in a teacup to some observers, others regarded it as a serious blow to the government's prestige.

The Ballot Act, 1872
There had been advocates of the secret ballot throughout the nineteenth century. Following the 1869 general election there were 111 petitions alleging malpractices and Gladstone decided that the time had come to end the confusion and corruption which was commonplace at the hustings. Although the Ballot Act ended the traditional method of open voting it did not end the opportunities for corrupt politicians to buy votes.

The Licensing Act, 1872
Many Liberals were concerned to reduce the evils of drunkenness which they believed stemmed from the huge numbers of ale houses and beer shops. Anyone who pleased could open an ale house and there were no restrictions on their opening hours. Bruce introduced his first Licensing Bill in the summer of 1871. It resulted in so much opposition that it had to be withdrawn. In 1872 he passed a weaker Licensing Act. The Act closed public houses in areas where there were too many, imposed limitations on opening hours and introduced regulations against adulteration.

The Act was enforced in spite of the fact that it led to rioting in many towns. Its opponents declared that it was an infringement of their liberty. In a debate in the House of Lords Dr Magee, the Bishop of Peterborough, declared that he would like to see 'England free better than England sober'. From 1871 onwards every public house that remained in existence seemed to be a centre for Conservative supporters. Gladstone always believed that the Act led to his defeat in 1874. He wrote to his brother, 'We have been bourne down in a torrent of gin and beer'.

The Judicature Act, 1873

In 1873 Lord Selborne (1812 – 95) passed the Judicature Act which joined the courts of Equity and Common Law. The seven courts which existed under the old system were united to form one Supreme Court of Judicature. The House of Lords objected to the Act for it abolished the appeal jurisdiction of that House. This objection was removed by Disraeli in 1876 when final appeal to the House of Lords was restored.

Why was Gladstone Defeated in the 1874 General Election?

Gladstone expected victory at the polls in 1874 but the Conservatives gained a majority of at least 48. There are several reasons why Gladstone's ministry, with excellent achievements to its credit, failed to win re-election. In the first place, the secret ballot helped the Irish party which returned 59 members pledged to pursue nationalist aims. Secondly, some Liberal supporters were so distressed by the government's measures on education and trade unionism that they stayed away from the polls. Thirdly, the Liberals were discredited by divisions amongst government leaders and by an inglorious record in foreign policy. The Licensing Act was another source of opposition to the Liberals. Finally, it must be noted that the Conservatives had not wasted their time in opposition. They had won seats steadily at by-elections and by 1874 they had candidates ready in every constituency they could hope to win.

Summary

Gladstone's first ministry brought much needed reforms to Ireland. The Protestant Church of Ireland was dis-established and the Land Act helped to remove some grievances, although it was criticized for not going far enough to meet the tenants' demands on the one hand, whilst landowners found fault with it on the other hand and believed that it was far too radical. Gladstone's record in foreign affairs was also criticized. He was blamed for the fact that Britain's standing in Europe did not seem to be as high as it had been in the days of Palmerston. At home Gladstone introduced far-reaching reforms which raised the standard of education and public health and strengthened the army. But his domestic policy led to criticism of the Liberals. Trade unionists felt that they had been badly treated and many people were bitterly opposed to the Licensing Act. For all these reasons Gladstone fell from office in 1874.

Exercises
1.   What were the chief elements of the Irish problem in the 1860s?
2.   Why did Galdstone want to 'pacify' Ireland?
3.   How did Gladstone attempt to solve the Irish problem from 1868 to 1874?
4.   Describe two incidents which illustrate the belief that Gladstone's foreign policy often seemed hesitant and ineffective.
5.   Describe two of Gladstone's domestic reforms which helped to reduce privilege in British society.
6.   Why did Gladstone lose the election of 1874?

19
Benjamin Disraeli, 1874 – 80

Disraeli was 70 years old when he began his second ministry in 1874. The aged Prime Minister suffered from almost constant ill health, but this did not prevent him from introducing many social reforms and becoming absorbed in foreign and imperial affairs. Disraeli helped to create the modern Conservative party, after a struggle with the party's right wing, which opposed many of his policies. He continually stressed the duties, rather than the privileges, of the governing classes, and developed a broadly-based political programme which appealed to all sections of society. Lord Salisbury gives us an insight into Disraeli's aims when he said, 'above all things, Disraeli wished to see England united, and powerful, and great'.

Early Life
Benjamin Disraeli was born in 1804. His background was Jewish and

literary. His grandfather was a Jewish immigrant who had prospered in business. His father was received into the Church of England and had written a book entitled *The Curiosities of Literature*. Disraeli had begun his career as a novelist, publishing *Vivian Grey* in 1826. His two best known works were *Coningsby* (1844) and *Sybil, or the Two Nations* (1845). Disraeli did not have the accepted background for a politician. As well as having Jewish origins, he was educated privately and did not attend university. He shocked many people by his love of flamboyant clothes. It took four attempts before he was returned to Parliament in 1837 as MP for Maidstone. He obtained this seat with the help of Mrs Wyndham Lewis whose family controlled it. When she became a widow Disraeli married her in 1839. Thereafter he held cabinet posts, including that of Chancellor of the Exchequer. As Leader of the Conservatives in the Commons he passed the 1867 Reform Act (see p.165). He was Prime Minister on Lord Derby's retirement for a short time in 1868.

1 Social Reform

With Disraeli's second ministry came the largest instalment of social reform introduced by any government in the nineteenth century. The reforms were intended to improve the conditions of the labouring classes. However, it would be inaccurate to conclude that the Conservatives deliberately abandoned *laissez faire* in favour of government intervention in social and economic life. Many of their reforms were permissive. There was an element of vote-catching in Disraeli's support for social reform and in many other aspects of Tory democracy, and therefore Disraeli cannot really be described as a committed social reformer.

Housing
One of the first reforms introduced by Disreali's government was the Artisans' Dwellings Act, 1875, which aimed to provide a better standard of housing for the poor. It gave local authorities the power to purchase and pull down slums and replace them with healthier buildings. The Act, however, was permissive and the result was that six years later only 10 of the 87 English and Welsh towns to which it applied had made any attempt to carry out its provisions.

Public Health
One of Disraeli's last acts as Prime Minister in 1868 had been to appoint a Royal Sanitary Commission. The commission reported in 1871 and the Liberals were the first to act upon it. When Disraeli

returned to power in 1874 one of his first priorities was to improve standards of public health. The Public Health Act, 1875, was largely a codification of previous legislation, placing the administration of public health in the hands of local authorities. The Act compelled local authorities to appoint medical officers of health to whom infectious diseases had to be notified. The authorities were also compelled to provide adequate drainage, sewage disposal and refuse collection. The water supply was no longer to be left in the hands of private companies. The authorities also had to provide public lavatories, control cellar dwellings and appoint inspectors of nuisances.

To the 1875 Act the Conservatives added in the same year the Sale of Food and Drugs Act, which prohibited harmful substances in food. In 1876 the Rivers Pollution Act attacked the problem of the pollution of rivers by industrial waste and sewage. The Enclosure of Commons Act, 1876, provided an additional bonus to the general welfare of the people by restricting the rights of landowners to absorb public land into their estates. This was followed by the Epping Forest Act, 1878, which saved the area for the enjoyment of all.

The Home Secretary, Richard Cross (1823 – 1914), was largely responsible for drafting these measures. He summarized the government's aims in the area of public health when he said, 'what the people of this country want almost as much as they want food is the air they breathe and the health which they enjoy'. His legislation laid the foundations of modern public health so thoroughly that no major changes were needed for over 60 years.

Conditions of Work

In 1874 the Conservatives passed the Factory Act which cut the 60 hour week laid down in 1850 to 56 hours. At last, the 10-hour day was achieved; working hours became 10 hours a day on week days and six on Saturdays.

In 1875 the Earl of Shaftesbury passed a Bill which forbade sweeps to carry on their trade without an annual licence from the police. The police were to enforce the laws regulating the use of chimney-sweep boys. One of the reforms for which the Earl of Shaftesbury had so long been fighting had at last been achieved.

Thanks to the work of Samuel Plimsoll (1824 – 98), MP for Derby, the Conservatives introduced the Merchant Shipping Act in 1876. The Act gave the Board of Trade powers to inspect ships and laid down regulations regarding accommodation for sailors on board ship. The principle of the load-line was introduced, but the responsibility for its positioning on the ship's hull was left to the ship owners until 1890 when it became the responsibility of the Board of Trade.

A further Factory Act in 1878 codified and rationalized all the factory legislation which had been passed since 1833. It abolished the distinction between factories and workshops as places where more or fewer than 50 persons were employed. It created a more sensible distinction between the use and non-use of mechanical power. This Act also gave added protection to industrial workers and was a response to the demands of the trade unions.

Disraeli took a keen interest in all this legislation and supported Cross in the face of many opponents within the Conservative party. He believed that the legislation would 'gain and retain the Conservatives the lasting affection of the working classes'. Disraeli was clearly seeking to gain votes in the urban areas and his strategy helped to create the 'Tory working man'.

Trade Unions

In 1875 Cross introduced the Conspiracy and Protection of Property Act and the Employers and Workmen Act (see p. 221). As a result of these reforms trade unions became a recognized element in society. This prompted Alexander MacDonald of the Amalgamated Society of Engineers to declare, 'the Conservative party has done more for the working class in five years than the Liberals have done in fifty.

Education

Sandon's Act of 1876 was a further step towards compulsory education (see p. 282). At the other end of the educational scale an Oxford and Cambridge Act was passed in 1877 (see p. 287).

Agriculture

The Agricultural Holdings Act, 1875, introduced personally by Disraeli, extended the Irish Land Act to English tenants by offering compensation for improvements. The Act was permissive and this did not please tenant farmers. Landlords however, were displeased because they resented interference with their property rights. The government did nothing to relieve distress in depressed areas of agriculture. Disraeli held firmly to the principle of free trade, even though the Americans were flooding Britain with cheap grain, because he knew that taxes on food would be unpopular in the towns.

Summary
Disraeli was always suspicious of state intervention in economic and social affairs and Conservative claims to be the party of social reform should not be blindly accepted. The flow of reforms stopped in 1877 with Disraeli's declining health and Irish tactics (see p.200) and more attention was paid to the pressing problems of overseas affairs. Disraeli took no interest in the details of the work on social reform except where trade union and factory legislation were concerned. Nevertheless, the growing prestige of the Conservative party indicates that Disraeli succeeded in creating a modern political party which catered for all sections of the population.

2 Foreign and Imperial Affairs

Disraeli's Principles of Foreign Policy
There is little doubt that Disraeli was an imperialist. He has also been described, rather disparagingly, as an opportunist in matters of foreign policy. Whilst this may be true of some of his policies, for example his purchase of the Suez Canal shares, it should not imply that Disraeli jumped from one policy to the next without basing his actions on any fixed principles. He declared that he based his foreign and imperial policies on the principles of *'Imperium et Libertas'* (Empire and Liberty). When Disraeli spoke of empire he did not mean that Britain should be solely concerned with the acquisition of colonies, rather that she should exert a responsible moral influence in the world. Since Britain had the richest empire in the world she had a duty to honour her obligations throughout the world and to act as a stabilizing influence in Europe. Disraeli declared, 'so long as the power and advice of England are felt in the councils of Europe, peace, I believe, will be maintained, and for a long period'.

The Suez Canal, 1875
The Suez Canal was opened in 1868 and in 1875 the Khedive of Egypt was forced to sell his holdings of Suez Canal Company shares to pay off his debts. Disraeli decided to buy the shares for Britain and he raised £4,000,000 from the House of Rothschild for the purchase. He acted in an unorthodox fashion, consulting few people, and he aroused the opposition of many Conservative and Liberal politicians. Disraeli disregarded the criticism for he realized that the possession of the Canal was vital to the development of Britain's empire. The Canal transferred to Egypt most of the strategic importance which had previously been attached to the Cape of Good

Hope. It reduced the cost of freight carriage by sea to Australia and New Zealand and made communication with India and the Far East shorter and safer. It also improved Britain's military and naval strength in the Middle and Far East. Although many politicians criticized the purchase of the Canal shares, the move was very popular with the people who regarded it as a great triumph for Disraeli.

The Royal Titles Bill, 1876

In 1876 Disraeli took a further step which he hoped would strengthen Britain's empire. In 1874 he had suggested that the Queen should assume the title Empress of India to mark the direct relationship between India and the Crown. Victoria was delighted but the suggestion was generally unpopular. Disraeli had a difficult time in forcing the measure through, but he achieved the satisfaction of knowing that it made him a great favourite with the Queen.

The Eastern Question

The most important aspect of Disraeli's foreign policy related to the Eastern question. The Treaty of Paris, 1856, had done little to strengthen the declining Turkish empire and Austria and Russia both hoped to expand at Turkey's expense. The Christian races in the Balkans, suffering from Turkish misrule, wished to be independent. Their aspirations, coupled with the corrupt and harsh government of the Turks, provided Russia and Austria with excuses for intervening in the Ottoman empire.

The Revolts Against Turkey, 1875 – 6

In 1875 the problem of the Christian subjects within the Turkish empire produced an international crisis when the Turkish provinces of Bosnia and Herzegovina rebelled. Their aim was to unite with Serbia and Montenegro which were under Turkish rule but had considerable independence. The rulers of Russia, Germany and Austria sent the Andrassy Note to Turkey, demanding reforms from the Sultan. Meanwhile, the revolt spread to Bulgaria and Macedonia. The three rulers then presented the Berlin Memorandum to Turkey, calling upon her to draw up an armistice with the rebels and introduce reforms.

Disraeli's Attitude

Disraeli rejected the proposals contained in the Berlin Memorandum. He had not been consulted before it had been drafted and he was anxious to develop an independent policy. He did not trust

Bismarck of Germany and was suspicious of Austria and Russia. He was determined to protect British interests in the Mediterranean. In 1876 the succession of a new Sultan, Abdul Hamid, led to the withdrawal of the Berlin Memorandum and Disraeli felt that he had achieved a considerable success.

The Bulgarian Horrors, 1876

In May 1876 the issue was complicated by a revolt of the Bulgars, followed by their wholesale massacre by Turkish forces known as the 'Bashi-Bazouks'. When news of the massacres appeared in the Liberal *Daily News* Disraeli declared that the atrocities were 'to a large extent inventions'. He believed that the revolt in Bulgaria could eventually give Russia access to the Black Sea and thereby threaten Britain's position. He was anxious to continue to support Turkey as he believed that her disintegration could only harm British interests.

At this point, Gladstone emerged from semi-retirement and issued a pamphlet entitled *The Bulgarian Horrors and the Question of the East*. On a tour of England he aroused hatred of the Turks and his campaign against them sabotaged Disraeli's policy.

Lord Salisbury (1830–1903) was sent to the Constantinople Conference, which recommended an armistice with the Serbs and a programme of reforms for Turkey. The Turks would not accept these proposals since they did not believe that Russia would declare war on them or that Britain would fail to support them in the remote event of war.

The Russo–Turkish War, 1877

Turkey's refusal to accept reforms was followed in April 1877 by a Russian declaration of war on Turkey. Disraeli declared Britain's neutrality, provided that Russia did not threaten the Suez Canal, Egypt or Constantinople. The popularity of Gladstone's attack on the Turks did not last long; events during the war caused a change of British opinion. When the Turks heroically defended Plevna British opinion began to turn in their favour and Disraeli resumed his support for Turkey. When Plevna eventually fell to the Russians they were able to reach Adrianople and threaten Constantinople. Disraeli immediately demanded an armistice. He ordered the British Mediterranean fleet to Constantinople and asked Parliament for £6,000,000 for military purposes. Faced with this opposition, Russia granted the Turks an armistice. However, the treaty which ended the war was the cause of another international crisis.

Fig.13 The Treaty of San Stefano, 3 March 1878

The Treaty of San Stefano, March 1878
By this treaty Rumania, Serbia and Montenegro became independent states. Russia gained Bessarabia from Rumania. The treaty led to the creation of 'Big Bulgaria' which stretched from the Aegean to the Adriatic (see Fig. 13, The Treaty of San Stefano). 'Big Bulgaria' could become a Russian satellite, allowing Russia to dominate the Balkans and threaten Constantinople. It provided Russia with an outlet to the Mediterranean. Britain and Austria demanded another conference and Bismarck invited the great powers to meet at Berlin. Russia, realizing that she was isolated, agreed to the congress which met in Berlin from 13 June to 13 July 1878.

The Treaty of Berlin, July 1878
By the treaty 'Big Bulgaria' was broken up and Turkey recovered sufficient territory to protect Constantinople. Northern Bulgaria became an independent principality, whilst in the south, Eastern

Fig. 14 The Treaty of Berlin, 13 July 1878

Rumelia was placed under Turkish control but had a Christian governor. Serbia and Montenegro were slightly enlarged and became independent. Austria was allowed to occupy and administer Bosnia and Herzegovina (see Fig. 14, The Treaty of Berlin). Britain gained Cyprus by guaranteeing to defend Turkey against any future Russian attacks and Turkey promised to treat her Christian subjects humanely.

What did Disraeli achieve at the Congress of Berlin?

There are differing views about the extent of Disraeli's achievements at the Congress of Berlin. He had succeeded in fending off Russia's threat to the Turkish empire. He had secured 'peace with honour' and increased his personal standing both at home and abroad. In addition to defending British interests in the Near East Disraeli claimed credit for destroying the *Dreikaiserbund* (League of Three Emperors — Germany, Austria and Russia).

Disraeli's critics claimed that he had restored thousands of Serbs and Greeks to Turkish rule. Other weaknesses of the settlement became apparent later. The division between Bulgaria and East Rumelia was undone within seven years when the two areas united.

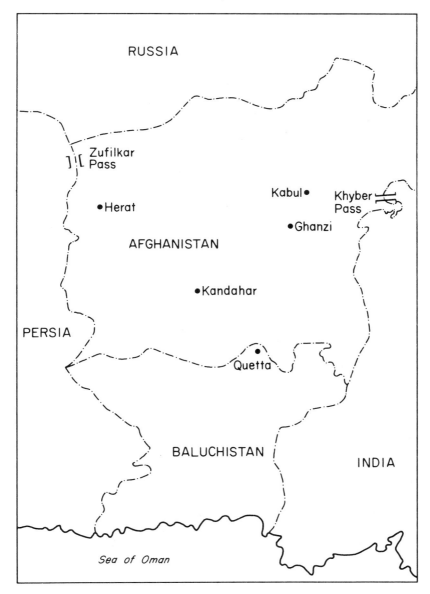

Fig.15 Afghanistan, 1880

The Turks did not keep their promises of good behaviour towards the Christians. Cyprus was of little value, for the centre of Britain's influence in the Middle East was soon to be Egypt, not Cyprus. In general, however, it may be said that whilst the Liberals disapproved of Disraeli's work at the Congress of Berlin, the country took pride in what was considered to be his greatest achievement.

Afghanistan, 1878
After the Congress of Berlin the Foreign Office continued to fear Russian expansion, this time in India. Afghanistan was regarded as a buffer state between Russia and India and Disraeli decided to secure India by gaining control of Afghanistan before Russia did so. Lord Lytton (1831 – 91) undertook this 'forward' policy in 1878 and demanded that a British mission should be received in Kabul. When the Amir hesitated Lytton sent three armies, led by General Roberts (1832 – 1914), against the capital. The Amir fled and his son signed a treaty of friendship with Britain. By the treaty Afghanistan received British protection, promised to conduct its foreign policy under British supervision, accepted a British Resident in Kabul and gave Britain control of her passes (see Fig. 15, Afghanistan 1880).

Soon after the treaty was signed there was a rebellion in Afghanistan. The Resident was murdered and the Amir fled to the British camp. General Roberts returned to Kabul, hanged the rebels and burned their villages. He then rescued a force at Kandahar, after a march of 313 miles through the mountains in 23 days. British setbacks in Afghanistan damaged Disraeli's popularity and, when Gladstone became Prime Minister in 1880, his 'forward' policy was reversed and British troops were withdrawn from Afghanistan.

South Africa
In 1878 Britain annexed the Transvaal, with the grudging consent of most of the Boer leaders, when news was received that the Zulus were about to attack it. The Zulus attacked in January 1879 and wiped out a British force at Isandhlwana in Zululand. However, in July the Zulu chief Cetewayo was defeated at Ulundi and the Transvaal seemed safe (see Fig. 16, South Africa). Then trouble arose when Disraeli sent Sir Garnet Wolseley to South Africa as High Commissioner. He gave the Transvaal the constitution of a crown colony, despite the fact that before annexation the Boers had been promised self-government. Disraeli was once more attacked for pursuing this 'forward' policy.

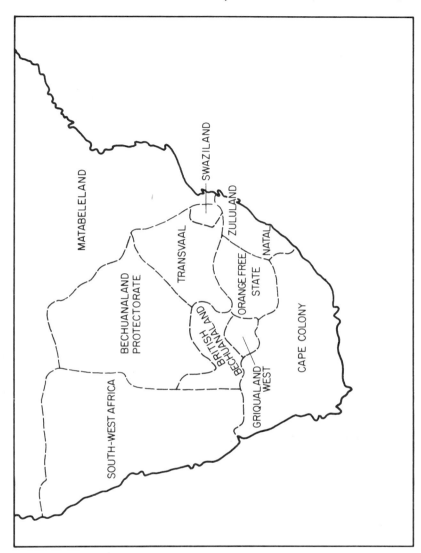

Fig.16 South Africa, 1868 – 80

Summary

For most of his second ministry Disraeli took more interest in foreign and imperial affairs than in social reform. Ironically, his government's social reforms were far less controversial than several of his foreign and imperial policies. He was criticized for his unorthodox purchase of the Suez Canal shares and for his policies in Afghanistan and South Africa. At the time, his work at the Congress of Berlin was seen as a great victory but the fruits of that victory did not turn out to be as great as his contemporaries might have expected. Nevertheless, Disraeli achieved much when he was 'at the top of the greasy pole' and he is remembered as one of the most colourful figures of the nineteenth century.

Exercises
1.   Describe legislation introduced by Disraeli which improved a) living conditions, b) working conditions.
2.   How did Disraeli help trade unions?
3.   Select and describe incidents from 1874 to 1880 which indicate that Disraeli seemed obsessed with a hatred and fear of Russia.
4.   Describe Disraeli's policies towards Afghanistan and South Africa.

20
Gladstone: The Later Ministries, 1880 – 94

Gladstone resigned the leadership of the Liberal party in 1875 and retired. Hartington (1833 – 1908) led the party for the next five years. Gladstone had emerged from retirement to publish *The Bulgarian Horrors and the Question of the East* in 1876 and in the following years he went on tours of Midlothian, criticizing Disraeli's foreign and imperial policies and calling for the establishment of a more Christian Europe. In the general election of 1880 the Liberals scored a great success, with a majority over the Conservatives and Irish combined of at least 42 seats.

Queen Victoria sent for Hartington and Granville and asked them to form a government. However, neither Hartington nor Granville dared to form a ministry to which Gladstone did not belong, now that he appeared to be out of retirement, and Gladstone made it clear that he was not prepared to serve under anyone. Public opinion looked to Gladstone as the head of the next government and Victoria, much as she disliked him for his attacks on Disraeli, was forced to send for him. Gladstone became Prime Minister for the second time on 23 April 1880. He remained in office for five years. He headed a third ministry in 1886 and a fourth in 1892, by which time the Grand Old Man was becoming deaf and blind with cataracts in both eyes.

The Divided Liberals, 1880–86

The Liberal party was far better organized to fight the 1880 election than it had been when it fought the election of 1874. Since then it had learned a lot about organization from the Conservatives. The Liberals' success in the 1880 election was due partly to the popularity of Gladstone's Midlothian campaign and partly to the large programme of social reforms which the radical wing of the party had promised the electorate. Of Gladstone's second administration Ensor says, 'never in the modern era has a triumphant House of Commons majority achieved so little'. There were many reasons for this failure. There was continuing economic unrest in the country and the new phenomenon of not one but two oppositions in the Commons — the Irish as well as the Conservatives — but above all the Liberals were weakened by divisions within their own party. On one side of the party were the Whigs, led by Lord Hartington, who disliked the tone of Gladstone's Midlothian campaign speeches and the rising influence within the party of the radicals. On the other side of the party were the radicals, led by Joseph Chamberlain (1830–1914), the Lord Mayor of Birmingham, who had organized the National Liberal Federation which helped the Liberals to gain office in 1880. They demanded a programme of social reform. These divisions grew during Gladstone's second ministry and the party eventually split in 1886.

1 Domestic Policy

Reforms

At the start of Gladstone's second ministry Ireland, and then Egypt, kept him too busy to attend to domestic matters. Ireland 'blocked the way' so that in the first three sessions no controversial legislation came before Parliament. This did not mean that there were no domestic reforms. The Burials Act, 1880, allowed Dissenters to hold their own burial services in Church of England graveyards. In the same year Chamberlain took up Plimsoll's work for sailors and passed a Seamans' Wages Act and a Grain Cargoes Act. In 1881 flogging was finally abolished in the army and navy.

The year 1882 brought two important reforms with far-reaching social consequences. The Married Women's Property Act granted married women the rights of separate ownership of property. The Settled Land Act broke down the barriers against land transfer and enabled settled land to be sold or let on long building leases. In 1883 Chamberlain passed two important measures which helped British commerce; they were the Bankruptcy Act and the Patents Act. A campaign against the Contagious Diseases Act led to their repeal in 1886. These Acts, passed in 1864, 1866 and 1869, had adopted for 18 garrison or dockyard towns a system of licensed and regulated prostitution. The abolition of the Acts led to the idea of a single standard of virtue for men and women and gave an impetus to the general movement for women's rights.

The Bradlaugh Controversy

When the new Parliament met in April 1880 Gladstone was confronted with the Bradlaugh incident which dragged on for five years and proved to be one of his most tiresome pre-occupations. Charles Bradlaugh (1833–91), a Liberal MP for Northampton, who was a well known atheist, was refused permission by the Commons either to affirm or to take the oath of allegiance when he came to Westminster. The Conservatives, who opposed Bradlaugh, implied that his supporters must sympathize with his beliefs; as well as being an atheist Bradlaugh advocated birth control. Although Gladstone detested Bradlaugh's opinions he loved liberty and did not think that a man's views should bar him from Parliament. Gladstone also respected democracy and could not ignore the wishes of the electors of Northampton to be represented by Bradlaugh, whom they continued to return to Westminster at a series of by-elections. Gladstone therefore defended Bradlaugh's right to sit in the Commons. He was opposed by Lord Randolph Churchill (1849–94) whose 'Fourth Party', a group of Conservatives dedicated to the ideals of Disraelian Tory democracy, used the Bradlaugh case as an instrument to oppose the Liberals and as a platform to gain attention. The dispute was not settled until after the next general election when a new speaker of the Commons allowed Bradlaugh to take the oath and his seat. In 1891 when Bradlaugh was on his death bed the Commons repented and agreed to delete their most savage resolutions against him from its journals.

Parliamentary Reform

Although the Liberals' reforms were welcomed by large numbers of people many radicals felt bitterly disappointed. They had listened to Chamberlain's speeches and been inspired by him. Some of the radicals' desire for reform was met in 1883, 1884 and 1885 by measures to reform Parliament. The costliness of the 1880 general election was testimony to the fact that the Ballot Act had not suppressed corruption. In 1883, acting on the recommendations of a Royal Commission, Gladstone passed the Corrupt and Illegal Practices Act. Severe penalties, including imprisonment, fines and exclusion from the Commons, were imposed on anyone who broke the law with respect to bribery, treating, impersonation, perjury and false expense returns. The Act restricted electoral expenditure. In England, Scotland and Wales candidates in the boroughs were limited to £250 where there were less than 2000 voters; where there were more than 2000 voters candidates could spend £380 plus £30 for each additional 1000 on the electoral register. In the counties the rate was £650 where the electorate was less than 2000; it was £710 where there were more than 2000 voters plus £60 for each additional 1000. As a result of this Act the old abuses died out.

In 1884, under pressure from Chamberlain, Gladstone embarked on an important measure of parliamentary reform. Radicals had been pressing for some years for the extension to householders in the countryside of the vote which the 1867 Reform Act had provided for householders in the towns. The Bill to secure this widening of the electorate passed the Commons fairly easily but when it reached the Lords it was set on one side, by a motion that the necessary redistribution of seats should first be effected. This obstructive attitude on the part of the Lords provoked an outburst of radical agitation and led to riots and demonstrations in large cities. This conflict between 'Peers and People' led radicals to call for the abolition of the power of the Lords and the slogan 'Mend them — or end them' became popular. The Queen urged compromise and in the end moderation prevailed. The Franchise Act passed both houses in 1884. It meant that the franchise in the counties became identical with that which the 1867 Reform Act had laid down for the boroughs. The electorate increased from three million to five million or nearly one in six of the whole population. The Irish electorate was trebled.

A third measure of parliamentary reform, the Redistribution Act, was passed in 1885. By this Act 79 towns with less than 15,000 residents lost their individual representation and were merged into adjoining constituencies. Thirty six towns with less than 50,000 residents lost one MP. This Act did away with the medieval notion that communities should be represented. Henceforth, with the exception of the University seats and the large boroughs with populations of between 50,000 and 165,000, all constituencies were single member seats. This involved the arbitrary division of shires and cities into separate constituencies, representing not a community with a common interest but administrative convenience. In the new constituencies the Liberals at first gained votes in the countryside whilst the Conservatives did better in the towns.

2 Foreign and Imperial Policy

In his Midlothian campaigns Gladstone had attacked the conduct of Disraeli's foreign policy, speaking out against his 'forward' policies in South Africa and Afghanistan and denouncing his treatment of the Balkan Christians. His original intention in taking office was to bring the Eastern question to a satisfactory conclusion and then to retire. Gladstone remained in office for five years and he found that once in office he could not necessarily carry out the policies he had advocated whilst in opposition.

The Eastern Question

One of Gladstone's first problems in foreign policy was to convince the Sultan of Turkey that he had to carry out the terms of the Treaty of Berlin which involved a loss of territory and that he could no longer rely on British support to evade this loss. Goschen (1831-1907) was sent as special ambassador to Constantinople and he secured the cession of Dulcigno to Montenego in 1880 and of Thessaly to Greece in 1881. This policy was not a triumph for Gladstonian principles of international politics, since the Sultan only surrendered his territory when faced with the direct threat of force from the Mediterranean fleet. British power alone, not the Concert of Europe, brought matters to a satisfactory conclusion. In addition, although he withdrew the 'military consuls' that Disraeli had begun to place in Asia Minor, he was not able to repudiate Disraeli's Cyprus Convention and hand the island over to Greece. The Queen disapproved most strongly of repudiation and it would have been most unpopular in the country at large.

South Africa
In his Midlothian speeches Gladstone had declared that he regarded the Transvaal, annexed in 1877, as valueless to the British empire. When he became Prime Minister the inhabitants of the Transvaal naturally expected to become independent. But Gladstone did not act hastily. He began to investigate a plan for a South African federation and in the summer and autumn of 1880 there were disputes about the form that such a federation should take. The Boers' patience ran out and they decided to fight to secure self-government. General Colley (1835 – 81) was sent to put down the rebellion and he was defeated in a number of minor battles, ending with defeat at Majuba Hill on 27 February 1881.

The British public thought that Majuba Hill was a disgraceful event and called for an expedition to teach the people of the Transvaal a lesson. Gladstone did not respond to these demands, instead he dealt with the Boers on equal terms. He did not wish to lose more lives and he did not wish to oppose the Boers' desire for independence. By the Convention of Pretoria, signed on 2 August 1881, the Transvaal was given independence except in the conduct of its relations with other states and in return the Transvaal recognized British suzerainty. Three years later a new convention was drawn up which modified these arrangements and omitted the word 'suzerainty' — this omission led to misunderstanding in the future and helped to bring about the Boer War of 1899 – 1902. Another factor which helped to make the war possible was that the Boers misinterpreted Gladstone's dealings with them as a sign of weakness. They felt that they had gained the convention by force and that Britain was a failing power.

Egypt
The Suez Canal had been built by French engineers with French capital and opened in 1869. It had increased the volume of European trade with India and the importance of Egypt which was still a province of the Turkish empire and was ruled by a Khedive who was subordinate to the Sultan of Turkey. The Egyptians had trouble administering the canal and this had led Disraeli in 1875 to purchase the Khedive's shares which amounted to 44 per cent of the total capital of the canal company. In 1876 Disraeli had agreed to joint Anglo-French intervention in Egypt's confused finances and a Dual Control over the Egyptian treasury was set up.

In 1881 Arabi Pasha, an army officer, organized a revolt against the Khedive and France and Britain sent their fleets to stand by in case the many Europeans in Egypt were threatened. In June 1882 the

Arabi's followers killed over 50 foreigners in Alexandria. Gladstone tried to persuade the powers of Europe to act in concert in Egypt but they refused. In the end even France refused to become involved in any action. The British fleet was left alone facing the Alexandrians, who were constructing batteries to fire upon it, and so Britain was compelled to bombard Alexandria on 11 July 1882 and destroy the batteries. A small British expeditionary force landed in Egypt, annihilated the Arabi's force, and captured its leader in the battle of Tel-el-Kebir on 13 September 1882.

British administrators, led by Sir Evelyn Baring (1841-1917), were sent to Egypt to introduce reforms. They tried to put an end to dirt, disease, crime and the slave trade. The British presence in Egypt led Bright to resign but Gladstone felt justified in occupying Egypt for a short time. In 1885 he secured a settlement of the Egyptian debt. This placed the country's finances and control of its administration under a board of six European powers. The whole Egyptian episode angered the French who had regarded Egypt as a zone of influence for nearly a century. It was a cause of hostility between Britain and France for the next 19 years.

The Sudan

Gladstone had viewed the occupation of Egypt as a temporary necessity to safeguard Europeans living there and to safeguard the canal. However, once there, developments in the Nile valley caused him more and more concern. In 1883 a new movement far up the Nile threatened Egypt's security. This was a religious movement and its fanatical head took the title of Madhi (he who is guided aright). Many of his followers regarded him as the Messiah of the Moslem world. In November 1883 an Egyptian army led by Colonel Hicks (1830-83) marched out into the desert to deal with him and was promptly wiped out. At this stage the British government decided to withdraw the occupants of the various Egyptian garrisons in the Sudan. In January 1884 Charles Gordon (1833-85) was chosen to go to the Sudan and assess the situation, finding out if it was safe to withdraw the garrisons. Hartington told Gordon to go to Khartoum and report on the evacuation of the 32,000 Egyptian troops in the area.

Shortly after Gordon reached Khartoum in February 1884 the Madhi's forces cut the telegraph lines between Khartoum and Cairo and thereafter telecommunications between Gordon and his superiors were limited. The situation was complicated for neither Gordon nor Gladstone understood the Mahdist movement. Gordon thought that it was merely a ruthless gang seeking power which he could easily suppress whilst Gladstone regarded it as a political movement of 'people . . . struggling rightly to be free'. This meant that what the government had intended to be a reconnaissance led by a single officer became a powerful expedition up the Nile to remove the officer who was not following instructions and was in danger. In August 1884 Sir Garnet Wolseley led a force up the Nile which defeated the Madhi in two battles. An advance party arrived at Khartoum on 28 January 1885. It was two days too late. Gordon was dead and the redcoats were fired on from Gordon's palace. (See the picture of the death of Gordon.)

There were bitter recriminations in Britain. The Conservatives attacked Gladstone for not sending help soon enough to Gordon whilst the Liberals attacked him for sending any help at all. The initials by which the Grand Old Man of the Liberal party were known were said to stand for 'Gordon's Only Murderer'. Gladstone admitted that he had been tortured by this affair. But he defended his actions in debate saying,

'We had no alternative in this Egyptian policy. Each step was inevitable; our decisions, sad and deplorable as they may have been in themselves, were yet inevitable in the circumstances, and at the moment when we were called upon to undertake them.'

Afghanistan
Gladstone's disapproval of Disraeli's 'forward' policy in Afghanistan can be seen in two famous sentences in one of his Midlothian speeches. He declared,

'Remember the rights of the savage as we call him. Remember that the happiness of his humble home, remember that the sanctity of life in the hill villages of Afghanistan among the winter snows, is as inviolable in the eye of Almighty God as can be your own.'

Gladstone did not continue the 'forward' policy but he was forced to turn his attention to Afghanistan in 1885. In March 1885 Russian and Afghan troops clashed in the remote border village of Penjdeh. The Amir did not take this incident seriously but in Britain many people called for a war to support Afghanistan. On 27 April Gladstone asked the Commons for £11 million to meet the Russian aggression but he also asked the Russians to consider arbitration. His proposal was accepted and the danger of war passed away.

3 Ireland and Home Rule

From the time when Gladstone went into opposition in 1874 until

The death of Gordon, 1884

1880 relations between England and Ireland deteriorated. Disraeli did nothing for Ireland and in the last three years of his ministry Irish MPs used delaying tactics in the Commons to make it impossible for him to do anything for England. They wanted to force MPs at Westminster to focus attention on Irish grievances. The economic depression of the late 1870s afflicted Ireland just as much as

England. There had been another Irish famine in 1879 and starvation and evictions were common.

Michael Davitt (1846–1906) and the Irish Land League

Michael Davitt was the child of Irish peasants. His family had been evicted onto the hillside when he was five years old. He had gone as a labouring child to Lancashire and had lost his arm in an accident at work when he was 11. He became attached to the Fenian movement and in 1870 he was sentenced to 15 years' hard labour for collecting arms. It was whilst he was in prison that he decided to try to obtain an economic rather than a political solution to Ireland's wrongs. He was released from prison in 1877 and, with the help of Parnell (1846–91), he founded the Irish Land League in 1879. Parnell became President of the Land League. The League's aim was to reduce exorbitant rents and to enable tenants to buy their holdings. Davitt intended the League to pressurize landlords by holding mass meetings in country towns. It did not preach violence but after almost every one of its meetings there were attacks on landlords' property and cattle. As the number of evictions grew, so did the number of attacks.

Charles Stuart Parnell

Davitt's aim was to unite the agitation for agrarian reform with the movement for Irish independence and to this end he worked closely with Charles Stuart Parnell. Parnell was an Anglo-Irish Protestant squire whose American mother had instilled a hatred of the English ruling class in him. He became an MP in 1875 and soon became the leader of the Irish nationalist party. This party removed Isaac Butt from the leadership of the Home Rule movement because he was not forceful enough. Parnell believed that Home Rule was the only solution to Ireland's problems.

When Gladstone became Prime Minister in 1880 he sought, as a temporary measure, to compensate tenants who were evicted because the last two years' harvests had been so bad that they could not pay their rents. His Compensation Bill was defeated in the House of Lords on 3 August 1880. Gladstone realized that he would have to prepare another Land Act. In the meantime Parnell organized a boycott against anyone taking over a farm from which a tenant had been evicted. Boycotting led to outrages committed by 'Captain Moonlight' and his followers.

The Co-ercion Act and the Second Land Act, 1881

Gladstone's government had allowed Disraeli's Co-ercion Act to lapse but the number of outrages grew. The Lord's rejection of the Compensation for Disturbance Bill meant that evictions continued and consequently so did the outrages. Gladstone's solution was to pass a Land Act but he knew that he would have difficulty in passing any Irish reform and so, to make the Act palatable, he decided to begin by passing a severe Co-ercion Act which suspended Habeas Corpus.

In 1881 Gladstone embarked on a four-month struggle to secure the Land Act. The Irish Land Act, 1881, gave the tenants much of what they had demanded. They achieved the 'Three Fs' — fair rent, fixity of tenure and free sale of land. The Land Act reduced rents enough to make an Irish agricultural revolution possible. The leaders of the Land League recognized the benefits of the Land Act but they regarded it simply as a concession which they had extracted from the government by force. They decided to apply more force to achieve the rest of their demands.

Parnell's Imprisonment and the Kilmainham Treaty, 1882

Parnell's reaction to the second Land Act disappointed Gladstone. Parnell did not really want Gladstone's reforms to work for if they did unrest would cease and he would be in a less strong position from which to press for Home Rule. Therefore the Land League decided to have nothing to do with the new rent courts and evictions and outrages continued. Parnell did not condemn the outrages. In a speech at Wexford he called Gladstone 'this masquerading knight-errant, this pretending champion of the rights of every other nation except those of the Irish nation'. The cabinet decided to arrest Parnell under the terms of the Co-ercion Act and on 13 October 1881 he was imprisoned in Kilmainham gaol.

Once in prison, Parnell became a martyr. In the six months following his arrest there were 14 murders and 61 attempted murders in the Irish countryside. By April 1882 Parnell wanted to leave prison and reassert his leadership over the anti-British movements in Ireland. He declared that he would support the Land Act and he was released. The Kilmainham Treaty, which was unofficial, embodied an understanding between Parnell and the cabinet that a Bill would be introduced at Westminster to deal with tenants whose rents were in arrears and in return Parnell would moderate the violence of the Land League. Forster, the Irish secretary, did not agree with the arrangements and he resigned. When he was released from prison Parnell exercised a moderating influence and for a time it seemed that all might be well in Ireland.

The Phoenix Park Murders, 1882

Gladstone sent Spencer (1835 – 1910) to Ireland as Viceroy and he appointed his nephew-in-law Lord Frederick Cavendish (1836 – 82) to the post of Lord Lieutenant. On 6 May 1882 Burke (1829 – 82), the head of the Irish executive, and Cavendish were stabbed to death in broad daylight in Phoenix Park. The murderers belonged to a secret society, the 'Invincibles', who had been trying for some weeks to kill Forster and had picked on Burke as a substitute. They killed Cavendish without knowing who he was. These murders put an end to an immediate Irish settlement. An even harsher Co-ercion Act was passed in 1882 but Gladstone stuck to his promise to Parnell and passed an Arrears Act which made the second Land Act workable.

In Ireland murders and outrages continued in spite of the Arrears Act, which cancelled arrears of rent in cases where tenants occupying land worth less than £30 a year were unable to pay. Meanwhile at Westminster the Irish nationalists obstructed proceedings in the Commons to try to force the government to deal exclusively with Irish affairs. In the end the government was forced to introduce the closure or 'guillotine' whereby a time for voting was announced before a debate began and voting took place come what may, even if all the issues involved had not been thoroughly discussed. In 1883 the Irish people raised £37,000, known as Parnell's 'Tribute', to help him pay his debts and in recognition of his services to Ireland. In 1885 Gladstone proposed to renew the Crimes Act of 1882; Parnell and a group of Irish MPs voted with the Conservatives to defeat the budget. Seventy Liberals, led by Hartington, abstained from voting and Gladstone resigned in June 1885.

The First Home Rule Bill, 1886

Gladstone hoped that Salisbury and the Conservatives who were in power in the winter of 1885 – 6 would introduce their own plans for a measure of Irish self-government. In fact Lord Randolph Churchill, a Conservative cabinet member, indicated to Parnell that the Conservatives would try to produce an acceptable answer to Irish demands for Home Rule. This pleased Gladstone who believed that Conservative proposals for Home Rule had far more chance of being accepted by the House of Lords than Liberal plans. In the end how-ever, the Conservatives did not offer any solution to the Irish problem. On 17 December 1885 Gladstone announced that he was in favour of Home Rule for Ireland. When Parliament reassembled in January 1886 Parnell and 85 Irish MPs voted with the Liberals against the Conservatives.

Gladstone began his third ministry in 1886 pledged to support

Home Rule but he led a weak and divided party. Hartington and the Whigs were afraid that Chamberlain's group of Liberals would come to dominate the Liberal party which would then concentrate more and more on radical reforms. In January 1886 Hartington and his followers left the Liberals and joined the Conservatives. At the same time Chamberlain and his followers resented Gladstone's announcement on Home Rule which had been made without consulting any of his colleagues. Chamberlain wanted to implement his unofficial programme and he believed that Home Rule would take time away from reform in England. In March 1886 Chamberlain and 40 supporters announced their opposition to Gladstone, declaring themselves to be Liberal Unionists — they were still Liberals but wished to maintain the union between England and Ireland.

In April 1886 Gladstone introduced his first Home Rule Bill in the Commons. The Bill proposed to establish a separate Parliament in Dublin to deal with Irish affairs, to end Irish representation at Westminster but to leave the control of foreign affairs, defence and external trade in the hands of the British government. The Bill was attacked by Salisbury, Hartington and Chamberlain and was defeated by 30 votes. Gladstone could have resigned but decided instead to fight an election on the issue. Voting took place in July and Gladstone, or rather Home Rule, was defeated. Lord Salisbury held office as Prime Minister from 1886 to 92.

The Second Home Rule Bill, 1893

Lord Salisbury was defeated in the election of July 1892 and Gladstone formed his fourth ministry. He still supported the idea of Home Rule but knew that it was not generally popular. In order to make Home Rule palatable to the British electorate he had agreed to an extensive programme of reform, adopted in conference at Newcastle. The Newcastle proposals included land reform, power for local bodies to forbid the sale of drink, triennial Parliaments, 'one man one vote', elected parish councils and Church disestablishment in Scotland and Wales. The Liberal cabinet included young men such as Asquith (1852 – 1928), Fowler (1830 – 1911), Bryce (1838 – 1922), Roseberry (1847 – 1929) and Campbell-Bannerman (1836 – 1908).

In February 1893 Gladstone introduced his second Home Rule Bill which contained similar provisions to those of 1886, except that 80 Irish MPs were to remain at Westminster. The Bill passed its third reading in the Commons on 1 September, but one week later the Lords rejected it by the largest majority ever recorded there. Gladstone urged his colleagues to agree to a dissolution on the issue of the 'peers against the people'. None of his colleagues would agree for they were getting some parts of the Newcastle programme enacted into law. On 1 March Gladstone made a speech warning that the Lords' opposition to Liberal Bills had produced a 'state of things, of which we are compelled to say that in our judgement it cannot continue'. Two days later he resigned.

Summary

When Gladstone died in 1898 he was recognized to have been the foremost Liberal of the nineteenth century. He had worked hard to solve Ireland's problems and had failed. He had championed the rights of smaller nations but once in office he was not always able to adhere to his principles so that the effects of his foreign policy were often the same as Disraeli's. In domestic policy several reforms were passed in Gladstone's later ministries although Gladstone himself was not usually directly concerned with them. Fear of drastic reforms led Hartington to leave the party whilst Gladstone's failure to make more of a commitment to reform led Chamberlain and the Liberal-Unionists to break from the party in 1886.

Exercises
1. Why did Gladstone and the Liberals win the election of 1880?
2. How did Gladstone's reforms of the 1880s help the development of democracy in Britain?
3. Describe Britain's policy under Gladstone (1880 – 86) towards South Africa, Egypt and the Sudan, and Afghanistan.
4. How did Gladstone tackle the Irish problem in the 1880s and 90s?
5. Why was Gladstone unable to solve the Irish problem?

21
Lord Salisbury: Conservatism and Imperialism, 1886 – 1905

Lord Salisbury became the leader of the Conservative party in 1880. He had been a member of the Derby ministry of 1867 but had resigned on the issue of parliamentary reform. Salisbury was the last Prime Minister in the House of Lords. He was aristocratic and aloof. He did not seem to understand the problems of ordinary people in Britain. Unlike Disraeli, he was not concerned with introducing sweeping domestic reforms and in this he had something in common with the Whigs who began to abandon the Liberal party after 1874. However, Salisbury and Disraeli did have something in common — they were both passionately interested in foreign and imperial affairs. Salisbury was Foreign Secretary for almost as many years as Palmerston had been. He held that office in 1878 – 80, 1885 – 6, 1887 – 92 and 1895 – 1900. He was Prime Minister for longer than anyone else since the passing of the 1832 Reform Act and held that post in June 1885 to February 1886, August 1886 – 92, and 1895 – 1902.

1 Foreign Policy

Salisbury's Principles of Foreign Policy

The phrase 'splendid isolation' is associated with Lord Salisbury's foreign policy but an examination of his policy shows that during the time that he was Foreign Secretary Britain did not follow a course of isolation. However, Lord Salisbury did not put his trust in alliances and other international schemes. He preferred instead to deal with each event as it arose in ways which best suited Britain's purpose. He was determined to safeguard Britain's industry and trade and to this end he wished to maintain the powerful position of Britain's navy. He was anxious to preserve world peace and did not want Europe to be dominated by any single power. Like many of his predecessors, he took an interest in developing the British empire, but he also supported the growth of independent democratic nations. When he first became Foreign Secretary Britain seemed most at risk by threats from Russia in the Balkans and Asia and from France in Egypt.

The Bulgarian Crisis, 1885

In 1885 the Bulgarians of Eastern Rumelia, supported by Prince Alexander of Bulgaria, united with the new Bulgarian state and thus breached the Treaty of Berlin, 1878. Salisbury wanted to prevent Russia from taking advantage of this situation and due to vigorous action on his part the great powers reached an agreement in January 1886 which recognized the union of the two provinces. Although Czar Alexander III accepted the agreement the issue was not immediately solved and subsequent Russian action led to a threat of general war. The Russians forced Prince Alexander to abdicate and sent a Russian general to control Bulgaria. The Bulgarians were supported by Austria, Britain and France and in the end the Russians backed down and accepted the Prince whom the Bulgarians had chosen as their ruler, Ferdinand of Coburg. Salisbury hoped that this outcome would prevent Russian advances in Bulgaria and in the Balkans in general.

The Mediterranean Agreements, 1887

Salisbury seriously doubted that the Sultan of Turkey had the ability to ward off future Russian aggression. He sought means of safeguarding British interests in the Mediterranean by concluding two Mediterranean Agreements with Italy and Austria in 1887. The first agreement was signed by Italy and Britain on 12 February and accepted by Austria on 24 March. In it the powers undertook to uphold the status quo in the Mediterranean, the Adriatic, the Aegean and the Black Sea. Italy accepted the British position in Egypt and Britain agreed to support Italy in North Africa. They agreed to adopt a common policy if Turkey were threatened and if Austria were attacked by Russia. Britain made it clear that she would not take part in an offensive war against France. The second Mediterranean Agreement was signed on 12 December 1887 and the three powers agreed to maintain the status quo in the East and in the Balkans and to support 'Turkish independence and integrity'.

Burma

Salisbury continued Britain's expansion in Burma which had begun in the 1820s. He conquered the remainder of Burma in 1886 and 10 years later forced the ruler of Siam to grant Britain spheres of influence in north and south Siam. France was also acquiring an empire in South East Asia and this led to further rivalry between France and Britain.

China

During the nineteenth century Britain had established strong trading links with China. By the end of the century other nations began to challenge Britain's position in that area. In 1897 Germany occupied the district around the port of Kiao-chow and in the following year Russia acquired Port Arthur. This led Salisbury to acquire Wei-Hai-Wei which was midway between the two. Britain also gained a virtual monopoly of trade in the Yangtze river valley. To avoid war in China Salisbury arranged spheres of influence for the European powers in that country.

The Sudan

Britain and France had long been rivals in Egypt and in 1898 the two countries clashed again in that area. Salisbury decided to reconquer the Sudan to forestall any moves into the area by France. In 1898 Sir Herbert Kitchener (1850 – 1916) defeated the Madhi's forces at Omdurman. When Kitchener entered Khartoum he heard that a French force led by Major Marchand had reached the Upper Nile and hoisted the French flag at Fashoda. France hoped to control the southern Sudan and thereby the upper reaches of the Nile. For a while neither side would give way. However, France was isolated and fearful of German action in Europe. In the end Marchand withdrew. The issue was settled in a satisfactory way as far as Britain was concerned. By the Anglo-French Convention of 1899 French and British spheres of influence in the Nile and Congo basins were defined. Britain was confirmed in her control of Egypt and the Sudan.

Turkey and a Change of Policy

In 1896 – 7 a crisis arose in Turkey when the Armenians demanded self-government and religious freedom within the empire. The Sultan responded to the Armenians' demands by massacring them. In Britain Gladstone called on the government to aid the Armenians but Salisbury took no decisive action. In 1897 events took a new turn when Greece supported Crete's demands for independence from Turkey. The Turks defeated Greece and Salisbury and the great powers intervened to prevent Greece from suffering at Turkey's hands; Crete was declared an autonomous state under Prince George of Greece.

   In the course of this crisis it became clear that British policy towards Turkey had changed. Salisbury was no longer prepared to defend Constantinople and the Straits at all costs. When the Austrian foreign minister tried to link renewal of the Mediterranean Agreements with a British promise to defend Constantinople Salisbury refused. Constantinople was no longer vital to the protection of the route to India. This could now be defended from Egypt.

Africa

Until the 1870s most European countries were not interested in the African interior. But in the next 30 years most of Africa was divided amongst the great powers. Salisbury did not involve the British government directly at first; he preferred to leave things in the hands of private chartered companies such as the Royal Niger Company, the British East Africa Company and the British South Africa Company. In 1890 Britain signed an agreement with Portugal which gave Britain control of Nyasaland. In the same year she signed an agreement with France which recognized British control of Zanzibar and French control of Madagascar. Finally in 1890, Britain and Germany signed an agreement which recognized British control of Uganda, Kenya and Zanzibar and German control of German East Africa, the Cameroons and South West Africa.

The Causes of the Boer War, 1899–1902

We have seen that the Dutch settlers left the Cape in 1836 and founded the Transvaal and Orange Free State. Britain recognized the independence of these two states in 1852 and 1854 respectively. Over the next 20 years the government of the Cape took steps to defend its people both from encroachment by the Boers and from native attacks. When the Transvaal was threatened by Zulu raids in the 1870s it was annexed by Disraeli on the condition that self-government would be restored when the crisis was over. Disraeli dealt with the crisis but failed to restore self-government. When Gladstone hesitated to meet the Boers' demands for independence the first Boer War broke out, 1880–81 (see p.197). It was ended by the Pretoria Convention, 1881, which restored independence to the Transvaal but placed the republic under British suzerainty. The Boers looked upon this as a great success. They had opposed a mighty colonial power and won. Three years later the London Convention was signed, allowing the Transvaal to call itself the South African Republic. The republic agreed to allow free trade and promised not to impose taxes on foreigners which were not imposed on its own citizens. It agreed not to sign treaties with foreign states or tribes without the consent of the British government. The London Convention differed from the Pretoria Convention in that it contained no mention of the word suzerainty.

The two conventions did not resolve the conflict between Britain and the Boers. Paul Kruger, the new president of the republic of South Africa, wanted to expand the territory of the Transvaal. In November 1884 a British force led by Sir Charles Warren (1840–1927) put an end to Boer advances into Bechuanaland. This hemmed the Transvaal in on the west. It then became hemmed in to the north by the chartered company's acquisition of Rhodesia. In 1894 Kruger obtained Swaziland as a protectorate but Britain kept Tongaland, the coastal strip between the Transvaal and the sea. This angered Kruger immensely for one of his aims was to obtain a port of his own.

In 1886 an extraordinarily rich goldfield was discovered at Witwatersrand in the Transvaal. A flood of foreigners who were mostly British moved into the area to exploit it. Kruger adopted a distinct attitude towards the newcomers, or Uitlanders, as they were called. He told them, 'We will not exclude you' but 'you shall have no votes and no rights and we shall so tax you . . . that a large part of what you get will pass to us'. The Uitlanders disliked this treatment and looked to Britain for help. Meanwhile, the increasing wealth of the Transvaal led Kruger to buy arms and to foster links with the Netherlands and Germany.

Britain had consented to the development of self-governing colonies in Cape Colony and Natal. From 1890 to 1896 Cecil Rhodes (1853 – 1902), who had made his fortune from the discovery of diamonds at Kimberley in 1870, was Prime Minister of the Cape. A strong supporter of the British empire, he wished to use his wealth to establish British control throughout southern Africa. He wanted Britain to control the entire continent and dreamt of building a railway from Cairo to the Cape. This could not be achieved without the co-operation of the Boer republics. Rhodes acquired a charter to extend his company's operations to the southern end of Lake Tanganyika. Then in 1893 he persuaded the British government to wage war on the Matebele tribe and when it was conquered half a million square miles were added to the British empire. Rhodes' British South Africa Company was given control of the area and distributed the land to white settlers. The territory was named Rhodesia.

Not surprisingly Kruger and Rhodes became political enemies. Just when Rhodes had reached the height of his power he was toppled by his part in the Jameson raid. Relations between the Boers and the Uitlanders had continued to deteriorate. In December 1895 Rhodes arranged that some of the leaders of the Uitlanders would organize an uprising in the Transvaal so that he could then send in an army to 'protect' British interests. His plan went badly wrong. No uprising took place but Jameson (1853 – 1917) led a raid into the Transvaal which was defeated. In Britain liberal opinion denounced the raid as an outrage and Rhodes was forced to resign. The German Kaiser sent a telegram congratulating Kruger on the defeat of the raid. The Boers' hatred of the British deepened whilst the British resented the Boers' success and the fact that they blocked hopes of a British advance to the north.

Between 1896 and 1899 all Britain's efforts to improve conditions for the Uitlanders failed. They petitioned Queen Victoria for help and anti-Boer feeling grew in Britain. Both Britain and the Transvaal began troop movements in 1899. In October 1899 the Boers sent an ultimatum to Britain, proposing the solution of the Uitlanders' problems by arbitration and demanding an end to British troop movements on the Transvaal borders. Britain rejected the ultimatum and found herself at war.

The Events of the Boer War, 1899–1902
Britain underestimated the strength of the Boers. They used guerilla tactics and had modern German weapons. However, Boer hopes that Germany or some other European power would come to their aid were not fulfilled. In Britain opinion was divided about the war. Several radicals and members of the new Labour party were opposed to the war and considered that Britain was bullying a small nation.

Britain entered the war in a rather carefree manner, not expecting an even contest with so small an opponent. In the first two weeks of the war Britain suffered a series of disastrous setbacks. The Boers immediately invaded Natal and the Cape. They laid siege to Kimberley, Mafeking and Ladysmith (see Fig. 17, The sieges of the Boer War). In December 1899 they inflicted three major defeats on Britain at Stormberg, Magersfontein and the Tugela River. These defeats led to changes in the British command. Lord Roberts was appointed supreme commander and Lord Kitchener became chief of staff. With 250,000 troops under his command Roberts overwhelmed the Boer forces led by Cronje. Early in 1900 Ladysmith and Kimberley were relieved. Mafeking held out for seven months under the command of Colonel Baden Powell and was relieved in May 1900. By June Roberts had occupied Bloemfontein, Johannesburg and Pretoria but the Boers fought on for another 18 months using guerilla tactics which the British found it very difficult to counter. In the end they built concentration camps to intern civilians suspected of helping the guerillas. The camps were so badly organized that one in five of the prisoners contracted diseases and died. This ruthless policy, together with the destruction of farms, eventually forced the Boers to abandon their struggle.

The End of the Boer War
In May 1902 a peace treaty was signed at Vereeniging. By this treaty

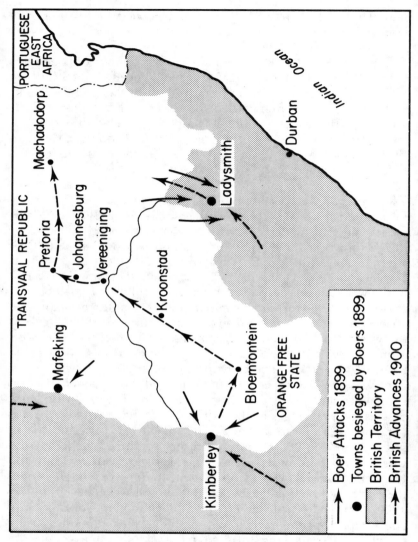

Fig.17 The Sieges of The Boer War, 1899–1902

the Transvaal and the Orange Free State became Crown colonies. They were promised the maintenance of Afrikaans as their official language and were given £3 million to compensate for losses they had suffered during the war. When the Liberals came into office they granted self-government to the Transvaal in 1906 and to the Orange Free State in 1907. In 1910 the Union of South Africa was created. These arrangements reflect a change in attitude towards the British empire.

The Death of Salisbury

When the Boer War was over a general election was held. The Conservatives were returned to power on a wave of patriotic fervour. Shortly afterwards Salisbury retired and he died in 1903. His nephew A.J. Balfour became Prime Minister. One of Balfour's achievements in foreign policy was the Entente Cordiale signed with France in 1904 (see p.243). This helped to cut down the isolation which Britain felt in Europe at the time of the Boer War.

2 Ireland

In the 1880s the Irish economy was depressed and distress was mounting. This led the Irish to adopt a 'Plan of Campaign' whereby they refused to pay landlords higher rents than local peasants' associations judged to be reasonable. In response to the 'Plan of Campaign' the landlords carried out more and more evictions. The peasants retaliated by boycotting, intimidation, arson, attacks on cattle and in some cases murder. As always the government's response to crime in Ireland was co-ercion. In the years of Conservative rule 1886–92 and 1895–1905 the government frequently resorted to the imposition of co-ercion in Ireland.

'Parnellism and Crime'

The Irish began to gain some support for their struggle in England in the 1880s, especially amongst the workers who believed that the Irish were fighting the sort of battle that trade unionists had fought for recognition earlier in the century. The Conservatives responded by trying to discredit Parnell and the Irish nationalist party. In this they were helped by *The Times* newspaper. *The Times* published a series of articles entitled 'Parnellism and Crime' in which they tried to show that the Irish nationalist party was connected with extremist organizations in Ireland. In 1887 *The Times* published a letter in which Parnell implied that Burke's murder in Phoenix Park was justified (see p.203). In the Commons Parnell denied that he had ever written the letter but he took no legal action against the newspaper. In July 1888 a Parnellite brought a libel action against *The Times* and when the Attorney-General read a number of other damaging letters, implicating Parnell in violence, the latter demanded an inquiry. During the hearing it was discovered that all the letters allegedly written by Parnell were forgeries. They had been written by an Irish journalist, Piggott. He confessed to what he had done and then fled the country and committed suicide. Parnell's reputation rose to new heights for he was seen to be the victim of a petty criminal and of a plot to discredit the Irish.

Parnell's Downfall

Just when it seemed that Parnell's character had been cleared the Irish leader received a far more serious blow. In 1890 Captain O'Shea brought a divorce case against his wife, citing Parnell as the co-respondent. Parnell did not defend himself during the case and the O'Shea lawyers destroyed his reputation. The case led many people to reconsider their views about Home Rule. Parnell seemed to have behaved so badly in his private life for so long that he could not be trusted to govern his country. Gladstone let it be known that he could no longer work with Parnell, the Irish Catholic bishops campaigned against him and his own party was split in its support of him. Parnell died suddenly in 1891. His party remained split for many years until John Redmond reunited it.

Reform

The downfall of Parnell and the divisions within the Irish nationalist movement led the British government to gain a much firmer grip on Ireland. The government also began to introduce reforms. In 1891 the Land Purchase Act provided money which tenants could borrow to buy their own farms. There were subsequent Land Purchase Acts and by 1910 250,000 tenants were affected by the scheme. County councils were established in Ireland in 1898 which gave the Irish greater participation in local administration. The Conservatives also set up the Congested Districts Board to improve conditions in the west of Ireland where the pressure of population on land was enormous. This, together with the construction of light railways in the west, made the Conservatives popular for a time in Ireland.

3 Domestic Policy

Since Lord Salisbury was primarily interested in foreign affairs he devoted little attention to domestic problems and social reform. His successor, Balfour, was also inactive in this area. Salisbury's chief domestic achievements came in the spheres of finance, local government and education.

Finance

The Chancellor of the Exchequer, Goschen, reduced income tax in his budgets of 1887 and 1888. He also reduced the taxes on tea and tobacco. He was faced with rising expenditure for local government and increases in the army and navy estimates. To meet these costs in 1889 he introduced an estate duty of one per cent on estates exceeding £10,000. Goschen is remembered for his conversion of the national debt in 1888 which brought the government an immediate saving in interest of £1,400,000.

The Local Government Act, 1888

In 1835 the Municipal Corporations Reform Act had brought a democratic system of local government to towns and cities but it had done nothing to reform the government of counties and parishes. In 1884 household suffrage was extended to these areas of the country and this made local government reform inevitable. Neither political party could ignore the demand that those who had votes for Parliament should also have votes for local government. Consequently, in 1888 the president of the local government board, C.T. Ritchie (1838–1906), passed the Local Government Act. The Act set up county councils, elected by the rate payers. Towns with a population of over 50,000 became county boroughs with the same powers as county councils. The Act also set up the London County Council which later assumed power over the 28 London boroughs established in 1899.

Legislation Affecting the Workforce

The Factory Act, 1891, increased the minimum age for employing children in factories to 11 and fixed the maximum hours of labour for women at 12, with one and a half hours for meals. In 1897 the Conservatives passed the Workmen's Compensation Act by which some work men who were injured at work or caught a disease as a result of their work could claim compensation from their employer. The Act did not cover seamen, agricultural workers or domestic servants. During Balfour's administration the government refused to reverse the Taff Vale decision (see p.225) which angered many trade unionists. Balfour's government passed the Unemployed Workmen's Act which allowed voluntary subscriptions to be used to create work for the unemployed. Many workers considered that this Act was an insult to the umemployed for it did little to help them.

Education

In 1889 the Conservatives passed the Technical Instruction Act, making the county and county borough councils responsible for that subject. In the following year the government ear-marked 'whisky money' to pay for the development of technical education. It abolished fees in elementary schools in 1891. Balfour was responsible for the Education Act, 1902, which abolished the school boards and established Local Education Authorities to administer elementary and secondary education. The religious schools of the Anglicans and Catholics retained their own religious teaching but were aided by money from the rates. This angered many Nonconformists who showed their opposition to the measure by trying to block the payment of rates for the religious schools.

Agriculture

Lord Salisbury was in office at a time of acute agricultural distress but he did little to aid the farmers. A Tithes Act was passed in 1891 which made tithes payable by the owner and not the occupier of the land. The Small Holdings Act, 1892, gave county councils the power to purchase land for the provision of small holdings.

Joseph Chamberlain and Tariff Reform

Joseph Chamberlain entered Parliament as a Liberal in 1876 but as we have seen he split the party in 1886 over the question of Home Rule for Ireland. He and his supporters campaigned for an 'unauthorized programme' of reforms, so named because it was unauthorized by the Liberals. The programme called for free education and the creation of small holdings for agricultural workers — or 'three acres and a cow'. Chamberlain also wished to establish a progressive income tax which would pay for welfare benefits such as old age pensions. Chamberlain differed from many radicals in his belief in the need to develop the British empire and strengthen its political and trading links. He believed that this was necessary to combat Britain's declining position in the world.

In the 1880s Britain found that she was no longer the foremost industrial nation. The German, French and American economies were all expanding at a much faster rate than Britain's. These countries had the benefit of new large machinery whereas much of Britain's machinery dated from the industrial revolution and was becoming obsolete. These countries had a much better system of technical education than Britain and their businessmen knew the value of marketing and advertising. British manufacturers felt that it was enough for an article to carry the tag 'made in Britain' and that no other sales technique was required. The governments of all Britain's trading rivals protected their developing industries with tariffs. The British government clung to a policy of free trade. As unemployment in Britain grew, so did the call for tariff reform.

Chamberlain became Colonial Secretary in Salisbury's government in 1895. He had studied conditions in Germany and the United States and he believed that a system of protective tariffs had enabled those countries to prosper. Meanwhile Britain had declined because she had neglected to introduce tariffs. In 1903 Chamberlain founded that Tariff Reform League and resigned from his government post. The League had a three point programme. Firstly, it called for a small import duty on food imports from foreign countries which would favour foods imported from the colonies which did not carry any duties. Secondly, there should be an import duty of 10 per cent on manufactured imports to weaken foreign competition and aid British industries. Thirdly, to help meet a possible rise in the cost of living, resulting from the imposition of tariffs, duties on tea, sugar and other articles of general consumption should be reduced. These measures would increase trade with the colonies who in turn would give preference to British exports. They would help to solve Britain's economic difficulties.

The Conservatives were divided on the subject of tariff reform. Although Balfour sympathized with Chamberlain's proposals he knew that they would lead to a rise in the cost of living and this made him reluctant to adopt tariff reform, knowing that it would be unpopular with the electorate. At a meeting of the unionist party those who supported free trade suffered a defeat. Shortly afterwards Balfour resigned and Campbell-Bannerman, the Liberal, formed a government. In 1906 he dissolved Parliament and fought a general election on the free trade issue. The Conservative party was decisively defeated in the election. Tariff reform was opposed by both the Liberal and the Labour party and the result of the election was a victory for free trade.

Summary
During his long career as Prime Minister Salisbury had paid scant attention to social reform. Although there were reforms in Ireland the Irish secretary, Balfour, had met any opposition in that country by a ruthless application of the Crimes Act. There had been much opposition to the campaign for tariff reform which split the Conservative party. A substantial number of people had been opposed to the Boer War. Although they had been considered unpatriotic at the time, after the war a popular feeling of revulsion against imperialism grew in Britain. Salisbury has been accused of isolationism in matters of foreign policy. He was not an isolationist and frequently worked in concert with other powers. Foreign policy was his chief love and it was in this field that he was most successful.

Exercises
1. Describe two aspects of Lord Salisbury's foreign policy which contradict the idea that he was committed to a policy of 'splendid isolation'.
2. Why was there such hostility between Britain and the Boers between 1886 and 1899?
3. Describe the major incidents of the Boer War. Explain what progress was made towards better relations between Britain and the Boers by 1914.
4. Why did the Irish problem remain unsolved in the 1890s?
5. Why were many sections of British society dissatisfied with the Conservative party by 1905?

22
Trade Unions and the Rise of the Labour Party, 1851 – 1914

Throughout the nineteenth century many different groups campaigned for better working and living conditions and universal suffrage. The Peterloo massacre, 1819, trade union activity in the 1830s, the struggle of the Chartists and those who supported the Co-operative movement, were all milestones, preparing the ground for the creation of a party to represent the interests of the working class in Parliament. As the century progressed, the trade union movement became closely linked with developments which led to the rise of the Labour party. It was also influenced by Social Democrats, the Fabians and many individuals such as Keir Hardie (1856 – 1915) who founded the Independent Labour Party. (See Fig. 18, The Formation of the Labour Party.)

'New Model' Unionism, 1851 – 75
In 1851 the Amalgamated Society of Engineers was founded. This union developed a number of characteristics which were imitated by many other unions and which collectively became known as 'new model' unions. 'New model' unions were large, national bodies,

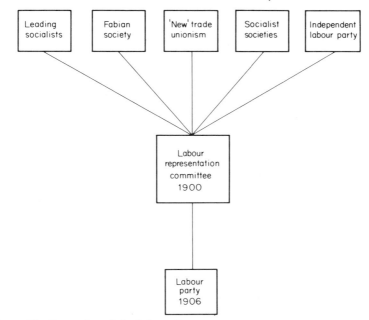

Fig.18 The Formation of the Labour Party

catering for skilled craftsmen. They charged high subscriptions; in return they provided many benefits for their members. The unions were well-organized with full-time paid officials. They were non-political; the Engineers' Union stated, 'we do not allow any political matter to be discussed'. 'New model' unions were not militant; they used the strike weapon only as a last resort.

The Legal Status of Trade Unions
Although trade unions became much stronger after 1851, they were still not allowed to 'molest', 'obstruct' or 'intimidate' others. The Conspiracy Act could still be enforced against them. In addition, according to a legal decision in the case of Hornby v Close, 1867, unions had no legal protection for their funds. Leading trade unionists were anxious to change this situation. They began a campaign to obtain political power for their members. They called for universal suffrage and vote by secret ballot; they were partly responsible for the passage of the 1867 Reform Act.

The Sheffield Outrages, 1866–7
The Sheffield outrages occurred in 1866 and 1867. They were acts of violence carried out by members of the Cutlers' Union against

non-unionists. So much opposition was aroused against unions that a Royal Commission was appointed to investigate the outrages and the whole position of trade unions. The unions tried to attract the attention of the commission to their non-militant policies and the benefits they provided for their members. The commission found that the events in Sheffield, and similar disturbances in Manchester, were not typical of union activities in general. Its final report proved quite favourable to trade unions, and recommended that they be given clear legal status.

The Parliamentary Reform Act, 1867
The 1867 Reform Act as we have seen gave the vote to all rate-paying householders and to lodgers paying a £10 rental in boroughs, and leaseholders paying £12 in the counties. The new voters were mainly skilled workers living in the towns. This Act made trade unionists more politically minded and they used their influence to try to obtain reforms which would benefit the working class.

The Trades Union Congress, 1868
Several officials of the 'new model' unions held regular meetings to discuss labour problems; they became known as the 'Junta'. They were the back-bone of the London Trades Council, founded in 1860. A number of conferences were held to co-ordinate the labour movement but the 'Junta' prevented progress by clinging to its own position of leadership. However, in 1868 the first conference, partially recognized by the 'Junta', met in Manchester. This was the origin of the Trades Union Congress, but it did not become a formal organization until some years later. The TUC became a powerful body, representing a number of unions and co-ordinating their activities.

The Labour Representation League, 1869
By 1869 the trade union movement was dissatisfied with the two existing political parties, neither of which had helped to strengthen the legal position of unions. The unions founded the Labour Representation League in 1869 with the aim of sending working men to Parliament to represent the interests of the working class.

Trade Union Law, 1871
In 1871 Gladstone's government decided to regularize the position of trade unions. On 29 June it passed two Acts — one pleased the unions, the other infuriated them. The Trade Union Act allowed unions to register in the same way as 'friendly' societies and so secure

full legal protection for their funds. The Criminal Law Amendment Act was very unpopular amongst trade unionists for it forbade peaceful picketing and repeated the old warnings against 'molestation', 'obstruction' and 'intimidation'. Men could be sent to prison not only for striking but for planning to strike.

The General Election, 1874

The Criminal Law Amendment Act united the trade union movement as it had never been united before. The 'Junta', which had previously only given luke-warm support to the TUC, summoned a congress to meet in London. The TUC elected a Parliamentary Committee which for the next few years concentrated on trying to persuade the government to repeal the Criminal Law Amendment Act. At the general election of 1874 trade unions put forward 13 candidates. Thomas Burt (1837 – 1922) and Alexander MacDonald, both officials of the Miners' Union, were elected to Westminster and paid by their union. The Liberal party was decisively defeated by the Conservatives and, while it would be an over-simplification to attach too much weight to the role of the TUC in bringing about this result, there can be little doubt that it did play a part.

The Conspiracy and Protection of Property Act, 1875

Disraeli, the new Prime Minister, felt obliged to placate the unions by repealing the Criminal Law Amendment Act. On 13 August 1875 he replaced it with the Conspiracy and Protection of Property Act. This gave the unions most of what they wanted. It legalized peaceful picketing. It also stated that no action taken by a group in the course of a trade dispute was to be punishable as a conspiracy unless it was already a crime when carried out by one person acting on his own.

Later in 1875 the Employers and Workmen Act removed the danger of fine and imprisonment for breach of contract by making it a civil, not a criminal, offence. In four years the legal position of trade unions had been revolutionized. A speaker at the TUC in 1875 claimed that the unions had been 'liberated from the last vestige of criminal laws specially appertaining to labour'.

Economic Depression, 1873 – 1900

Soon after 1870 Britain was plunged into the worst economic depression of the nineteenth century. Unemployment rose from one per cent in 1875 to 10 per cent in 1885. Rising unemployment led to the adoption of new policies by trade unions. Since the government seemed unable or unwilling to help the poor several trade unionists were prepared to take matters into their own hands.

The 'New' Unions, 1875 – 1914

The economic depression which hit agriculture and industry after 1873 led to dissatisfaction not only with the government but also with the 'new model' unions. Many trade unions began to take on new characteristics and, after a time, 'new' unions emerged. They catered for semi-skilled and unskilled workers, including women, and consequently charged low subscriptions. The 'new' unions expected the state to provide welfare benefits. They were interested in politics, many of their members were socialists, and they were militant. 'New' union members were determined to make full use of manhood suffrage and, when the existing political parties did not seem to have their interests at heart, it was only a matter of time before they began to call for the formation of a new party.

Trade Union Militancy

Two strikes carried out in the late 1880s highlight the nature of the 'new' unions. In 1888 the women working at Bryant and May's match factory in London went on strike as a protest against their conditions of work. Their cause was supported by several influential middle-class women including Mrs Annie Besant. She appealed for money for the match girls since they had no strike fund. The strikers won their case and returned to improved conditions in the factory.

In the following year the London dockers went on strike; they demanded sixpence an hour — the dockers' 'tanner'. The dockers were led by John Burns, Ben Tillet (1860 – 1943) and Tom Mann (1856 – 1941). Within three days 10,000 men were on strike and within a week the Port of London was closed. Each day the dockers marched through London; they were well organized and this contributed to their success. They were supported by sympathizers in London and received much needed funds from trade unionists in Australia. Within four weeks their aims were achieved and they returned to work. At the end of the strike the Dock, Wharf, Riverside and General Labourers' Union was established. Tom Mann was its first president and by the end of November 1889 it had 30,000 members.

The success of these two strikes encouraged other unskilled workers to join trade unions. It also led to a call for working class representation in Parliament. At first, most trade unionists wanted to sponsor MPs rather than create an entirely new party.

Karl Marx (1818 – 83)

Karl Marx was an intellectual and a radical. His teachings influenced some trade unionists and other groups which helped to create the labour party. Marx became a journalist and in 1843 he left Germany for Paris where he met Friedrich Engels (1820 – 95). The two men issued the *Communist Manifesto* in 1848 and Marx settled in London in 1849. *Das Kapital* was published in 1867; in this work Marx developed in great detail the economic theories put forward in the *Communist Manifesto*. In his writings he put forward the view that the class struggle was inevitable. He declared that a new capitalist society had come into existence during the industrial revolution which resulted in workers being exploited by the manufacturers. Marx believed that the workers were bound to engage in a class struggle with their employers, the capitalists. Since the capitalists would not willingly give up their wealth and power the workers would have to unite to overthrow the existing economic and social order. Several people attributed the growing trade union militancy of the closing years of the nineteenth century to the spread of Marx's teachings.

The Social Democratic Federation, 1881

Trade unions were only one group which helped to create the Labour party, the members of the Social Democratic Federation were another. The SDF was founded in 1881 by Henry Hyndman (1842 – 1921), a wealthy Marxist. The Federation wished to change the character of Britain's government and had a very wide programme. Its aims included: votes for all adults; the abolition of the House of Lords; payment for MPs; an eight-hour working day; free education; government housing schemes; progressive taxation; self-government for Ireland; state ownership of land, railways and mines.

The SDF concentrated its efforts amongst London's unemployed. In 1886 it clashed with a Fair Trade meeting in Trafalgar Square and, when turned away by the police, its members marched up Pall Mall, smashing the club windows. Violence errupted again in the following year at a demonstration in Trafalgar Square — on what came to be known as 'Bloody Sunday'. The leaders of the SDF tended to quarrel amongst themselves about how their programme should be achieved. A few years after it had helped to form the Labour party the SDF split up and its influence on the labour movement ceased.

Leading Socialists

Many influential socialists emerged in the late nineteenth century.

One man whose influence was widely felt was Robert Blatchford. He started the weekly socialist newspaper, the *Clarion*, in 1891 with a capital of £400. He soon sold 40,000 copies of each issue. The *Clarion* used the language of ordinary people, calling for the nationalization of the country's wealth, William Morris (1834–96) was another socialist whose influence was felt in many aspects of nineteenth-century life. He was a poet and a craftsman who joined the SDF and sold its newspaper *Justice* on street corners. Eventually, he broke away from the SDF and formed the Socialist League, through which he continued to preach socialism. The Christian Socialists were a group who worked hard to combat social evils (see p.291). They attacked capitalism, declaring that socialism was the truest form of Christianity.

The Fabian Society, 1884

The Fabian Society was founded in 1884 by a number of middle-class intellectuals. They hoped to 'make thinking people socialistic'. At first they hoped that their ideas would influence the Liberal and Conservative parties. Amongst their members were the Webbs, George Bernard Shaw (1856–1950) and H.G. Wells, who contributed to essays and pamphlets which had a very wide circulation. The Fabians took part in local affairs and joined trade unions. Soon after the foundation of the Fabian Society its members began to realize that it was not enough simply to influence existing political parties and they called for the creation of a new party. The Fabians believed that ideas of revolution were out of date and that a socialist system should be achieved through the ballot box. The Society did not have a large membership but its influence was widely felt and it helped to prepare the ground for the creation of the Labour party.

The Independent Labour Party, 1893

James Keir Hardie founded the Independent Labour Party in 1893. He came from a poor family and had little formal education. He became interested in politics whilst working in a mine and was appointed secretary of the Scottish Miners' Federation. At first Keir Hardie supported the Liberal party but he soon came to realize that a new party was needed to speak for the working class. This led to the creation of the ILP. The ILP soon had a large membership. Its members toured the country, preaching socialism and conducting a campaign inspired by idealism. In 1895 28 ILP candidates stood for election. They were all defeated and Keir Hardie became convinced that only with the official support of the trade unions could an independent Labour party hope to be successful. Every attempt to secure the support of the TUC failed until the Congress of 1899.

The Labour Representation Committee, 1900

As a result of a resolution passed by the TUC in 1899 which called for 'a distinct labour group in Parliament' the Labour Representation Committee was founded in 1900. It was not yet a Labour party but was, according to a writer in the *Clarion*, 'a little cloud, no bigger than a man's hand, which may grow into a United Labour Party'. The Labour Representation Committee's aim was to finance MPs to represent the interests of the working class. Its creation was a great step forward, yet it passed almost unnoticed and it was a long time before the trade unions fully accepted it. At the end of 1900 only 40 out of 1200 unions had affiliated to the LRC for many unions still wished to sponsor their own MPs who would devote themselves solely to union business.

Early Labour MPs

At the 'Khaki' election, 1900, the LRC put up 15 candidates. They had no funds and their opposition to the Boer War made them unpopular. It is not surprising that only two members were returned, Keir Hardie and Richard Bell. This poor result confirmed many trade unionists in their belief that the LRC could be of little use to them. However, in the following year a legal decision was taken which made the unions change their minds and draw nearer to the new party.

The Taff Vale Case, 1901

In 1900 there was a strike on the Taff Vale railway in South Wales. The general manager of the railway company decided to prosecute the Amalgamated Society of Railway Servants for the losses the company had sustained as a result of the strike. In 1901 he lost the case but then took it to the House of Lords who ruled that the union was liable for damages amounting to £23,000. This decision was a great blow to the unions because it meant that they could no longer afford to go on strike. More unions became affiliated to the LRC in an attempt to reverse the Taff Vale decision. In 1903 it was decided that each union member should contribute one penny per year into a parliamentary fund to pay MPs a salary of £200 per year. This decision meant that the trade unions effectively became the paymasters of the labour movement.

The 1906 General Election

At the general election in January 1906 the LRC had 50 candidates; 29 were elected and, in an elated mood, the LRC changed its name to the Labour party. Keir Hardie was elected chairman of the parliamentary party. Overall, the Liberals achieved an enormous majority in the new Parliament.

The Trade Disputes Act, 1906

The 29 Labour MPs, together with many Liberal MPs, were determined that the Taff Vale judgement should be reversed. In 1906 the Liberals passed the Trade Disputes Act, giving the unions most of what they wanted. It stated that unions could not be sued for damages caused by a strike and trade union members were given protection in picketing and in carrying out procedures essential to a strike.

The Osborne Judgement, 1908

The elation of 1906 was short-lived. In 1908 W.V. Osborne, a branch secretary of the Amalgamated Society of Railway Servants and a member of the Liberal party, questioned the right of his union to give financial support to the Labour party. He took the matter to law and the case eventually went before the House of Lords who declared that Osborne was right and that the Amalgamated Society had acted unlawfully in spending its funds on political objects. The Osborne judgement dismayed the trade union movement. It restricted union activities and threatened to kill the Labour party in its infancy by depriving it of its chief means of financial support.

Trade Union Militancy

In the years before the First World War trade union militancy increased (see p.236). There were a large number of strikes and in 1913 the miners, railwaymen and transport workers formed the Triple Alliance with the aim of carrying out a general strike if necessary. Many of the strikes were caused by low wages at a time of rising prices and several of the strikers were influenced by the doctrine of syndicalism. Syndicalism taught that trade unions should operate as an offensive weapon against capitalism. They should bring about revolution by incessant strikes, culminating in a general strike which would overthrow the existing social, economic and political order.

The Trade Union Act, 1913

In 1911 a salary was paid to MPs for the first time but this did not stop the trade unionists and Labour MPs from wanting to reverse the

Osborne judgement. They were successful in 1913 when the Trade Union Act was passed. The Act stated that a trade union was allowed to take part in political activities provided that a majority of its members had agreed to this and that political payments were put into a separate fund. Any union member who did not want to contribute to the fund could contract out of it.

Summary

A new political party came into existence with the new century. Its supporters came from the ranks of the 'new' trade unions, the socialist societies, the Fabian Society and the Independent Labour Party. The Labour party represented working class opinion in the House of Commons and within a few years of its foundation had been so successful that everyone realized that it was a force to be reckoned with.

Exercises

1. Trace the development of a) 'new model' unions after 1850 and b) 'new' unions after 1875.
2. What were the differences between 'new model' unions and 'new' unions?
3. What part did trade unions play in establishing the Labour party?
4. What role did James Keir Hardie play in the early history of the Labour party?
5. How did the Fabians contribute to the rise of the Labour party?
6. Explain how the Liberal government of 1906–14 helped the Labour party.

23
The Liberal Government, 1906 – 14

In 1906 Sir Henry Campbell-Bannerman formed a Liberal government. He appointed Lloyd George (1863 – 1945) to the Board of Trade and Herbert Asquith became Chancellor of the Exchequer. Sir Edward Grey (1862 – 1933) took charge of the Foreign Office and Richard Haldane (1856 – 1928) was in charge at the War Office. Bannerman retired in 1908, owing to ill health, and Asquith became Prime Minister. Lloyd George took over the Treasury and Winston Churchill (1874 – 1965) took over at the Board of Trade. From 1906 to 1914 the Liberals' achievements were considerable. They laid the foundation of the modern welfare state, gained a great victory over the House of Lords and reformed the armed forces. However, in some areas they were not so successful. They faced serious opposition from militant trade unionists, from suffragettes and from Ulster Unionists.

1 The Constitutional Crisis

When the Liberals were returned to office in 1906 with a huge majority it soon became apparent that they would face opposition from the House of Lords. Although the Conservatives had lost the election Balfour refused to accept defeat; he was determined to use Unionist peers to destroy the Liberals' legislative programme. There were 401 Liberals and 29 Labour MPs in the Commons. Of the 602 peers in the House of Lords only 83 were Liberals. As the House of Commons became more representative of the nation as a whole people began to resent the political power of the House of Lords. Feelings rose when the Lords rejected several Bills and a bitter constitutional crisis occurred in 1909.

The Early Struggle, 1906 – 08
In 1906 the Lords amended the Education Bill which was designed to remedy Nonconformist grievances against the 1902 Act. The government rejected the Lord's amendments and withdrew the Bill.

Next, the Lords drastically altered the Plural Voting Bill which would have restricted to one vote those electors who previously had several. The government was forced to withdraw the Bill. In 1907 four Land Bills designed to meet the Liberal and Labour demands for land reform were either rejected or radically altered by the Lords. In 1908 the Lords attacked the Licensing Bill which sought to reduce the number of public houses so that in any area they would not exceed a fixed ratio of the population. With each set-back the Liberals were failing to live up to expectations. They began to suffer defeats at by-elections in 1908. They sought ways to restore their popularity and Lloyd George's solution was the People's Budget.

The People's Budget, 1909–10

Lloyd George became Chancellor of the Exchequer in 1908. He needed to find new sources of revenue to meet the cost of defence and social welfare. He introduced the People's Budget on 29 April 1909, calling it a 'war' budget. 'It was for raising money for waging implacable warfare against poverty and squalidness', he declared. For the most part he relied on traditional sources of raising government revenue, but there were two controversial proposals — the introduction of super tax on incomes over £3000 and of land value duties to be paid whenever land changed hands. At the end of November the Lords rejected the budget. In so doing they challenged the Commons' power of the purse, something they had not done for over 250 years. Asquith immediately dissolved Parliament, arguing that the Lords had acted unconstitutionally.

The Parliament Act, 1911

A general election was held in January 1910 with the Liberals gaining 275 seats, the Conservatives 273, Labour 40 and the Irish Nationalists 82. The Liberals sought support from the Irish MPs and the Lords passed the controversial budget in 1910. In return for their support the Irish asked for Home Rule. In addition they demanded a Bill to curb the power of the House of Lords. They argued that if the Lords had been prepared to reject a budget they would be equally prepared to reject proposals for Home Rule as they had done so in the past.

King George V came to the throne in May 1910 and invited all the political leaders to a round-table conference at Buckingham Palace to sort out their differences. From May to November there were 21 meetings to find a solution to the constitutional crisis. The conference failed and Asquith drafted a Parliament Bill designed to curb the power of the House of Lords. It passed through the Commons and was rejected by the Lords.

The Lords' rejection of the Bill led to another general election in December 1910 and once more the issue before the electorate was who should govern the country — 'peers or people'? The result was

PUNCH, OR THE LONDON CHARIVARI.—August 2, 1911.

THE OLD TROJAN.

Lord Lansdowne. "DON'T LUG THAT INFERNAL MACHINE INTO THE CITADEL. THE THING'S FULL OF ENEMIES."

Lord Halsbury. "I KNOW. THAT'S WHERE MY HEROISM COMES IN."

The Trojan Horse was the liberals' answer to their constitutional struggle with the House of Lords

very similar to the January result. Liberals and Unionists each won 272 seats, Irish Nationalists 84 and Labour 42. Once more the Liberals introduced the Parliament Bill. It was passed by the Commons and, after a struggle, the Lords decided to pass the Bill rather than face the threat of the creation of 500 new Liberal peers which George V had promised to do if the measure was once more rejected. (See the cartoon — The Old Trojan.)

On 9 August 1911 the Lords approved the Parliament Bill by 131 votes to 114. The Parliament Act removed the Lords' ability to veto legislation, allowing it a suspensory veto of two years. It provided that the Lords should lose all power to reject or amend money Bills. The life of Parliament was reduced from seven to five years. As a result the wishes of the House of Commons could only be denied for a limited period by the Lords. The Liberals could now proceed with their programme of reforms.

2 Social Reform

In the nineteenth century the Liberal party believed in the minimum of state intervention as the best means of preserving individual liberty. However, by 1906 the Liberals seemed to hold the opposite view, believing that increased state intervention enlarged liberty. This change in attitude resulted from a change in the government's awareness of social problems. The government was made aware of these problems by the publication of investigations and statistics. Charles Booth's (1840 – 1916) work *Life and Labour of the People in London* and Seebohm Rowntree's study of York entitled *Poverty: A Study of Town Life* showed that one quarter of Britain's population was living in poverty. It was clear that private charities were insufficient and that the state should intervene. Moreover, the 'new' Liberals represented by Lloyd George and Winston Churchill saw the political necessity of winning working-class votes, especially after the birth of the Labour party. They believed in securing a minimum standard of living for all, or as Churchill declared, 'a line below which we shall not allow persons to live and labour'.

Children
The first Liberal reform affecting children was the Education (Provision of Meals) Act, 1906. The Act stated that Local Education Authorities could continue to use the existing voluntary services which provided meals, where these existed, or provide their own school meals at the cost of a halfpenny rate. By 1910, 9,000,000

meals were provided annually and the figure reached 14,000,000 in 1914. In 1907 the Education (Administrative Provisions) Act was passed, providing medical inspection in schools. In addition to marking the beginning of the construction of the welfare state, these Acts helped to dispel some of the alarm which had been created by the poor physical condition of recruits during the Boer War.

In 1907 the government introduced Borstals and the probation service. It set up Juvenile Courts to deal with young people accused of crime. In 1908 the Liberals passed the Children Act which came to be known as the 'Children's Charter'. This charter covered the legal rights of children, including such matters as the protection of infant life and the prevention of cruelty to children. The sale of alcohol, tobacco and fireworks to children was forbidden. Hours of work for children were severely restricted.

Old People

The Liberals passed the Old Age Pension Act in 1908 which gave people aged 70 or over a pension of five shillings per week, payable every Friday at the Post Office, provided they received less than £21 a year from other sources. In 1909 650,000 people applied for pensions and this figure rose to over 970,000 by 1914. Many people declared that the pension scheme was insufficient and Churchill admitted that the government had not been able to go far enough. He declared, 'We have not pretended to carry the toiler on to dry land. What we have done is to strap a lifebelt around him'.

Wage Earners

The Liberals introduced several reforms to help wage earners. As a result of the Workmen's Compensation Act, 1906, employers were compelled to pay compensation to any workman earning less than £250 a year who was injured at work.

One of the first problems Winston Churchill tackled on taking office at the Board of Trade was that of 'sweated labour'. In several occupations not covered by factory legislation people worked long hours in filthy conditions for very little pay. Many of the workers in the 'sweated' trades were women engaged in dressmaking, lace-making, chain-making and brush-making. The Trade Boards Act, 1909, set up trade boards consisting of equal numbers of employers, employees and officials for several of the 'sweated' trades. The boards fixed minimum rates of pay and any employer who paid less than the minimum was to be fined. Factory inspectors were responsible for administering the Trade Boards Act which covered 200,000 workers.

Another problem which Churchill had to tackle was that of unemployment. In 1908 unemployment rose to 7.2%. Churchill realized that something would have to be done to help the unemployed and to stop working men voting Labour. His views were influenced by W.H. Beveridge who published *Unemployment: A Problem of Industry* in 1909 in which he called for the introduction of unemployment insurance and labour exchanges. In September 1910 83 exchanges were opened.

The scheme for unemployment insurance was delayed for two years by the constitutional crisis arising from the People's Budget. During these two years Churchill and his advisers continued to plan the measure. Beveridge wanted the state to provide cover against unemployment and his views were echoed by the Webbs in the *Minority Report of the Royal Commission on the Poor Laws* in which they called for non-contributory aid for the unemployed. Churchill favoured a compulsory contributory insurance scheme as he did not believe that the Liberals were ready to finance welfare out of general taxation.

The unemployment insurance scheme formed Part II of Lloyd George's National Insurance Bill, 1911. It provided unemployment benefit for workers in building and the engineering and shipbuilding trades, which were known for high unemployment. The scheme was run by the trade unions and labour exchanges. A weekly levy of two pence halfpenny was raised from both the employer and the employee to which the state added a contribution. This provided the insured worker with seven shillings a week when unemployed. He received one week's benefit for every five contributions he had paid and there was a limit of 15 weeks' unemployment benefit in any single year.

The Sick
The most ambitious of all Liberal measures was the Insurance against Loss of Health and for the Prevention and Cure of Sickness Bill which was incorporated in the National Insurance Act, Part I. It was introduced by Lloyd George to combat the inadequate provision of medical care. Until he took action the rich were able to pay for expert medical advice and treatment whereas the poor were not. Lloyd George wanted the state to intervene to help the sick and he took the German scheme as his model.

The National Insurance Bill was introduced on 4 May 1911 and received the royal assent on 16 December 1911. It imposed a compulsory weekly insurance payment against loss of health at the rate of four pence per employee, three pence per employer and two pence from the state on all workers earning less than £160 per annum and on all manual labourers between the ages of 16 and 60. In return the insured worker received medical treatment from a general practitioner with free medicine, sickness benefit of 10 shillings a week for 13 weeks and five shillings a week for the next 13 weeks, with five shillings a week disability benefit and the right to treatment in a sanatorium. These benefits were administered by 'approved societies' which included friendly societies, trade unions and insurance companies.

The health insurance scheme was attacked by many people. It was unpopular with the workers who were suspicious of increasing state intervention and who resented the compulsory contributions. Friendly societies, insurance companies, trade unions and the British Medical Association all attacked the scheme and had to be won over by Lloyd George. By 1914 opposition to the health insurance scheme had died down and 13,000,000 people were insured. The state had provided for its citizens what they were unable or unwilling to provide for themselves.

Trade Unions

The Trade Disputes Act, 1906, reversed the Taff Vale decision and safeguarded union funds from damages arising from strikes. However, many trade unionists suffered a setback as a result of the Osborne judgement which prevented unions from using their funds to support candidates for Parliament. The Liberals helped to remove a trade union grievance and furthered the cause of democracy when in 1911 they passed a law which granted MPs a salary of £400 a year. In 1913 the Trade Union Act reversed the Osborne judgement (see p.226).

3 Social Unrest, 1910-14

In their period of office from 1906 to 1911 the Liberals achieved a large measure of success in social and constitutional reform. However, in the years immediately before the outbreak of the First World War they seemed to lose their momentum. They failed to introduce votes for women and this led the suffragettes to carry out militant tactics which were far more violent than any which had been used before. Their failure to come to terms with the demands of the workers led the workers to turn away from parliamentary methods to direct action in the form of strikes and demonstrations.

Votes for Women

In the second half of the nineteenth century women began to obtain a measure of social and political emancipation. They gained rights under the Married Women's Property Act, wider opportunities in education and the right to take part in local affairs. From 1834 onwards women could vote in municipal elections; from 1870 they could vote for and be elected to the new school boards; in 1880 they were given the vote for the new county councils and from 1894 they were allowed to sit on district and parish councils. A natural consequence of these developments would have been votes for women in parliamentary elections. Between 1867 and 1906 the House of Commons voted in principle in favour of female suffrage on four occasions. However, no government gave serious consideration to votes for women. Liberal leaders believed that if women were given the vote on the same qualifications as men — the household suffrage — they would be bound to vote Conservative because of their age and possessions. On the other hand, whilst Conservative leaders were in favour of votes for women, their backbenchers were hostile. It was therefore left to private members to introduce female suffrage. Without government approval their Bills had little chance of success.

In 1904 the Women's Social and Political Union was founded by Mrs Emmeline Pankhurst and her daughter, Christabel. Its aim was the 'immediate enfranchisement' of women. In 1906 the society began an all-out attack on the Liberal government, promising militancy until the women's demands were met. As time went by and votes for women seemed no nearer the suffragettes employed violent tactics such as interrupting meetings, smashing windows and chaining themselves to railings. They began prison hunger strikes in 1908 and the government retaliated with forcible feeding to keep the prisoners alive. Militancy gained more publicity for the cause of women's suffrage than years of peaceful agitation could have done.

The suffragettes suspended their militant activities during 1910 – 11 when an all-party Conciliation Committee was trying to work out an acceptable women's suffrage Bill. Its failure led to a revival of suffragette militancy, including arson and bombing. On Derby Day 1913 a suffragette, Emily Davison, threw herself under the King's horse and was killed. There were other suffragette 'martyrs' who went on hunger strike in prison. In response the government introduced what was known as the 'Cat and Mouse Act' in 1913 which enabled the Home Secretary to release any prisoner whose health deteriorated in prison and to rearrest her on recovery.

The tactics of the suffragettes aroused horror and pity in some and disgust in others. They did not gain women the vote.

Industrial Unrest

From 1910 to 1914 there was acute industrial strife in Britain. The fundamental reasons for labour unrest were economic. From 1909 to 1913 wages lagged behind the rise in the cost of living and this caused trade unionists to seek wage increases. At the same time there was a marked increase in the power of trade unions. The Trade Disputes Act, 1906, strengthened their position. Furthermore a substantial number of workers were becoming disillusioned with the traditional methods of gaining improvements and were turning to direct action of the type associated with syndicalism.

In 1907 a call by the Railway Servants' Union for a national strike in support of higher wages and union recognition so alarmed the government that they intervened and prevented the strike from taking place. A compromise acceptable to both sides was reached. In 1908 there was a general slump in trade and more time was lost through industrial stoppages than in any of the previous 10 years. In 1909 – 10 there were miners' strikes in Yorkshire, South Wales, Northumberland and Durham. The strike at Tonnypandy in South Wales resulted in rioting which was quelled by police and troop movements. In 1911 there were strikes among Southampton seamen and dockers and unrest spread to transport workers in other ports. Troops were used in many places and rioters were killed in Liverpool and Llenelly. In the same year there was another threat of a national rail strike but Lloyd George found a peace formula. Militancy continued in 1912. In February the Miners' Federation went on strike. Unrest continued in 1913 and 1914 with strikes in the Midlands and a long struggle between the tramway employers and the Irish Transport Workers' Union in Dublin. Bitter industrial strife continued until the outbreak of war.

4 Ireland

Home Rule for Ireland had been Liberal policy in the general election of 1910. Once the Parliament Act was passed in 1911 it seemed that Home Rule could be achieved by constitutional means. However, Liberal and nationalist hopes were dashed by a rebellion in Ulster. The government failed to find a solution to the Ulster problem. The Liberals appeared to be totally helpless as Ireland drifted towards civil war — an event which was only forestalled by the outbreak of the First World War.

Ulster

The people of Ulster formed a distinct and separate group from the population of the rest of Ireland. Their Protestant religion and industrial wealth distinguished them from the less prosperous southern Irish Catholics who depended on agriculture for their livelihood. In the late nineteenth century when Gladstone's two Home Rule Bills took no account of Ulster's special position, Ulstermen feared that 'Home Rule would mean Rome Rule' and they were determined to oppose this. The Ulster Defence Union resisted the idea of Home Rule and from 1905 onwards the Ulster Unionist Council took up the fight against Home Rule.

The revival of Home Rule in 1910 made the Ulster unionists even more determined. They were led by Sir Edward Carson, a Dublin Protestant lawyer and an MP. He opposed the Home Rule Bill in Parliament whilst at the same time he prepared Ulster for resistance if Home Rule became law. He prepared a provisional government for Ulster, backed by armed volunteers. The Conservative and Unionist party supported Carson's moves. In July 1912 Bonar Law asserted that the Ulstermen 'would be justified in resisting (Home Rule) by all means in their power, including force'. The Conservative and Unionist leaders can be criticized for inciting civil strife in Ireland. At the same time Asquith can be blamed for his government's lack of decision.

Asquith's Failures, 1912 – 14

The Liberals introduced the third Home Rule Bill in 1912. Asquith knew that he could neither abandon Home Rule nor co-erce Ulster into accepting it. He tried to amend the Home Rule proposals so that Ulster was not included but Redmond, the leader of the Irish nationalists, would not agree to this. Meanwhile, the situation in Ireland continued to deteriorate. The delay in achieving Home Rule had weakened Redmond's leadership and the extremist policies of Sinn Fein were gaining support. Directed by the Irish Republican Brotherhood, the Irish Volunteers appeared as a rival military force to that in Ulster. Although Redmond was embarrassed by the existence of the Irish Volunteers their existence made it impossible for him to make concessions to Asquith. The result was that two private armies faced each other in Ireland. By the end of 1913 Asquith introduced an Amending Bill which proposed that any county in Ulster could vote to be excluded from the Home Rule Act for six years after which it would be brought in. Redmond reluctantly accepted this compromise but Carson rejected the Bill. The government seemed to have lost control of the situation.

The Curragh Incident, 1914
When Carson rejected the Amending Bill it became clear that since a constitutional settlement to the problem of Ulster seemed impossible the Liberals would have to impose a military solution. At this stage the government discovered that the British army officers were strongly pro-Ulster in their sympathies. When the government tried to use the army to reinforce its position in Northern Ireland a brigade at the Curragh refused to move and the government backed down. This episode, known as the Curragh incident, illustrates the Liberals' total failure during this crisis.

On the eve of the First World War a final attempt was made to find a solution by postponing the inclusion of Ulster under the proposed Irish government. However, an all-party conference on the subject broke down on 24 July 1914. On 18 September the Home Rule Bill finally became law. It was accompanied by a Bill to suspend its operation until the end of the European war. Civil war in Ireland was averted but the problem of Ulster had not been solved.

5 Reform of the Armed Forces

When the Liberals came into office in 1906 both the army and the navy were in need of reform. In 1905 Lord Roberts told the House of Lords, 'our armed forces, as a body, are as absolutely unfitted and unprepared for war as they were in 1899 – 1900'. As international tension mounted Britain had to be prepared to help her new ally, France, in the event of a German attack on her.

Navy Reform
Britain depended on her navy for defence. But after the passage of several German Navy Bills Britain's supremacy at sea was severely challenged and reforms were necessary. Sir John Fisher (1841 – 1920), First Sea Lord from 1904 to 1910, carried out reforms upon the principles of 'economy and efficiency'. He had begun his work before 1904 by reforming the recruitment and training of officers and cadets. He also improved sailors' pay and living conditions, whilst at the same time making discipline less brutal. All these measures raised morale in the navy. After 1904 Fisher transformed the reserve fleet, making sure that it was ready for war and achieving a more economical use of man power. Next he redistributed the fleet which he concentrated in the North Sea and the Channel rather than the Mediterranean (see p.244). He kept up to date with technical improvements and built the first *Dreadnought* by December 1906. This gave Britain a lead in the design of ships and improved her posi-

tion as a naval power. There were political objections to increased naval expenditure, but after 1909 demands for economies were ignored by a government determined to maintain its lead over Germany.

Army Reform

When Richard Haldane took over the War Office in 1906 he was determined to introduce radical reforms in the army. Like Fisher, his reforms were achieved in a most economical manner. He transformed the home field army and reserves, creating in 1907 a British Expeditionary Force which could be mobilized quickly in the event of war. Changes were made in the Reserve; the Territorial army was created to carry out operations anywhere in Britain, but not abroad. Further changes included the creation of Officer Training Corps in universities and schools and the retraining of army personnel in tactics, staff work and administration.

Summary

Between 1906 and 1914 the Liberals carried out great political, social and defence reforms. They transformed the constitution, built the foundations of the welfare state and ensured that Britain was prepared for conflict on a world scale. However, their treatment of the Irish question and of votes for women was at fault. In addition the Liberals were losing their links with the working classes who were beginning to give their support to the Labour party.

Exercises

1. Give an account of the worsening relationship between the House of Lords and the Liberals from 1906 to 1908.
2. Why were there two general elections in 1910?
3. How did the Parliament Act, 1911, make the government more democratic?
4. Indicate how Liberal reforms helped a) children, b) trade unions, c) working people.
5. What attempts did Asquith make to solve the Irish problem? Why did he fail?
6. Show how the Liberals prepared the armed forces for the First World War.

24
Britain and the Origins of the First World War

On 5 August 1914 British people awoke to find themselves at war. For a considerable length of time events in Europe had been out of control and people waited for a war which no responsible statesmen wanted. In his London office Sir Edward Grey, the Foreign Secretary, was filled with despair and could be heard repeating over and over to himself, 'I hate war'. At the same time Bethman Hollweg, the German Chancellor, confided to a friend that he did not know how Europe had been plunged into war. From the time war broke out a debate started about its origins. It is difficult to separate the tangle of events leading to war, they do not fit neatly into categories. However, in any examination of the origins of the 'Great War' the system of European alliances, the rising tide of nationalism, colonial rivalry and relations between Britain and Germany must be examined.

The System of European Alliances

In 1871, with the creation of the German Empire, a new power emerged in Europe. Prussia had united the German states and Bismarck, formerly the Prussian Minister-President, became Chancellor of Germany. He tried to protect the infant empire with a system of defensive alliances. The Dual Alliance was signed between Germany and Austria in 1879. Another alliance was concluded between these two countries and Russia in 1881 and yet another between the Dual Alliance partners and Italy in 1882, leading to the formation of the Triple Alliance. As the century drew to a close Bismarck's successors dropped the Russian alliance. The Italian alliance proved to be of little value so that Germany realized that in any future struggle she would have to rely on the Austrian empire for help.

There was a rival alliance in Europe, centred upon France who had suffered a humiliating defeat in the Franco-Prussian War, 1870, and had lost the two provinces of Alsace and Lorraine. Some Frenchmen hoped for a war of revenge against Germany but this was not the

French government's policy. France and Russia signed an alliance in 1894 which, like the German alliances, was a defensive alliance — a safeguard against future attack.

British Isolation In Europe

For most of the nineteenth century Britain's diplomatic activity was connected with the defence of the British empire. Britain had not wished to become entangled in a system of European alliances. However, by 1901 Britain found herself totally isolated. Britain and France were at loggerheads in Africa. Russia had always been a threat to Britain's position in India, and to this was added in the late nineteenth century Russian expansion in Manchuria and northern China which threatened Britain's China trade. There was colonial rivalry between Britain and Germany in Africa and the Far East. In addition, Salisbury's refusal to guarantee the defence of Constantinople led Austria to sever the links made at the time of the Mediterranean Agreements of the 1880s. This meant that Britain no longer needed Italian co-operation in her policy towards Russia over the Straits, in addition to which Britain had consistently refused to guarantee Italy against a possible French attack. Several politicians began to believe that Britain had manoeuvred herself into a very dangerous situation.

The Anglo-Japanese Alliance, 1902

By 1901 Britain was isolated. This in itself was not necessarily significant. What was significant was that Britain had lost confidence in her ability to defend herself unaided. The British government sought an alliance with Germany to check Russian advances in Asia but the Germans were not enthusiastic. As a substitute, on 30 January 1902 Britain signed a defensive alliance with Japan. Britain and Japan claimed to be motivated 'solely by a desire to maintain the status quo and general peace in the Far East' and to maintain 'the independence and territorial integrity of China'. Britain acknowledged Japanese aims to control Korea and Japan recognized British interests in China. Both countries agreed to remain neutral in the event of war between one of the signatories and another power and to come to the aid of each other in the event of a war between one of them and two other powers. The alliance had a life-span of five years. In 1904 Japan was highly successful in a war against Russia. The British government anxiously watched this episode, wondering whether or not it would become involved. In fact Britain was not called upon to take part in the war but this did not leave the British government feeling any easier. Some other means of defending her empire seemed necessary.

Anglo-German Rivalry

Before Britain signed the Anglo-Japanese alliance she had sought an agreement with Germany. From 1898 to 1901 Britain sought to draw closer to Germany. By the Anglo-German Agreement, 1898, the two countries reached an agreement about the Portuguese colonies in Africa and by the Anglo-German China Agreement, 1900, they reached some agreement about China. No other agreements were reached. Germany was not willing to support Britain against Russia in the Far East unless Britain joined the Triple Alliance and assumed all the responsibilities of being an ally. Britain was not willing to join the Triple Alliance and risk the possibility of being involved in a war against France for the sake of German support in the Far East.

Tension between Britain and Germany had existed before Britain sought an alliance with Germany and the failure to reach an agreement heightened the tension. Since 1870 the German economy had been expanding at a rapid rate. There was economic rivalry between the two countries as Germany began to capture former British markets. Britain and Germany were also colonial rivals and occurrences connected with South Africa turned many British people against the Germans. The Kaiser had offered friendship to the Boers in the Kruger telegram, 1896, following the failure of the Jameson Raid and during the Boer War German newspapers published many anti-British articles. In the late nineteenth century Germany had the strongest army in Europe, backed by Europe's greatest iron, steel and chemical industries. She then decided to build a navy and rivalry between Britain and Germany was most pronounced in the field of naval expansion.

Anglo-German naval rivalry began in 1895 when the Kiel Canal was opened, linking the Baltic and its German ports with the North Sea. Between 1898 and 1908 the German Parliament voted for a number of Navy Bills to create a powerful German navy. Then in 1906 it was announced that the Kiel Canal was to be widened to accommodate large battleships. Britain claimed that Germany had no need of a navy for purposes of defence. Churchill called the German navy 'a luxury' whilst the British navy was 'a necessity'. The British public came to the conclusion that the only reason Germany was developing a navy was to attack Britain or her empire. They were alarmed by speeches and articles in the German press proclaiming German racial superiority and the glory of war. This led Britain to engage in an arms race with the Germans. Britain maintained a lead over Germany by building the *Dreadnought* (see p.238).

The Entente Cordiale, 1904

Soon after it signed the alliance with Japan the British government considered an alternative method of resolving Britain's differences with Russia. An arrangement with Russia was sought which would clarify British and Russian interests in Asia. Instead of negotiating with the Russians directly it was decided to make an indirect approach, to establish friendly relations with France and then use that country as a bridge to form an agreement with Russia. This was the origin of the Anglo-French Entente, 1904, by which the two countries recognized each other's colonial interests in Africa. France agreed to recognize the British occupation of Egypt whilst Britain supported French measures to preserve order in Morocco. Whilst this entente was not as binding as an alliance, the two countries agreed to support the interests they had recognized if this became necessary.

The Triple Entente, 1907

British hopes were fulfilled in 1907 when a similar agreement was reached with Russia. Britain and Russia agreed to respect each other's spheres of influence in Central Asia. The British government congratulated itself on having solved its imperial defence worries. At the same time, however, Britain had exposed herself to involvement in future European strife.

Crises in Africa

Britain was called upon to support French interests shortly after she had signed the Entente Cordiale. In 1905 the German government challenged the increasing French control of Morocco. The Kaiser sailed to Tangier in a warship and in a speech he demanded that Moroccan independence be respected. The result was an international conference held in Algeciras in January 1906 to consider the Moroccan question. The conference supported the French government. A protocol of the conference was signed on 7 April 1906 in which the Sultan retained his rule in Morocco, but France controlled the Moroccan Bank and France and Spain jointly controlled the Moroccan police. The Kaiser was defeated but the matter was not resolved for he was determined to fight on this issue in the future.

Germany had suffered a setback at the Algeciras conference but this did not stop her from intervening in Morocco again in 1911. There had been a rebellion against the sultan of Morocco and the French had sent troops to protect the lives and property of Europeans in the area. The Germans sent a gunboat, the *Panther*, to Agadir to protect German interests even though there were no Germans in the area. In a speech at the Mansion House, London, Lloyd George

244 British History 1760 – 1914

denounced Germany's action and hinted that Britain would be prepared to go to war on the issue. The Agadir crisis was resolved by a conference in Paris which confirmed France as the paramount power in Morocco, Algeria and Tunisia, and confirmed Britain's special position in Egypt. Germany was given land in the French Congo in return for the 'rights' which the Kaiser claimed to be giving up in Morocco.

Anglo-French Military Conversations

From 1906 onwards there were military conversations between Britain and France. Plans were made for the British army to be sent to fight alongside the French and for the French navy to take over the defence of the Mediterranean, releasing the British navy for action in the North Sea in the event of war in Europe. The entente had no sooner been made than it began to change its purpose. There is no doubt that Germany's attitude towards Morocco and the growing trouble in the Balkans contributed to this change.

Crises in the Balkans

Throughout the nineteenth century there had been many occasions when the Turkish empire seemed on the verge of collapse. Small independent states had been created in the Balkans which were determined to maintain their independence. In the twentieth century international tension grew when the existence of these small states was threatened. In 1908 Austria seized control of Bosnia and Herzegovina. The Serbs asked Russia, who had traditionally championed the rights of the subject nations in the Balkans, for help to ward off Austrian advances. But Russia was not in a strong position. She was recovering from defeat in the Japanese war and both France and Britain advised her to tread carefully in the Balkans and not to commit herself to Serbia. As a result Austria retained Bosnia and Herzegovina which gave her confidence to extend her influence further in the Balkans. Serbia felt betrayed and angry. She was determined to seek revenge against Austria in the future. At the same time Russia was determined that she would not dismiss any future calls for help in the Balkans. Austria and Russia seemed bent on a collision course in the Balkans.

As Turkish misrule continued so did trouble in the Balkans. Serbia, Greece, Bulgaria, and Montenegro formed a Balkan League which attacked and defeated Turkey in 1912. In 1913 a conference met in London to try to resolve the situation in the Balkans. The outcome of the conference was the creation of another small independent state, Albania.

Within one month the Bulgarians were at war with all their former allies, plus Rumania, because they did not agree with the decisions made at the end of the first Balkan War. The Bulgarians claimed part of Macedonia which the Serbs refused to give up. With so much opposition against her, Bulgaria was quickly defeated in the second Balkan War. The Treaty of Bucharest ended the war. By the terms of the treaty Bulgaria lost Thrace to Turkey and part of Dubruja to Rumania. Serbia gained northern Macedonia and Greece gained southern Macedonia. Montenegro was enlarged.

The Sarajevo Assassination, 1914

Serbia had been successful in the Balkan Wars and she had helped to break up the decaying Turkish empire. Her ambition was to create a large Slav kingdom by freeing the 17,000,000 Serbs within the Austro-Hungarian empire and uniting with them. In this the Serbs had the backing of Russia. Naturally, Austria was opposed to these plans. The struggle between Serbia and Austria came to a head on 28 June 1914 when a Serb patriot assassinated the heir to the Austrian throne in the town of Sarajevo. The Austrian government was determined to be revenged against Serbia and to show its strength. It declared that the Serbian government was responsible for the assassination in so far as the government had permitted anti-Austrian propaganda and terrorist activities to be carried out from Serbia. On 23 July the Austrian government presented Serbia with an ultimatum calling on her to suppress all anti-Austrian activity and dismiss all Serbian officials to whom Austria objected. In addition, Austrian officials were to be permitted to enter Serbia to investigate Serbian guilt in the murder and to supervise the suppression of anti-Austrian societies. Serbia agreed to the first two demands. Acceptance of the third would have led to a virtual loss of her independence and Serbia offered to submit this point to arbitration at the Hague tribunal. Austria brushed aside all attempts to find a peaceful solution. Sir Edward Grey's proposal to hold a conference in London to discuss the Serbian situation was dismissed. On 28 July 1914 Austria declared war on Serbia.

The Russians tried to come to an agreement with the Austrians on behalf of the Serbs. When the discussions failed Russia began to mobilize her army on 30 July. Germany promptly sent a demand to Russia, urging the Russian government to countermand its mobilization order. Russia refused and on 1 August Germany declared war on Russia.

The Invasion of Belgium

When Germany declared war on Russia she calculated that France would come to Russia's aid. However, although France had issued mobilization orders on the same day as the Germans she did not make any move to support Russia. Nevertheless, on 3 August Germany declared war on France and on the following day she began moving her troops through Belgium. Britain became involved at this stage. She had been responsible for the treaty of 1839 by which the great powers of Europe had guaranteed Belgian neutrality (see p. 147). In accordance with that undertaking Britain demanded that German troops be withdrawn from Belgium. When the Germans did not reply to Britain's ultimatum she declared war on Germany.

Summary
Towards the end of the nineteenth century tensions mounted in Europe. A system of two hostile alliances was created whereby Austria, Germany and Italy were ranged against Britain, France and Russia. In Africa and the Balkans members of the Triple Alliance were opposed to members of the Triple Entente. Tension was reflected in an arms race between Germany and Britain to add to the existing economic and colonial rivalry between the two countries. Responsibility for the outbreak of the war has been endlessly debated. The German historian Hermann Lutz apportions the blame evenly. He declared,
    'All the powers in 1914 put their own interests, true or supposed, and their own ambitions before the peace of the world. . . .
    No belligerent except Belgium was blameless and none was the sole culprit.'

Exercises
1. Describe the circumstances in which Britain in the early years of the twentieth century signed treaties of friendship with a) Japan, b) France, and c) Russia.
2. Why was Britain unable to sign a similar treaty with Germany?
3. Explain how crises in a) Africa and b) the Balkans threatened the peace of Europe in the early years of the twentieth century.
4. What was the immediate reason for Britain's entry into the First World War?

25
The British Empire

1 India

The East India Company

The British East India Company had a monopoly of trade between Britain and India. The company controlled a number of trading posts in India and imported spices, cotton and silk into Britain with huge profits for the company's shareholders. By 1763 the company had rid India of its European rivals and it controlled the provinces of the Carnatic, whose capital was Madras, and Bengal, whose capital was Calcutta. In 1764, following the defeat of a combined revolt of the princes of Bengal and Oudh, the company took control of the province of Oudh. Ten years after the Treaty of Paris, 1763, the East India Company was the most powerful force in India.

The East India Company was not purely a trading company. In the East it was assuming powers of government and in Britain it was an important finance house. The company had its own private army. Its directors were amongst the wealthiest men of the day and they were able to dispense patronage. They could find a place in the company for the son of a relative or friend which might be poorly paid but which offered him the chance of becoming rich by engaging in private trade in India. By 1767 the British government had begun to demand a share of the power and the wealth of this company.

Lord North's Regulating Act, 1773

As the East India Company expanded it was faced with increased administrative costs and falling profits. In 1772 the company was on the verge of bankruptcy and had to ask the British government for help. Lord North appointed two committees to study India in 1772 and 1773, but they were bedevilled by personal rivalries. The government's solution to the company's problems was Lord North's Regulating Act, 1773. The Act was a compromise for it established a system to regulate the work of the East India Company, but the government did not take power for itself in India. The Act stated

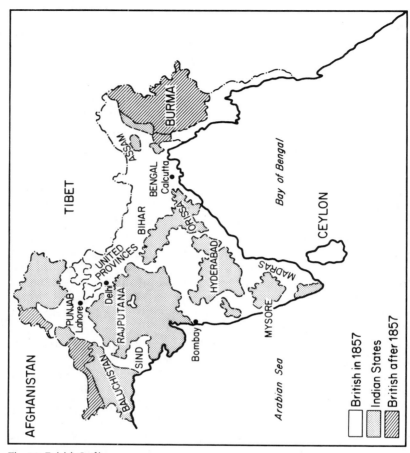

Fig.19 British India

that the company had to appoint a Governor General to oversee all the districts controlled by the company, and the government appointed a council of four men who were to advise and control the Governor General. The Act also stated that British judges were to be sent to India to administer the legal system.

Warren Hastings

Warren Hastings, an employee of the East India Company, was the first Governor General and he held office from 1773 to 1784. He established a civil service and dismissed the native tax collectors, replacing them with British collectors who were forbidden to take bribes. During Hastings' time in India Britain's influence and territory was consolidated. He sent a British army to Bombay to fight against the Mahratta tribes of central India. Bombay was saved by his action and the company's influence was extended in the western provinces. In 1780 the King of Mysore, Hyder Ali, attacked the Carnatic. Hastings sent a British army, led by Sir Eyre Coote (1762–1823), to defend the province. In 1781 Hyder Ali was defeated at Porto Novo and the Carnatic was secured.

Although Hastings made considerable progress in India he was handicapped by the council of four men sent out under the terms of the Regulating Act to supervise him. They believed that the company was dishonest and tyrannical. They often opposed his plans and it was they who organized his impeachment (see p.53). When he helped the ruler of Oudh to regain some of his treasure which had been seized by his female relations Hastings was accused of accepting rewards for doing this. He was also accused of bribe-taking and being needlessly cruel in his suppression of Indian opposition.

The India Act, 1784

William Pitt passed the India Act in 1784. It stated that trading should be separated from the governing of India. The British government was to set up a Board of Control which would appoint a Governor General and other officials to rule India. The Act also gave the Governor General the power to over-rule his council.

The Marquess of Wellesley (1760–1842)

The Marquis of Wellesley, brother of the future Duke of Wellington, was Governor General of India from 1797 to 1805. He removed sources of danger and extended British power so that British supremacy in India was widely recognized. He concluded alliances with some of the weaker native rulers, making the company responsible for the defence of their states and in return gaining control of their trade. In 1799 at the battle of Seringapatam he defeated Tipu of Mysore, who had been intriguing with the French. After the battle he annexed the land on the east and west coasts and appointed a puppet ruler over the rest of Mysore. He forced the ruler of Hyderabad to dismiss his army and join an alliance with Britain.

He also conquered large areas around Bombay. Then between 1801 and 1805 he broke the power of the Maratha chieftains who had carried out many raids in central India.

British Expansion

It was left to the Marquess of Hastings (1754–1826) to complete the destruction of the Marathas in 1816–19. He annexed Poon and captured Nepal. By the mid 1820s the whole of central and southern India was under British control. Only the Punjab and Sind remained outside Britain's control. In 1823 Britain began an attack on Burma and in 1839 the Governor General, Lord Auckland (1784–1849) tried to impose a puppet ruler on Afghanistan. He was overthrown within two years and the country remained unsubdued and a prey to Russian influence. In 1843 Britain conquered Sind and in 1849 she annexed the Punjab. By 1850 Britain ruled about 200,000,000 Indians (see Fig. 19, British India).

Lord Bentinck (1774–1839)

The Governor General had the task of governing India's huge population with less than 800 officers. They had to deal with the practices of human sacrifice, slavery, the drowning of the aged, suttee (the practice by which widows of high caste Hindus were burnt alive on their husband's funeral pyre), and thuggee (a practice by which members of a religious sect robbed and murdered travellers as sacrifices to the goddess Kali). Lord Bentinck, Governor General from 1828 to 1835, carried out a campaign against suttee and thuggee. He also introduced the English education system to India, founded the Calcutta Medical College and began to establish a unified system of law. During his term of office the India Act, 1833, forbade the East India Company to engage in trade and gave it a purely administrative and political role.

Lord Dalhousie (1812–60)

During the time of Lord Dalhousie, who was Governor General from 1848 to 1856, westernization began in earnest. Roads and canals were built and the Indian railway was planned with the first line from Bombay to Thana opened in 1853. The electric telegraph and a postal system were introduced. There was a new education scheme and engineering colleges were founded. Dalhousie also embarked on a campaign known as the 'doctrine of lapse' which annoyed several of the native rulers. This doctrine stated that on the death of a native ruler who had no heir, and would no longer be allowed to adopt one, his family's rule would 'lapse' and the company would take over his territory. As a result of this policy Dalhousie gained seven states and deposed the ruler of Oudh, seizing that territory for Britain.

The Indian Mutiny, 1857

Whilst Dalhousie's policies were not a direct cause of the Indian Mutiny, 1857, they did lead to a state of unrest in India. Unrest grew in 1856 and 1857 when a number of agitators told superstitious Indians that the Dowlah, who had been responsible for killing 123 Europeans in the 'Black Hole' of Calcutta a century ago, would return to drive the British out of India. Unrest was growing amongst the native troops, or sepoys, in the Indian army who resented the fact that they had been sent abroad to fight since this infringed their caste system. Travel to Burma had offended the caste system, as did the indiscriminate mixing of the castes in railway carriages. Many Indians believed the rumours which were being spread by agitators that the British planned to suppress the Hindu and Moslem religions and impose Christianity on India. A final cause of discontent was aroused in the sepoys when the new Enfield rifle was introduced. The user of the rifle had to bite off the ends of the cartridges before inserting them into the rifle. These cartridges were greased with animal fat. Some Hindus believed that the fat came from the cow, — their sacred animal. At the same time some Moslems believed the rumours that the fat came from the pig which they regarded as an unclean animal. They rioted and were supported by large numbers of the native population.

During the mutiny there were uprisings in Calcutta and Meerut. Sepoys marched to Delhi and Nana Sahib, a Mahratta chief, massacred the English population at Cawnpore and captured Lucknow. General Havelock (1795 – 1857) recaptured Lucknow but it was then besieged and had to be rescued by a force led by Sir Colin Campbell (1792 – 1863). The immediate suppression of the Mutiny was barbaric. In the course of the mutiny the Governor General, Stratford Canning (1812 – 62), instructed the civil servants that once it had been suppressed there should be no reprisals against the native population. When the mutiny was over Europeans cut themselves off as much as possible from the native population which led to still more difficulties in the future.

The India Act, 1858

This Act abolished the East India Company. Henceforth India was to be ruled directly by the British government. A council of India with 15 members was established and the Crown appointed the Governor General.

The Indian Economy and the National Congress

When the mutiny had been suppressed the British government decided to slacken the pace of reform in India. However, there was heavy British investment in the Indian economy. New railways and factories were built. In 1881 the India Factory Act was passed to abolish the same types of abuses which had existed in English factories at the time of the industrial revolution. In 1885 the Indian National Congress was founded. The Congress agitated against the British domination of the Indian economy and civil service. At its annual meetings Indian grievances were discussed. At first its support came from middle-class Indians, but in the early years of the twentieth century it gained wider support.

Gladstone and India, 1880 – 94

During Gladstone's second ministry steps were taken which it was hoped would lead ultimately to Indian self-government. Representative methods of government, modelled on British lines, were introduced by the Viceroy, Lord Ripon (1827 – 1909). Local committees, elected by the taxpayers, were given powers over education, health and public works. The India Councils Act, 1892, extended the system of elections to the councils of the provinces and to some of the councils which dealt with legislation for the whole of India.

The Morley – Minto Reforms, 1909

The Liberal government of 1906 to 1914 was responsible for guiding India further along the path to self-government. Lord Morley (1838 – 1923), the Secretary of State for India, and Lord Minto (1845 – 1914), the Viceroy, introduced provincial representative councils. The councils of Bengal, Bombay and Madras were to have elected Indian majorities and the Legislative Council for all India was to have a larger Indian representation. There were to be Indian members of the Viceroy's Executive Council and the Secretary of State's council in England. These councils were advisory bodies with no legislative powers and this led some members of the Indian National Congress to demand strong action against British rule.

2 Australia and New Zealand

Transportation to Australia

Between 1768 and 1779 Captain Cook (1728 – 79) explored the

Australian coast and took possession of New South Wales. When Britain lost the American colonies she turned to Australia as an outlet for her convicts. In 1788 Captain Phillip (1738–1814) established a penal colony in Sydney and further penal colonies were established in Tasmania, Hobart, Brisbane and Melbourne. In 1793 the first free settlers arrived in New South Wales and worked their land with convict labour. The number of free settlers increased in the 1830s and 40s when the British government gave grants to emigrants and the voyage to Australia dropped to only 140 days — it had originally taken eight months. The free settlers called on the government to stop transportation. No more convicts were sent to New South Wales after 1840 and in 1866 the practice ceased completely when the convict settlement in western Australia was closed. The ending of transportation encouraged more British people to emigrate and between 1851 and 1861 Australia's population increased from 405,000 to 1,145,000.

The Australian Economy

Australian settlers began to move away from the coast and open up the interior. Rich land was discovered in the valleys of the Darling and the Murray and merino sheep farming began on a large scale. Western Australia was founded in 1829. Gibbon Wakefield (1796–1862) led the movement for the establishment of a new colony in South Australia which was established in 1836. In 1850 Victoria and Queensland became separate colonies. In 1851 gold was discovered near the Australian settlement of Bathurst. This led to a gold rush and in 1852 84,000 immigrants flooded into Melbourne. The Australian economy depended initially on sheep and gold. They brought wealth to the country and led to the establishment of banks and insurance companies. As Australia prospered she began to import manufactured goods from Britain and exports to Australia became a very important part of Britain's trade.

The Government of Australia

From the moment they began to prosper the Australian states sought self-government. New South Wales became a crown colony in 1826 under the control of a Governor General, who nominated the council, and the British government. A further step was made towards self-government in New South Wales when in 1842 two-thirds of the council was elected. In 1850 Victoria and Queensland separated from New South Wales and elections to the council were introduced. In 1855 government responsible to an elected assembly was established in New South Wales, Victoria, South Australia and

Tasmania. There was a similar development in Queensland in 1859 and in Western Australia in 1890. Moves towards the union of Australian states into a federation culminated in 1901 when the Federal Constitution, set out in the Commonwealth of Australia Act, was adopted. To overcome the rivalry between the states a new capital, Canberra, was built to house the federal Parliament.

Early Settlers in New Zealand
Captain Cook annexed New Zealand for Britain in 1769. At first the British government ignored the country but the islands attracted settlers, traders and escaped criminals. In 1838 Gibbon Wakefield founded the New Zealand Company to colonize the islands. He believed that colonies were beneficial to Britain, not only because they could absorb surplus population, but also because they would lead to a valuable expansion of trade for Britain. The New Zealand Company planned to sell land and use the money to bring out selected emigrants from Britain in an orderly fashion. At first the government did not particularly approve of this scheme, but when the Whigs heard that a French company was planning to colonize the islands it changed course and negotiations began with the Maoris of New Zealand.

The Treaty of Waitangi, 1840
In 1840 the Governor of New South Wales, Captain Hobson, signed the Treaty of Waitangi with the native Maori chiefs. By the treaty Britain gained sovereignty in New Zealand but the Maoris were guaranteed undisturbed possession of their lands and estates. It was agreed that Britain should have the right to purchase any native lands which were to be sold. This agreement never worked properly and the New Zealand Company constantly ignored the Maori's rights. In 1848 the Maoris on the north island rebelled.

The New Zealand Economy and Government
As in Australia, gold and sheep were important items in New Zealand's economy. By 1859 her wool exports to Britain were valued at £317,000. By 1870 her total exports amounted to £4,700,000. Sir Charles Grey was Governor of New Zealand from 1845 to 1853 and he purchased the South Island for the British Crown and dissolved the New Zealand Company. In 1852 the New Zealand federation was founded, joining the six main areas of settlement and in 1856 self-government was introduced, with the Maoris excluded from the franchise. In 1878 the federation and the provincial assemblies were

abandoned and New Zealand was ruled by a single Parliament at Wellington, (see Fig. 20, Australia and New Zealand).

The Maori Wars

In the 1850s the influx of migrants to New Zealand reached new heights. The settlers took over land at a rate which alarmed the Maoris and between 1860 and 1870 there were continuous battles over land sales between the settlers and the Maoris on the North Island. The Maoris could not hope to be successful against the superior British forces and their numbers were rapidly reduced by western diseases brought to the islands by the settlers to which the Maoris were not immune. When Grey became Governor for a second time he reached a settlement which secured half of the North Island for the Maoris.

3 South Africa

In 1815 at the Congress of Vienna Britain gained the Cape of Good Hope from the Dutch. British settlers went out to the Cape where they found the Boers, Dutch settlers, who had been there since the seventeenth century and who used slaves to work their farms. They also found African tribesmen, called Kaffirs, who had been gradually moving south from central Africa. It was not long before the Boers were dissatisfied with British rule. They resented the use of English instead of Dutch as the official language, and they also resented the fact that when Boers clashed with the Kaffirs British missionaries often urged the government to support the Kaffirs. The abolition of slavery in the British empire in 1833 caused further resentment.

All these factors led to the Great Trek in 1836 when 5000 Boers left Cape Province and sought a new life north east of the Orange river. Some of the Boers settled in Natal but moved on when Britain annexed this area in 1843. They set up new states and two of them, the Transvaal and the Orange Free State were recognized by the British as independent Boer republics. (What happened to these two republics subsequently is described on p.209.)

4 Canada

The Quebec Act, 1774

Britain had acquired Canada from France in 1763 at the end of the Seven Years' War. In 1774 the Quebec Act was passed in an attempt

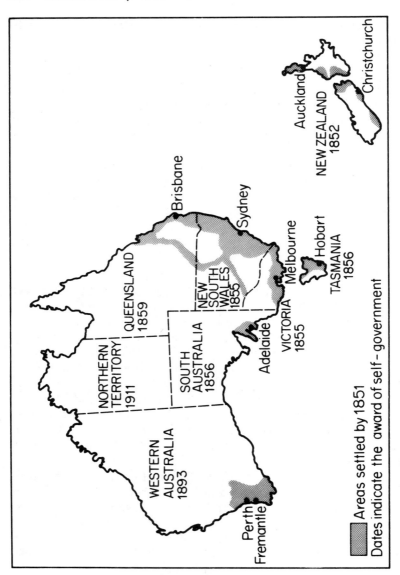

Fig.20 Australia and New Zealand

to gain the loyalty of French Canadians. It established a nominated council of Canadians to advise the British Governor of Canada. It recognized French law but introduced English criminal law, and it protected the lands and titles of the Roman Catholic church in Canada.

The Canada Constitutional Act, 1791

When the American War of Independence ended, new problems were created in Canada with the influx of loyalists from the 13 colonies. The loyalists, together with immigrants from Britain, tended to settle in Upper Canada. The English clashed with the French Canadians, and in 1791 Pitt passed the Canada Constitutional Act which created two provinces — Upper Canada (Ontario), which was English, and Lower Canada (Quebec), which was French. One Governor was appointed for the two provinces and each had a separate Lieutenant Governor with an executive council. Each province had a nominated legislative council and an elected assembly, which could present laws to the Lieutenant Governor but could only pass them if the British government agreed. In Upper Canada English civil law as well as criminal law was established, whilst in Lower Canada French civil law was retained, though alongside English criminal law.

The 1837 Rebellion and Lord Durham's Report

In 1837 rebellions took place in both Upper and Lower Canada for both provinces were dissatisfied with the system of government established in 1791. The English settlers resented the Governor's power to over-rule the wishes of the local assembly. In Lower Canada the French Catholics resented the fact that an English speaking Protestant Governor had the right to over-rule their decisions. Settlers in both provinces had economic grievances and they felt that land was being unfairly distributed.

The rebellions were suppressed and Melbourne sent Lord Durham (1792 – 1840) to investigate conditions in Canada. Durham's assistants were Gibbon Wakefield and Charles Buller (1806 – 48). He produced a report in 1839 which recommended that Upper and Lower Canada should be united, and that there should be a greater measure of self-government for Canada. At first there was some opposition to his recommendations, for people believed that if Canada was allowed political freedom the British empire would be weakened.

The Canada Act, 1840

This Act united Upper and Lower Canada and established a nominated Legislative Council with life members and a House of Assembly with an equal number of members from each province.

Gradually the British government began to implement Lord Durham's proposals. By 1847 Lord Elgin (1811–63), the Governor of Canada, chose his ministers from the majority in the House of Assembly and accepted all the Assembly's measures. Responsible government came to Nova Scotia in 1846 and to New Brunswick and Newfoundland in 1847.

The Dominion of Canada, 1867

At the Quebec Conference held in October 1864 there were discussions amongst the republics of the Canadas (Ontario and Quebec) and the Maritime Provinces (New Brunswick, Nova Scotia, Newfoundland and Prince Edward Island) about a federal scheme for Canada. This was followed in 1866 by a conference in London. In 1867 the Canadas, New Brunswick and Nova Scotia united to form the Dominion of Canada. Manitoba joined the federation in 1870, British Columbia in 1871, Prince Edward Island in 1873 and Alberta and Saskatchewan in 1905. All the tasks of government were carried out by the federal government in the new capital of Ottawa.

Summary

Britain's empire expanded rapidly in the nineteenth century. Initially much of the expansion was brought about by the work of private chartered companies. The East India Company gained control of most of India by 1850. Some of the first people to go to Australia were convicts, but thousands of settlers arrived there in the nineteenth century. New Zealand and South Africa were colonized with the help of private chartered companies, inspired by Gibbon Wakefield who was also responsible for the expansion of the empire in Canada. The British empire brought great wealth to Britain but it also brought the government many responsibilities.

Exercises

1. Trace and explain the growth of British power in India from 1760 to 1833.
2. What caused the Indian mutiny, 1857? How far was British power in India more firmly based after the mutiny?
3. Describe the contribution made by Gibbon Wakefield to the development of the British empire.
4. Show the importance of Britain's empire in the nineteenth century from the point of view of trade.

26
Scientific Development

During the nineteenth century remarkable progress was made in the physical and biological sciences. British scientists kept in touch with fellow scientists abroad so that to a large extent the development of the sciences was international. Scientific discoveries affected every aspect of the nation's life. They helped the economy to prosper, cast new light on the nature of the universe and improved standards of health. Scientists projected a feeling of optimism and made great claims for the power of science. In 1802 Sir Humphry Davy contrasted men living in former times 'in a state of nature, at the mercy of the elements', with nineteenth-century civilized men 'informed by science and able to modify and change the beings surrounding them'.

1 Physical and Biological Sciences

In the early years of the nineteenth century there were few facilities in Britain for the study of science. The Royal Institution, founded in London in 1799 by private subscription, aimed to publicize new ideas and run courses of lectures and experiments. Similar foundations were set up in other cities, and unless a student was wealthy enough to equip his own laboratory he depended on these private societies to carry out experiments. There was no state institution for scientific research or teaching until the Royal School of Mines was founded in 1851. This lack of facilities makes the scientific discoveries of the early nineteenth century all the more remarkable.

Joseph Black (1728–99)
Joseph Black pioneered the chemistry of gases and formulated the theory of specific and latent heat. All his experiments were logically conducted and he stressed the need to test all theories by the use of the balance. Black founded a chemical society for his students, one of the first chemical organizations to exist.

John Dalton (1766 – 1844)

Another chemist, John Dalton, rose from very humble origins to be internationally famous for the formulation of the atomic theory. The theory explained chemical reactions and was based on the concept that the atoms of different elements are distinguished by differences in their weights. The theory indicated that there was a mathematical order in chemistry which could be expressed in equations and it opened up new fields of experiment.

Sir Humphry Davy (1778 – 1829)

Sir Humphry Davy pioneered electrochemistry, splitting up compounds by electrolysis. He is famous for his discovery of sodium and potassium and the invention of the miners' safety lamp. It is said that his greatest achievement was the 'discovery' of his brilliant assistant, Michael Faraday.

Michael Faraday (1791 – 1867)

Michael Faraday discovered benzene. He studied the process of electrolysis and discovered electromagnetic induction which led him to invent the dynamo. Electric motors stem from Faraday's discoveries. He was also the main architect of the classical field theory.

Charles Darwin (1809 – 82) and Evolution

Until the mid-eighteenth century most people accepted the Biblical description of creation and had no doubt that the world was created in six days. The first attack on this theory of the universe came from geologists. James Hulton (1726 – 96), in his work *Theory of the Earth*, argued that the earth's features had been formed by a very gradual action of natural forces. William Smith (1769 – 1839) demonstrated that the age of rocks was revealed by their fossil content. At the same time Charles Lyell (1797 – 1875) was providing proof against the theory that the world was created suddenly. He declared that the facts of the earth's surface could only be explained by the action of slow upheavals followed by denudation. Other work contradicted the Biblical theory that every animal and plant produced offspring identical to itself. Erasmus Darwin (1731 – 1800), Charles Darwin's grandfather, maintained that the struggle for existence caused organisms to acquire new characteristics which they passed on to their offspring. Many scientists were using the term 'evolution' long before Charles Darwin published *The Origin of Species by Natural Selection* in 1859.

Darwin's views about what Herbert Spencer called 'the survival of the fittest' were the result of years of painstaking research. From

1831 to 36 Darwin was a naturalist on board *HMS Beagle*. During this voyage he studied thousands of animals and plants and noted the differences which existed between species on neighbouring islands in the Pacific. In September 1838 he read the *Essay on the Principle of Population* by T.R. Malthus (1766–1834), which argued that population increase outstripped the rate of increase of food, resulting in hardship, misery and death for the poor. Darwin saw that this argument, translated to the case of animals and plants in nature, explained why the less efficiently adapted died whilst the better adapted flourished. He completed his theory of natural selection almost 20 years before it was published.

At first Darwin's theory of evolution was attacked on all sides, especially by churchmen. People were shocked to discover that man appeared to be only a superior animal with ape-like ancestors. Eventually conflict died down and Darwin's views were generally accepted. For his magnificient work Darwin received many honours from foreign governments, but nothing from the British government except burial in Westminster Abbey.

Astronomy
Whilst the government ignored many branches of science it was quick to recognize the practical importance of astronomy. The growth of overseas possessions and trade led to the foundation of observatories outside Britain. In 1829 a Royal Observatory was opened at the Cape of Good Hope. From the Royal Observatory at Greenwich British observers made important discoveries about navigation and time-keeping. For many years the largest telescope in the world belonged to William Parsons, third Earl of Rosse (1800–67). Rosse, a distinguished astronomer and President of the Royal Society from 1848 to 1854, constructed a six-foot reflecting telescope at his family seat in Ireland. The telescope had no rival and attracted many distinguished astronomers and mathematicians. Later in the century developments in photography and spectroscopy widened the scope of astronomy. William Higgins (1824–1910), the pioneer of astrophysics, used spectroscopy to measure the velocity of stars.

James Prescott Joule (1818–89)
Joule studied under John Dalton and is celebrated for his establishment of the mechanical theory of heat. He laid the foundations for the theory of the conservation of energy which states that energy is never lost but only converted from one form to another. In all his work he combined patience, experimental skill and great accuracy.

William Thomson (1824 – 1907)
William Thomson, later Lord Kelvin, made many contributions to experimental and theoretical physics. A child prodigy, he matriculated at Glasgow University at the age of 10. He worked with Joule and, together with Michael Faraday, was jointly responsible for the theory of the electromagnetic field.

James Clerk Maxwell (1831 – 79)
Maxwell is remembered as the creator of the electromagnetic theory of light. In a few differential equations he expressed the whole science of electromagnetism and related this to light, showing that electromagnetic waves travel through space in the same way as light waves. Maxwell's discoveries had practical results, leading to the development of radio telegraphy, television and radar. In 1871 he became the first Cavendish professor of experimental physics at Cambridge University where he designed the new Cavendish laboratory, which was to become the seat of some of the most important discoveries in modern physics.

Joseph Thomson (1856 – 1940)
Joseph J. Thomson discovered the electron. Working as a physicist in the Cavendish laboratory, he discovered that the particles, which he called electrons, passing through a cathode tube were charged with negative electricity. He succeeded in measuring their velocity and mass. His work with vacuum tubes had practical results, including the development of flourescent lighting and electronic valves. Thomson received the Nobel prize for physics in 1906.

2 Medical Science

The contrast between modern medical knowledge and the ignorance of the early nineteenth century is difficult to imagine. Antiseptics and anaesthetics have been developed only in the last 120 years. Until Pasteur discovered microbes in 1857 the true cause of infection was not known. The mass of Britain's population lived in squalid, overcrowded conditions and throughout the country infant mortality never fell below 150 out of every 1000 babies born. The standard of health was raised by improvements in housing and public health reform, but some of the greatest benefits to health came from medical discovery.

Scientific Surgery
John Hunter (1728 – 93) is regarded as the founder of scientific

surgery in Britain. After being employed as a cabinet-maker he began to assist his brother William, the anatomist, with dissections in London. Such was the interest in dissection that the demand for corpses was met by bodysnatching from graveyards. Hunter became a surgeon at St George's Hospital and in 1776 became surgeon-extraordinary to George III.

Vaccination

One of John Hunter's pupils, Edward Jenner (1749 – 1823), was the pioneer of vaccination. As a boy in Gloucestershire he learned of the belief that those who had contracted cowpox were immune to small-pox. When he became a medical practitioner he tested this theory in three ways. Firstly, he innoculated a healthy boy with cowpox pus and found that it was not then possible to infect him with smallpox. Secondly, he showed that 10 people who were known to have had cowpox were naturally immune to smallpox. Finally, he demon-strated that cowpox could be transferred from person to person, carrying immunity to smallpox with it.

Jenner's findings were readily accepted and by 1800 100,000 people had been vaccinated against smallpox and the practice spread throughout Europe and North America. In 1806 President Thomas Jefferson of the United States wrote to Jenner: 'Future generations will know by history only that the loathesome smallpox existed and by you has been eliminated'. As a result of vaccination the death rate from smallpox in Britain fell from 4000 per million in the eighteenth century to 90 per million after 1872 when vaccination was generally enforced.

Vaccination against smallpox was followed by vaccination against other diseases. The French scientist Louis Pasteur (1822 – 95) dis-covered vaccines for anthrax and rabies. He also developed the germ theory of fermentation and disease. He established the role of micro-organisms in causing fermentation. Pasteur's discoveries led to the development of pasteurization — a process which is now applied to many perishable foodstuffs.

Anaesthetics

At the beginning of the nineteenth century surgery consisted mainly of amputations, the setting of fractures and the removal of surface tumours — all things which were obvious without diagnosis. Operating theatres resembled slaughter-houses. The patient, drugged with brandy, was held down whilst the surgeon performed his task with the greatest possible speed. The discovery of anaes-thetics revolutionized surgery and diminished the terrible sufferings of surgical patients. In 1846 W.T.G. Morton, an American dentist, showed the value of ether as an anaesthetic on a patient who was to have a tumour removed from his neck. Although this represented a major advance in surgery ether was not an ideal anaesthetic and this led to a search for other agents. Dr J.Y. Simpson (1811–70) began to use chloroform as an anaesthetic in obstetric surgery. With the use of chloroform operations increased in number and scope.

Antiseptics

At first the boon of anaesthesia was offset by the scourge of sepsis. Post-operative infections and gangrene were common in all hospitals where surgical wards were filled with the stench of putrefying flesh. It is hardly surprising that infection was widespread since operating theatres were filthy and the surgeons always operated in the oldest frock-coats they possessed. In Britain 40 per cent of all patients who had amputations for compound fractures died of gangrene. Joseph Lister (1827–1912) studied this problem in Glasgow where he was professor of surgery. He learned from Pasteur that putrefaction is fermentation and that this is caused by the entry of micro-organisms into the fermentable matter. Lister decided to destroy the organisms in the air and in the wound. After many experiments he found that carbolic acid was a suitable antiseptic. Lister was soon recognized as the founder of antiseptic surgery and his methods spread quickly throughout Europe.

The Conquest of Malaria

In the nineteenth century several doctors worked in distant parts of the British empire, studying tropical diseases. Ronald Ross (1857–1932), the son of an Indian army officer, became famous for his pioneering work on the life cycle of the malarial parasite which lived in the stomach of the mosquito. As a result of his discoveries malarial fever was overcome by the use of drugs and the destruction of malarial breeding grounds. Ross was awarded the Nobel prize in 1902 for his malarial studies.

The Medical Profession

The British Medical Association was founded in 1854 and the Medical Act, 1858, created a general council of medical education and registration. The council had the power to keep a register of qualified practitioners and to approve the institutions conferring medical qualifications. Henceforth, quacks and cranks had less opportunity to harm the public. Throughout the nineteenth century branches of medicine and surgery became more specialized.

Standards in the profession were raised by the invention in 1797 of the clinical thermometer and the stethoscope in c1819. Both implements led to improvements in diagnosis. The hypodermic syringe was invented in 1855.

Nursing

The great revolutions in antiseptics and anaesthetics came at the same time as the revival of sisterhoods devoted to medical and social work. After her experiences in the Crimean War Florence Nightingale returned to apply her principles of cleanliness and care to English hospitals. As a result of her agitation professional health visiting, to care for the sick and newborn babies in their homes, began in 1892. In the early years of the nineteenth century midwives were untrained and often dirty and drunken. In 1902 the Midwives Act created a Central Midwives Board to register trained midwives whom it examined and to forbid women attending confinements unless they held a certificate or acted under the direction of a doctor.

Summary

During the nineteenth century British scientists made important discoveries which greatly benefited the country. Their work had practical results. Britain's economy and British society benefited from the discoveries leading to the development of electrical machinery and wireless telegraphy. The health of the nation was improved by the discoveries of vaccination, anaesthetics and antiseptics. The work of Britain's scientists was internationally recognized and several were awarded Nobel prizes.

Exercises

1. Why was Michael Faraday's work so important?
2. What is evolution? Why did Darwin's views shock people when they were first published?
3. What contribution did Jenner make to improving the nation's health?
4. Describe the improvements made in the treatment of surgical patients in the nineteenth century.

27
Transport and Communications

In the first half of the eighteenth century most people did not travel far from their homes. Communication networks were primitive and many parts of the country were isolated. There were three methods of industrial transport — by coastal navigation, by river and by road using pack horses or horsedrawn carts. Transport was a costly, slow process. Reforms were gradually introduced and by the end of the following century the transport and communications revolution was complete. Cheap, swift travel was available by road, rail and steamship. Through the use of the telegraph, telephone and wireless systems Britain was in contact with different parts of the world.

1 Roads

The Poor State of the Roads
In 1760 the state of British roads was appalling. The parish was responsible for their upkeep, but it did not usually feel inclined to work on roads which strangers used more often then the native inhabitants. Consequently, the fine Roman roads had fallen into decay, becoming dusty in summer and like quagmires in winter. The industrial revolution and the growth of towns gave rise to increasing use of roads which in turn added to and revealed the necessity for improvement. The government realized that as well as benefiting the economy a good road network was also necessary for political and military purposes. Many people began to examine ways in which travel by road could be improved.

Turnpike Trusts
The solution to the vexed question of travel by road was to extend the turnpike method of road building and maintenance which was first adopted in 1663. A turnpike road was usually planned and financed by a group of interested people who hoped to benefit from the improved road. They secured permission from Parliament to collect tolls from all users of the road in question and in return they

agreed to repair the road and keep it in good order. Between 1751 and 1790 Parliament passed 1600 Turnpike Acts and by 1820 there were 20,000 miles of turnpike roads.

Although the turnpike system greatly improved the country's roads it did not provide a perfect answer to the demand for better roads and it was not without its critics. The turnpike system had three shortcomings. Firstly, there was no obligation on the trustees to spend a fixed sum from the tolls they received on the upkeep of the roads. In many cases turnpike roads were left in a poor state of repair. Secondly, because a trust often covered only a short stretch of road, travellers on long journeys were sometimes obliged to pay several tolls which made their journey very expensive. Most of the roads were not connected with each other and were often built in a haphazard, meandering way rather than taking a direct route. Thirdly, the turnpike system did not recognize the needs of purely local travellers whose daily journey might take them past a toll booth. In some areas resentment of turnpike trusts led to riots and the demolition of toll gates and booths. Turnpike trusts were not a complete success because they were a piece-meal and purely local answer to the problem of road transport.

Civil Engineers

Several trustees employed skilled engineers to carry out the planning and construction of turnpike trusts. John Metcalfe (1717–1810) was the first road builder in Britain since Roman times. He built roads in Yorkshire and constructed 180 miles of road across the Pennines. His roads and bridges withstood the harsh weather conditions of the region and in times of flood his bridges were usually the only ones standing. Metcalfe paid attention to gradient and drainage. He laid firm foundations and laid 'metal' roads composed of stone or gravel closely packed together.

Thomas Telford (1757–1834) began by constructing canals and went on to become a famous road builder. The greatest of all his achievements was the London to Holyhead road, including the Menai suspension bridge. Telford introduced definite principles of road building, paying attention to the foundations, drainage, camber and gradient of the road. He tried to make his roads as direct as possible. In particular he believed that there should be a most careful selection and preparation of materials to be used in road building. Metcalfe's roads had relied on local materials. They tended to be soft and sandy and subject to swift erosion. Telford's roads were more substantial and his work can still be seen today.

Another great civil engineer, and a great rival of Telford's, was

John McAdam (1756 – 1836). Unlike Telford, McAdam believed that it was not the foundation but the surface which was the most important factor in road building. The surface should be smooth and solid and capable of carrying a great weight. For this purpose he used small stones and allowed them to bind themselves together under the weight of the traffic until complete packing had taken place. He did not use a binding material because he believed that this prevented packing. Thanks to the work of these and other civil engineers Britain had 20,000 miles of good road by 1830.

Road Traffic

The new and better roads led to increased travel and traffic. The period from the 1780s to the 1830s was the golden age of the stage coach which provided quicker travel than ever before. The new roads brought order and regularity to road travel. Many of the new stage coaches had armed guards and swift horses which deterred highwaymen. Travel became safer and stage coach services expanded. Hundreds of coaching inns opened to cater for the increasing number of passengers.

Once the roads were improved John Palmer (1742 – 1818) of Bath suggested that there should be a regular mail service. By 1784 the carriage of mail by coach had started. Within a decade the country was criss-crossed by mail coaches and by 1800 400 towns received post daily. In the towns hansom cabs appeared in 1834 and horse-drawn trams in the 1860s.

After 1830 roads, like canals, suffered competition from the railways and many turnpike trusts and coaching companies were ruined. Railway companies tried to prevent the application of steam power to road transport and in 1865 they obtained the passage of the Red Flag Act, which restricted the speed of mechanically powered road vehicles to two miles per hour in towns and five miles per hour in the countryside. Powered vehicles had to be accompanied by three men, one of whom had to walk ahead with a red flag. The internal combustion engine, invented in the 1880s, revolutionized road transport. The Red Flag Act was repealed in 1896, allowing cars to travel at 12 miles per hour and this, together with improved road surfaces, made travel by motor car more enjoyable. The Motor Car Act, 1903, raised the speed limit to 20 miles per hour and introduced the compulsory registration and licensing of cars.

2 Canals

Early Canal Development

In the early eighteenth century the carriage of heavy goods to and from the ports depended to a large extent on river navigation. From the late seventeenth century onwards long stretches of river were improved. Weirs, silt and obstructions were removed, bends straightened and banks strengthened. The logical step from improving existing rivers was the creation of artificial ones. Canals had existed for centuries in some countries and were widely used in Holland and France. It was probably because Britain had a good network of navigable rivers that she was slow in constructing canals. Eventually industrial expansion, especially in the coal, cotton and pottery industries, created a demand for canals in Britain. The first artificial waterway, the Sankey canal, was constructed between 1755 and 1757 to link St Helens with the river Mersey.

The Duke of Bridgewater (1736–1803) and James Brindley (1716–72)

Britain's first major canal was the brainchild of the third Duke of Bridgewater. He wanted to bring his estates and coal mines at Worsley into contact with the growing town of Manchester, which offered a rich market for agricultural products and coal. James Brindley, an illiterate millwright, designed and supervised the construction of the Bridgewater canal, which ran from the Duke's coalmines at Worsley to Manchester — a distance of about eight miles. Opened in 1761, the canal was a great success and immediately became the wonder of the nation. Brindley planned a national network of waterways, joining all the major ports and towns. He went on to build over 360 miles of canals including the Grand Trunk canal.

Canal Construction

Canal construction was a costly business and was usually financed by a joint stock company with many shareholders. Once the initial capital had been raised and the route surveyed, the canal promoters applied to Parliament for powers of compulsory purchase of the land and the power to run and maintain the completed canal. Once Parliament granted permission the engineers took over. Gangs of labourers known as navigators, and then simply as 'navvies', built the canals. As soon as a section of the canal was completed it was opened to traffic. A toll was charged for each barge which used the canal. By the 1790s the pace of canal construction had accelerated and 'canal mania' swept the country. At their fullest extent there were 2500 miles of canal in Britain.

The Major Canals

In the second half of the eighteenth century canals were constructed which linked all Britain's major ports. In addition, several short canals were built to serve the particular needs of Lancashire, the West Midlands and Birmingham. The Bridgewater canal was extended to Runcorn in 1767. It linked Manchester and Liverpool and carried cotton, food and passengers. The Grand Trunk, or Mersey – Trent canal was completed in 1777 and carried clay to the Staffordshire potteries. It also helped the development of the Cheshire chemical industry and the brewing industry of Burton-on-Trent. In 1805 the Grand Junction and Oxford canal was completed. It linked the Midlands and London, enabling goods imported through London to be distributed and carrying the food produced in the Home Counties to the Midlands. The last major canal, the Leeds to Liverpool canal, was constructed between 1769 and 1810. It carried cotton, wool and passengers. (See Fig. 21, Britain's Inland Waterways.) Since there was a navigable river from Leeds to Hull goods could now be transported right across the country by inland waterway.

The Decline of Canals

The development of railways was the chief cause of canal decline. Railways provided cheap, quick and easy travel and they attracted traffic away from canals. Canal companies fought competition from the railways for as long as they could, but the new railway companies gradually bought controlling shares in most of the canal companies and by 1846 they owned half of Britain's canals. As it was in their interests to be rid of canal competition the new owners neglected the canals and traffic declined rapidly.

3 Railways

The Origin of Railways

The locomotive was invented in the early years of the nineteenth century and soon after this railways as we know them today were built. However, railways existed long before 1800 and can be traced back to the seventeenth century. They were first built in the mining areas of Britain, using horses for haulage. At first the rails were wooden but cast iron rails were in general use by 1800. These early

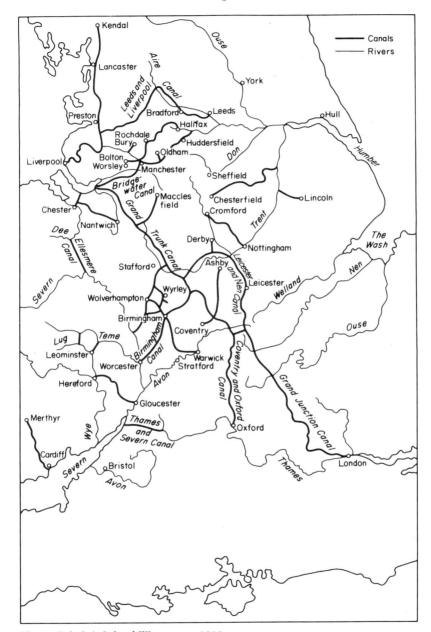

Fig. 21 Britain's Inland Waterways, 1800

railways carried coal, stone and other heavy goods from the mines to
the nearest road, river, canal or port.

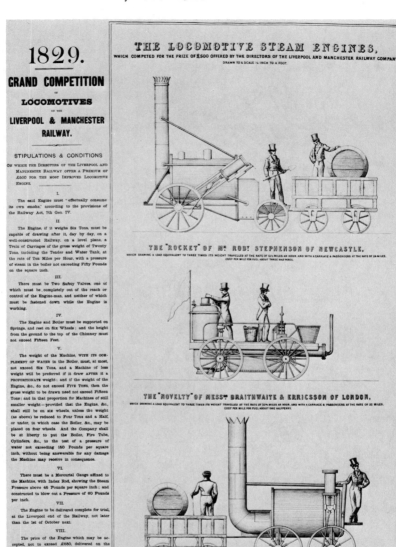

A poster for the Rainhill Trials

Experiments with locomotion were carried out in mining areas at the start of · the nineteenth century. William Murdoch (1754–1839), Watt's assistant in Cornwall, experimented with a model steam carriage. Richard Trevithick (1771–1833) produced some of the earliest locomotives, but after one of his engines exploded and another overturned he abandoned his experiments. John Blenkinsop (1783–1831), of the firm of Fenton, Murray and Woods of Leeds, made a number of locomotives in 1812. His engines were built with cogged wheels to fit into toothed rails. At about the same time on Tyneside William Hedley (1779–1843) started to build locomotives which ran on smooth rails.

George Stephenson (1781–1848)
George Stephenson did not invent the locomotive but he played a vital part in its development. In 1812 he was appointed engine-wright in a colliery near Newcastle. There, in 1814, he produced his first locomotive which was built to draw coals to the Tyne. In the next few years all his attention was focused on railways. He examined everything from the improvement of the locomotive to the construction of the track. He supported the use of wrought iron instead of cast iron rails and he suggested the idea of a groove to keep the wheels on the track. Stephenson was appointed engineer of the Stockton to Darlington railway, which opened in 1825 using five of his engines.

The start of large scale public railways in Britain is marked by the construction of the Liverpool to Manchester line. Even at this stage in railway development it was still open to question whether the locomotive could compete successfully with the horse or with a stationary steam engine. The directors of the railway held the Rainhill trials in October 1830 to determine what type of engine they should adopt (see the poster advertising the trials). The trials were won by George Stephenson's 'Rocket' which reached a speed of 30 miles per hour. Stephenson's success ensured the adoption of the locomotive as the normal method of haulage on the railways. The Liverpool to Manchester railway, opened in September 1830, proved a great success. In the first three years it carried an average of 1100 passengers a day.

Railway Expansion
The success of the Liverpool to Manchester railway led to a period of frenzied railway building. The London and Birmingham railway and the Grand Junction railway were both started in 1833. They were followed by the construction of the London and Southampton

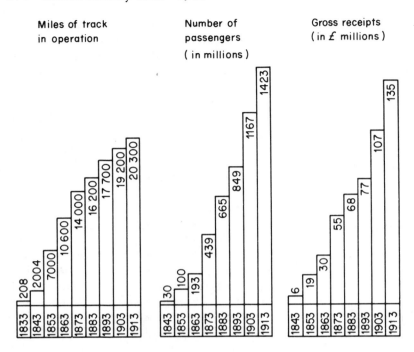

Fig.22 The Expansion of Railways

railway and the Great Western railway which ran from London to Bristol. Between 1825 and 1835 54 railway Acts were passed and by 1843 London was linked by rail to York, Bristol, Lancaster, Dover, Birmingham, Southampton and Brighton. The boom in railway expansion was marred only by the railway 'mania' of 1845 when several speculative companies were formed which laid very little track and lost thousands of pounds. By 1850 8000 miles of track covered Britain and most of the major railway routes were complete. By 1900 the railway network extended to the remotest parts of Britain. Railways offered dining and sleeping car services and provided a comfortable and efficient service (See Fig. 22, The Expansion of Railways.)

The Importance of Railways

Railways contributed to Britain's economic prosperity. They produced an increased demand for the products of the iron, coal and steel industries. They encouraged the development of mechanical and civil engineering and helped to encourage the growth of large businesses. Mass production became worthwhile once Britain had an adequate transport system. Trains provided a quick, cheap means of transport. Bulky manufactured items and food could be moved quickly all over the country. The result was an expansion in domestic and overseas markets. Railways themselves proved to be a valuable export. The construction and operation of railways gave work to thousands of men. They helped to increase labour mobility and the Railway Act, 1844, brought travel by train within the price range of everyone (see p. 140). For the first time in their lives many town dwellers visited the countryside and the coast. The railways created new towns such as Crewe and Swindon and played a part in the expansion of the suburbs of many large cities.

4 Transport by Sea

Throughout the eighteenth century Britain's main 'highway' was the sea which was used far more than might be expected for the transport of passengers as well as goods. Large numbers of small craft were engaged in trade around the coast. Their principal cargoes were coal, slate, clay and grain — all items whose weight and bulk made transport by road difficult and expensive. As industry expanded Britain's external trade increased and British shipping found it difficult to cope with the increased volume of traffic.

In the eighteenth century transport by sea was interrupted in bad weather and in time of war and the goods carried were subject to heavy duties. British sailing vessels were small and heavy and travelled extremely slowly. Docking and harbour facilities were poor and life at sea was dangerous. In the nineteenth century changes in ship design came from the United States. Voyages were speeded up for the vessels now had a much greater length in proportion to their breadth and travelled quickly. Clippers came into use in Britain after 1840 and were renowned for bringing the tea crop from China. As the nineteenth century progressed docking facilities were improved. Safety at sea was improved by the construction of lighthouses, the introduction of a lifeboat organization and the Plimsoll line (see p. 182).

From Sail to Steam

British shipping was revolutionized by the change from sail to steam. The first successful use of steam came in 1802 when the *Charlotte Dundas*, a steam tug, sailed on the Forth – Clyde canal pulling two boats behind it. The next development was the work of Henry Bell who built the *Comet* in 1812. At first it was used on the Forth – Clyde canal but it proved to be so successful that it was also used along the coast. Regular steam boat services around the coast and across the Channel followed. The first Atlantic crossing under steam came in 1833 when the *Royal William*, a Canadian vessel, made the voyage in 20 days. In 1839 Samuel Cunard (1787 – 1865) obtained the first government contract to carry mail across the Atlantic. Steamships were a great improvement over sailing ships. They could carry more cargo, were independent of the weather, could take the shortest routes and consequently could make many more trips per year than sailing ships.

From Wood to Iron

Side by side with the change from sail to steam came the change from wooden to iron ships. John Wilkinson was one of the first to experiment with the construction of iron ships (see p.19). At first there was some resistance to the change from wooden to iron ships for iron ships were heavier, rode lower in the water and therefore carried less cargo than wooden ships. In 1822 the first iron ship was used on the Thames. Brunel's (1806 – 59) *Great Western* was the first iron steam boat to cross the Atlantic in 1838. In 1865 the Cunard company converted entirely to iron and steamships and other companies followed its example. By 1900 iron ships had been replaced by steel ones.

Technical Progress

The introduction of screw propulsion in 1839 and the invention of the expansion engine in 1854 by John Elder (1824 – 69) both contributed to fuel economy which cut the cost of shipping. In 1897 steam turbines were introduced, adding speed and comfort to sea voyages. In the years before the First World War oil began to replace coal and it was adopted as the general fuel throughout the British navy.

5 Telecommunications

The Telegraph

The era of modern telecommunications began in the 1830s with the invention of the electrical telegraph. Sir Charles Wheatstone (1802 – 75) and Sir William Cooke (1806 – 79) invented the needle telegraph system in which electronically controlled needles pointed to letters of the alphabet on a dial. The telegraph enabled messages to be sent quickly. It was first used by railway companies and then by the Stock Exchange and by Reuter's news agency in London. Cables were laid across the Channel and the Atlantic and in 1870 a line was opened between Britain and India. Eventually, the Morse dot-dash system, invented in the United States in the 1830s, replaced the needle system everywhere except on the railways. In 1870 the Post Office took control of private telegraph companies.

The Telephone
The next step in telecommunications came in 1876 when the first transmission of the human voice was made by Alexander Graham Bell (1874 – 1922) in America. The telephone was soon introduced in England and in 1878 the first telephone exchange was opened. At first telephones were operated by private companies but the Post Office gradually took control. By 1912 there were 700,000 telephones in Britain. The telephone had a profound effect on business and social life.

The Wireless
Clerk-Maxwell (1831 – 79) had worked on the basic theory of the wireless (see p.262). Towards the end of the nineteenth century the Italian Marconi (1874 – 1937) invented wireless telegraphy. In 1895 he sent a Morse code message over a distance of one mile. In the following year he came to England and demonstrated his apparatus on Salisbury Plain to officials of the army, navy and Post Office. In 1901 the first wireless telegraph message was sent across the Atlantic. The Wireless Telegraphy Act, 1904, stated that the installation and working of wireless in Britain had to be covered by a licence from the Postmaster General. In the same year Sir John Flemming (1849 – 1945) invented the thermonic valve which enabled the rapid development of wireless. Wireless telegraphy and telephony became an invaluable communications device.

Summary
For most of the eighteenth century Britain did not have an adequate transport system. Many parts of the country were isolated and, consequently, trade suffered. By 1800 a transport revolution was under way. Eventually, muddy tracks were replaced by macadam roads and wooden sailing vessels were replaced by steel steamers. Canals and railways linked many cities and brought new life to remote areas. Towards the end of the nineteenth century there were dramatic improvements in telecommunications which led to improvements in business and the expansion of the Post Office.

Exercises
1. How did Turnpike trusts improve the state of Britain's roads?

2. Identify Britain's major canals and explain how they helped the country's economy.
3. Describe the growth of railway networks in Britain between 1825 and 1850.
4. How did railways help a) the economy, b) the development of society?
5. Describe the changes which took place in transport by sea in the nineteenth century.
6. How did improvements in telecommunications help a) business, b) the armed forces?

28
Education

In the second half of the eighteenth century Britain had several educational institutions. There were elementary or primary schools, together with several types of secondary schools. In England there were only two universities — Oxford and Cambridge, but in some areas of the country further education could be obtained in Nonconformist Academies or Mechanics' Institutes. The state did not control any of these institutions which were run by private individuals, often with guidance from the Church of England. Attendance at an educational institution was neither compulsory nor free. By the early twentieth century the picture had changed dramatically. The state had stepped in to provide free, compulsory education on secular lines. Following government inquiries secondary schools and universities had been reformed. By 1914 Britain possessed a modern education system which matched those of its European rivals in every respect, except perhaps in the provision of scientific education.

1 Elementary Education

Early Schools
In 1760 there were several different types of elementary school. One thing which many of these schools had in common was the emphasis

they placed on religious instruction which it was thought would have a civilizing and stabilizing effect on the poor. There were several 'Dame Schools', usually run by an elderly woman who charged a small weekly fee and did not provide more than a very basic education. Private day schools, often run by men who were unfit for any other work, provided the rudiments of knowledge to all those children whose parents could pay a small weekly fee. In 1698 the Society for Promoting Christian Knowledge had founded charity schools to encourage the children of the poor to develop habits of industry and lead God-fearing lives. Charity schools were attached to the parish and did not charge fees. In 1760 they were educating 30,000 children. In Wales the SPCK helped 'Circulating Schools' in which teachers travelled the country teaching children and adults to read the Bible and catechism. Free education for the poor was also provided by the schools of industry which taught handicrafts, religious instruction and sometimes reading. Finally, poor children received an elementary education in Sunday schools, popularized by Robert Raikes (1735 – 1811), which emphasized religious and social training. In these schools children were taught to read so that they could read the Bible but other forms of learning were generally discouraged.

The Monitorial System

Although there were several types of elementary school in the eighteenth century most children received no education whatsoever. This situation began to change in the early nineteenth century when Andrew Bell (1753 – 1832) and Joseph Lancaster (1778 – 1838) popularized a scheme known as the monitorial system. Under this scheme the headmaster taught the monitors who then taught the rest of the pupils after they had been split into manageable groups. The technique was mechanical and the subject matter was elementary but the system was cheap for, with the aid of monitors, one teacher could teach hundreds of children.

Disagreements about religious instruction between Bell and Lancaster led to the foundation of two rival societies. In 1811 the 'National Society for Promoting the Education of the Poor in the Principles of the Established Church throughout England and Wales' was founded to promote Bell's ideas. In 1814 the British and Foreign Schools Society was founded and, according to Lancaster's principles, it provided elementary education for children of any denomination. Monitorial schools helped to popularize elementary education. Lancaster and Bell left their mark on the system. As a result, throughout the nineteenth century, elementary education was fettered by mechanical methods, low standards, religious rivalry and an obsession with cheapness.

The Government Grant to Education, 1833

In 1833 the Whigs awarded £20,000 for the erection of elementary school houses. This was the first government grant in aid of education and it was paid to the National Society, which we have seen was sponsored by the Church of England, and to the British and Foreign Schools Society sponsored by the Nonconformists. The Whigs drew up conditions to regulate the scheme. To qualify for government aid local subscriptions from the societies had to equal half the grant made in any particular case. Once built, the society was responsible for maintaining the school. Preference was given to applications from large cities for schools wishing to accommodate over 400 children. The government grant was significant but initially its effects were limited. It tended to encourage schools in comparatively well-to-do areas, neglecting the poorer areas and country districts. It laid down no building standards and there were no inspectors.

The Newcastle Commission, 1858

By the mid-nineteenth century it was evident that voluntary effort was not catering adequately for the educational needs of the country. Many schemes for improvement were put forward. In 1856 the Education Department was created by an order in council, which indicates that the importance of education was generally recognized. In 1858 a Royal Commission was appointed under the chairmanship of the Duke of Newcastle (1811–64) to 'inquire into the Present State of Popular Education in England, and to consider and report what measures, if any, are required for the Extension of sound and cheap Elementary Instruction to all Classes of the People'.

The commission estimated that one in eight of the population was attending school. This was an improvement on conditions in 1800 when only one in 21 children had attended school. However, although more children went to school the commission found that they did not attend school for more than a few years, that their attendance was irregular and that their education was superficial. Teachers tended to devote more time to their older pupils, leaving the younger ones in the hands of pupil-teachers who had replaced monitors. The commission reported in 1861 and recommended 'the extension of sound and cheap elementary education'. It believed that the government grant had not been used effectively and to ensure that this did not happen in the future the commission recommended that there should be regular attendance, better teaching and a wider curriculum.

The Revised Code, 1862

The Newcastle Commission recommended that the state should pay a grant for each pupil and pupil-teacher to all elementary schools which had a satisfactory report from Her Majesty's Inspectors. These grants should be supplemented by local grants from the rates subject to the satisfactory performance by the pupils in an examination. Robert Lowe, who had been appointed Vice-President of the Education Department in 1859, was responsible for introducing the Revised Code in 1862. The Code incorporated the commissioners' recommendations and contained some of Lowe's own ideas. He retorted to anyone who criticized the Code, 'If it is not cheap, it shall be efficient; if it is not efficient it shall be cheap'.

Under the Code grants were awarded to schools on the basis of regular attendance and subject to the results of an examination of each child in the 'three Rs' by an Inspector. Thus began the system of 'payment by results' which lasted for the next 40 years. The Revised Code cut the cost of education and led to a rise in average attendance at school but the curriculum narrowed and the annual examination led to increasing pressure on the children, mechanical teaching and rote-learning.

The Education Act, 1870

In 1870 W.E. Forster, Vice-President of the privy council Committee for Education, secured the passage of the Education Act. The Act allowed churches to continue providing their own schools and increased their grants. Where churches had failed to provide schools, local school boards were to be set up to build and run additional schools. Forster pointed out that the aim of the Act was 'to complete the present voluntary system, to fill up gaps . . . not to destroy the existing system in introducing a new one'. The new school boards were to be elected by the rate-payers. They received a grant from the government and were also empowered to levy a local rate for their schools. Board schools were not allowed to provide denominational religious teaching.

Ensor calls Forster's measure 'the great English Education Act'. It has been called 'the greatest achievement of Gladstone's first administration'. It was in keeping with Liberal philosophy for whilst it had far-reaching social consequences, the state only intervened in education. It did not take over the administration of education and thus kept within the sphere of self-help. The Education Act attacked privilege and the right of the church to control education.

Free, Compulsory Education

The 1870 Education Act had not made education free or compulsory, but it had given school boards the power to compel attendance if they wished by introducing a by-law. Fees of needy children could be refunded. Lord Sandon's Act (1886) stated that it was the duty of parents to send their children to school between the ages of five and 10. School attendance committees were set up in areas where no school boards existed to ensure that children received 'efficient elementary instruction in reading, writing and arithmetic'. In 1880 Mundella's Act compelled all school boards and school attendance committees which had not already done so to frame by-laws to enforce attendance at school. For children between the ages of five and 10 attendance was obligatory. Between the ages of 10 and 14 exemptions could be obtained, based on proficiency or attendance. Mundella's Act did not abolish fees. This was done in 1891 when a grant of 10 shillings per head was introduced which made elementary education virtually free.

The Education Act, 1902

This Act abolished the school boards. They were replaced by county and county borough councils which became responsible for both secondary and elementary education. Local Education Authorities had to supply elementary education in what had been board schools and to erect new schools where they were needed.

2 Secondary Education

Grammar Schools

Grammar, or endowed, schools originated in Britain in Roman times as schools where classical languages were taught. Many had been founded for the benefit of poor students but by the eighteenth century most of their pupils were fee payers. In the early years of the nineteenth century the narrow curriculum found in these schools was beginning to be criticized. Sydney Smith wrote an essay which was published in 1809 entitled *Too Much Latin and Greek* in which he declared,

'A young Englishman goes to school at six or seven years old; and remains in the course of education until twenty-three or twenty-four years of age. In all that time his sole and exclusive occupation is learning Latin and Greek; he has scarcely a notion that there is any other kind of excellence.'

Many of the charters of the endowed grammar schools compelled them to stick rigidly to Latin and Greek. In 1805 the Leeds Grammar School tried to widen its curriculum but was forbidden to do so in a legal judgement by Lord Eldon. It was not until 1840 that the Grammar Schools Act enabled the courts t o interpret the grammar school charters more liberally which allowed the schools to introduce a wider selection of subjects.

Public Schools

In the early years of the nineteenth century there were nine 'Great' or public schools to which the upper classes sent their sons from all parts of the country. The curriculum in these schools was narrowly classical, discipline was harsh and, despite the high fees, living conditions were poor. The schools were reformed in the mid-nineteenth century, thanks to the work of several reforming headmasters like Dr Arnold (1795–1842), and in an attempt to meet competition from newer schools. Public schools began to offer a wider range of subjects, discipline became more humane, organized games were introduced to occupy the boys in their leisure time and the senior pupils had study bedrooms. New schools like Wellington sprang up in the mid-nineteenth century. They catered for the growing demand for public school places for the sons of the wealthy middle class, and they tended to provide a wide curriculum.

Private Schools

For those middle-class boys who did not attend grammar or public schools there were the private schools, often run by a clergyman headmaster. We obtain a good picture of these schools from the writings of Thackeray and Dickens, and Mr Squeer's Dotheboys Hall was quite typical of some of the private schools of the period. These schools were often modelled on endowed schools and had a classical curriculum, but since they often catered for merchants' sons arithmetic, history, geography and modern languages were taught in some of them. There were also private schools for girls which concentrated on teaching refinements such as music and dancing, which would enhance a girl's chances in the marriage market.

The Clarendon Commission, 1861–4

In 1861 Lord Palmerston's government established a Royal Commission, chaired by Lord Clarendon (1800–70), to examine the revenues, management and curriculum of the nine great public schools — Eton, Winchester, Westminster, Harrow, Charterhouse, Rugby, Shrewsbury, Merchant Taylors' and St Paul's. The commission reported in 1864 and praised the discipline and moral tone of the schools, but criticized their narrow curriculum and poor teaching methods. The commission called for reform of the schools' governing bodies and curricula. It was followed by the Public Schools Act, 1868, which required each school to submit a scheme for a more representative governing body, which would have charge of the school fees, the curriculum and the appointment and dismissal of the headmaster.

The Schools Inquiry Commission, 1864–8

In 1864 the Schools Inquiry Commission was set up, under Lord Taunton's (1798–1869) chairmanship, to investigate the schools which had not been considered by the Newcastle and Clarendon Commissions — schools other than elementary and public schools. The commissioners visited 942 schools and issued their report in 1868. They called for three types of school to be made available. The first should have a leaving age of 18 and cater for the sons of parents of ample means, with a curriculum which included the classics, modern languages and mathematics. The second should have a leaving age of 16 and cater for the sons of less well-to-do parents who wanted their boys to enter the professions, e.g. the army, engineering and medicine. The third school, with a leaving age of 14, would cater for the sons of tenant farmers and tradesmen and would provide a general education. A central authority would administer the schools, but they would be left as much as possible under local control. A system of exams would ensure that standards were high. In 1869 Gladstone's government passed the Endowed Schools Act which took little account of the commissioners' report. The Act was confined to the problem of educational endowments. Three commissioners were appointed to try to make better use of the educational endowments even extending, where possible, the benefit of endowments to girls' schools.

The Balfour Act, 1902

As has been seen Balfour's 1902 Education Act gave county and county borough councils the responsibility for secondary education. Where the provision for secondary education in an area was insufficient the Local Education Authorities had to remedy this. They were given the power to aid secondary schools from the rates and this included endowed schools as well as new schools. Secondary school fees were retained, but in 1907 rate aid was extended in the form of scholarships to those who could not afford fees in accordance with the stipulation that 'ample provision be made by every Local Authority for enabling selected children of poorer parents to climb the education ladder'.

3 Higher Education

University Education
Until the 1830s Oxford and Cambridge were the only universities in England. Instead of being places of learning they had become a preserve for the idle rich who often spent their time hunting and gambling rather than studying. The universities had a classical curriculum which was often badly taught and they were open only to male members of the Church of England. In the later stages of the eighteenth century the curriculum had begun to expand with new professorships in scientific subjects at Cambridge whilst at Oxford the Radcliffe Observatory was founded in 1772. But changes were slow.

Nonconformist Academies
Protestant Dissenters and Roman Catholics were excluded by law from Oxford and Cambridge. Dissenters who wished to give their sons a further education sent them to Nonconformist Academies. In general, these Academies provided a higher standard of education than the universities. Many of their courses lasted for four years and included not only the classics but mathematics, natural science and sometimes medicine. These Academies were so efficient that members of the Church of England often sent their sons to them in preference to Oxford and Cambridge.

Mechanics' Institutes
In the early years of the nineteenth century most working-class people had very little elementary education and no secondary education; they did not even think of higher education. Yet some members of the working class received a higher technical education at Mechanics' Institutes. George Birkbeck (1776 – 1841) who had a degree in medicine, began lecturing to Glasgow artisans in 1799 and Mechanics' Institutes soon spread to every part of the country. They catered for the new artisans — the engineers and mechanics — to whom knowledge would be of daily use.

Teacher Training
When the state began to provide elementary education it required a

supply of teachers for the new schools. Sir James Kay Shuttleworth (1804 – 77) had introduced the pupil-teacher system to replace monitors. Pupil-teachers were promising elementary school pupils aged 13 who were apprenticed to the head teacher for five years. He gave them what amounted to a secondary education course in the evenings and in return they taught in the elementary school during the day. When they were 18 they could sit for a Queen's Scholarship, which entitled them to a three-year course in a teacher training college. This provided them with an element of higher education, although most of the courses at these colleges were narrow because the standard of their entrants was not high and because they did not want elementary teachers to become too distant from those they were destined to teach. In the later nineteenth century universities began to provide facilities for the training of secondary school teachers.

The Science and Art Department, 1854

At the Great Exhibition of 1851 England discovered that other European nations were ahead of her in the field of applied science. As a result of this discovery the Science and Art Department came into being in 1854 and it administered parliamentary grants to encourage the teaching of art and more particularly science in Britain. At first scientific subjects were taught mainly at evening classes, and in 1859 the department started an examination for science teachers. In spite of the work of the Science and Art Department Britain continued to lag behind her continental neighbours in the field of applied science.

New Universities

In a letter to *The Times* which appeared on 9 February 1825 Thomas Campbell (1777 – 1844) called for a 'Great London University' to provide education for 'the middling rich' on a non-residential basis. There followed a meeting chaired by the Lord Mayor, and in 1828 University College was opened in Gower Street. It was an undenominational institution and it tended to concentrate on modern studies and science. As a balance to what Arnold called 'that Godless institution in Gower Street' King's College, a Church of England establishment, was founded in London in 1831. In 1836 London University was founded with the power to grant degrees for students studying at University College and King's College. In the second half of the nineteenth century new universities were founded in several of Britain's major cities.

University Reform

As the nineteenth century progressed Oxford and Cambridge Universities began to reform themselves in response to the competition they were encountering from the new universities. They adopted new courses and more imaginative teaching methods. A Royal Commission was established to investigate Oxford and Cambridge and it reported in 1852. Its recommendations formed the basis of the Oxford University Act of 1854 and the Cambridge University Act of 1856. As a result of these Acts a modernization programme began. Further reform came in 1871 when the University Tests Act opened all teaching posts at Oxford and Cambridge to men of any religious creed. In 1877 an Oxford and Cambridge Act abolished life-fellowships and introduced prize-scholarships for research. New professorships were founded. College revenues were made more readily available for purposes of teaching and learning. Celibacy was no longer required for Fellows. These reforms transformed Oxford and Cambridge into modern universities.

Summary

Between 1760 and 1914 there was a transformation of education in Britain. In 1760 there was no state provision of education and large sections of the population were illiterate. Gradually in the nineteenth century the state began to intervene to provide elementary education. By 1902 free, compulsory education was available for all. Britain's secondary schools were reformed but remained fee-paying institutions, although scholarships became available for clever children. The Universities of Oxford and Cambridge were reformed and new universities and teacher training colleges were founded. Educational provision was expensive and any extension of the state system always had its critics. However, there was a general realization that unless Britain had a satisfactory education system she could not hope to compete in the world. This realization unfortunately did not prevent other countries of Europe from maintaining a lead over Britain in the field of scientific education.

Exercises

1. Describe the development of state education in Britain referring in your answer to the following dates: 1870, 1880, 1891 and 1902.
2. How were a) grammar schools, b) public schools reformed in the nineteenth century?
3. What provision was there for higher education in 1800?
4. How were teachers trained in the nineteenth century?

29
Religious Beliefs

In 1760 the Church of England was the established church of the country. It was wealthy and privileged and supported by most of the upper class. There were a number of Roman Catholics in Britain who did not enjoy full civil rights and a significant number of Protestant Dissenters who also lacked full civil rights. In Scotland Presbyterianism was the dominant religion and in Wales there were more Dissenters than members of the Church of England. In the countryside the poor attended church on a regular basis but in the towns their attendance was erratic. In the nineteenth century, whilst religious practice was the hall-mark of respectability for the middle class, working-class attendance at church continued to decline to a point where areas of many cities were regarded as pagan dens of iniquity.

Reform and the Church of England

The Church of England's institutions and administrative machinery had not been reformed since the Middle Ages. The Church was weakened by absenteeism and pluralism. Nearly half of the clergy in 1827 were absentees. Where clergy were present they were often poor and the worst paid clergymen often worked in the poorest districts of England where the greatest resources were needed. As the nineteenth century progressed the Church ceased to attract as many people into the clergy. Other professions such as the civil service and the law offered interesting and well-paid alternatives.

The Church of England made a serious attempt to remedy its deficiencies in the nineteenth century. To diminish absenteeism two Acts of 1813 and 1817 enforced the duty of maintaining a curate and, in a parish whose value was over £300, a resident curate. They tried to secure that except in poor parishes curates had to be paid a minimum salary of £80 a year. However, it was a constant struggle to ensure that all curates were paid and, since there were no clerical pensions or provisions for sickness, many curates lived in fear of old age and ill health. To remedy the deficiency of churches a parliamentary grant of 1818 gave £1 million for the building of new churches.

When the Whigs came into office in 1830 Dissenters asked them to remove some of the disabilities against them. When Sir Robert Peel briefly replaced the Whigs in office he laid the foundations for a number of reforms, so that the measures which followed the Whigs' return to government were agreed between the two parties. Peel introduced the measure on which the Whig Tithe Commutation Act, 1836, was based, whereby tithes paid by farmers to the Church of England were replaced by a rent charge based on the average price of corn for the previous seven years. Peel had prepared a Dissenters' Marriage Bill and an Act of 1836 established a civil register of births, marriages and deaths, and enabled marriages to be celebrated in places of worship other than an Anglican church, provided that a registrar was present. In addition charters were granted to University College, London, and to the University of London giving them the authority to grant degrees irrespective of the religion of their students. A further reform came when the Ecclesiastical Commission was set up in 1835, which had the power to reorganize the Church's financial position, to abolish sinecures, and to use the money to supplement poor livings or to create new parishes. The commissioners were helped by voluntary bodies such as the Church Pastoral Aid Society.

The Whigs were also concerned with the Church of Ireland. In 1833 they passed a measure which abolished the church 'cess' or rate in Ireland and replaced it by a tax on clerical stipends. They suppressed 10 sees and dispensed with parish clergy who had no Protestant parishioners. They also enabled tenants of the bishops to demand leases in perpetuity so that they could avoid any subsequent increases in their rents. The Irish Tithes Act of 1838 operated on similar lines to the British one of 1836.

When Peel became Prime Minister in 1841 he continued to be interested in church reform. In 1843 he passed a measure to help urban areas, whereby ecclesiastical districts were created and clergymen appointed to serve them before a parish church was built. As Prime Minister he made a much more responsible use of ecclesiastical patronage than others had done and he gave freely of his own fortune for church extension. Between 1800 and 1860 over 3000 new Anglican churches were built, and £11 million was raised by voluntary subscription. The numbers of clergy increased and abuses declined dramatically. However, all the efforts of the Church of England failed to keep pace with the growth of population. In the first half of the nineteenth century the population increased by 100 per cent, the number of churches by 25 per cent.

The Methodists

John Wesley is remembered as a man who tried to revitalize the Church of England. He founded the Methodist movement whose members tried to live simple religious lives 'according to the method laid down in the Bible'. He travelled across the country preaching hundreds of sermons, often in the open air, to huge crowds. Other influential preachers included Wesley's brother, Charles (1707 – 88) and George Whitefield (1714 – 70). Several Methodist preachers travelled abroad, particularly to North America.

Wesley intended that his missions would revive religious fervour. He did not expect Methodists to act independently of the Church of England. However, the Methodist societies which sprang up in many parts of the country soon began building their own chapels. This was necessary in places where no church existed and in areas where Methodists were refused Holy Communion in Anglican churches. As the number of Methodists increased Wesley needed priests to administer Holy Communion to them. When no bishop could be found who was willing to ordain Methodists Wesley took the task upon himself. From 1784 onwards, although Wesley would never accept it, the Methodists operated outside the Anglican fold. Wesley's great contribution was to inject enthusiasm into religion. Although this offended many conservative members of the religious establishment it gave ordinary people hope and a sense of purpose. Its radical critics claimed that it may even have stopped revolution in Britain.

The Evangelical Movement

In the early nineteenth century the most active members of the Church of England were the Evangelicals. They led strict, pious lives and were often involved in public affairs. William Wilberforce and the Earl of Shaftesbury were Evangelicals. The rich members of the movement used their wealth to good purpose and they helped to spread the gospel by example rather than by preaching. The Evangelicals constantly stressed the need for a renewal of personal religion. They were centred at Clapham and Cambridge where they did a great deal to found new institutions within the church and to revive old associations. They founded the Religious Tract Society and the Church Missionary Society in 1799. They were also responsible for the foundation of the British and Foreign Bible Society. The Evangelical movement was responsible for a considerable religious revival. However, the Evangelicals neglected theology and history. They held narrowly to a literal interpretation of the Bible and much of their zeal came from a belief that unconverted sinners would burn in Hell for eternity.

The Oxford Movement

The Evangelicals had no serious rivals in the Church of England for nearly 20 years after 1815. Then, as their influence declined, a high church party rose to importance. This group emphasized the importance of the priesthood and of church doctrine and it led to the Oxford Movement. In 1833 John Henry Newman (1801 – 90), John Keble (1792 – 1866), Richard Froude (1803 – 36) and Edward Pusey (1800 – 82), who were Oxford dons, formed an Association of Friends of the Church and decided to publish a number of *Tracts for the Times*. The *Tracts* were addressed mainly to the clergy and they asserted clerical authority and insisted upon doctrines which had been condemned in England at the time of the Reformation. This led them to be condemned as Papists. In February 1841 Newman issued *Tract Ninety* in which he tried to prove that there was nothing in the Thirty-Nine Articles, to which every Anglican clergyman was bound to subscribe, which contradicted Roman Catholic belief. An immediate outcry followed and Newman gave up his fellowship and his position as Vicar of St Mary's, Oxford. Four years later he entered the Roman Catholic church, and in 1879 he was made a cardinal.

The Oxford movement had a great effect on the Church of England. It encouraged a greater care for external order and ceremonial in the church. There was a revival of interest in church architecture and ritual. This emphasis on externals alienated public opinion. Laymen seemed to be ignored by the clergy who were raised to new heights of importance. Church unity was broken and there was a deepening gulf between the high church and low church parties.

The Christian Socialists

Unlike the supporters of the Oxford movement, the Christian socialists showed churchmen that Christianity was a way of life, not a series of intellectual propositions. Amongst the leaders of the Christian socialists were Charles Kingsley (1819 – 75) and Frederick Maurice (1805 – 72) who published a series of *Tracts for Priests and People* in 1854. In his novels Kingsley reached a public which had not been touched by the Oxford Movement. Christian socialists emphasized the social rather than the intellectual aspects of religion, and they worked hard to bridge the gap which existed between the working class and organized religion.

Religious Practice

In the early years of the nineteenth century Britain appeared to be very religious. The bulk of the nation was Christian and it was dangerous to attack religion in public. Robert Owen's reputation suffered when he publicized his atheistic views. Many public discussions were religious in tone and MPs frequently used Biblical language in parliamentary debates. Popular literature often had a sentimental Christian background. On Sundays the nation seemed to be at prayer; church bells called the people to morning, afternoon and evening service, shops were closed and recreation was forbidden.

The assumption that Britain was a religious nation was shattered by a census conducted in mid-century. On Sunday 31 March 1851 worshippers were counted at morning, afternoon and evening services. Out of a population of nearly 18 million, only seven million went to church. Over five million more people could have attended church but did not. It came as a great shock to many to learn that about half the population were not practising Christians. The census showed that of those who attended a service 52 per cent were Church of England whilst 48 per cent went elsewhere. This caused bitter controversy for Dissenters claimed that a church which could only attract a little more than half of those who went to church had no right to claim to be the church of the nation. The Church of England answered sharply, questioning the accuracy of the figures. There followed a period of bitterness, almost a state of war, between the Church of England and Dissent which affected many aspects of Victorian life and had a profound influence on the country's educational system.

Religion and the Working Classes

In 1846 Engels pronounced that amongst the British working class there was a complete indifference to religion. It was not that the Church had lost the urban masses, it had never captured them. This view was portrayed by Disraeli in *Sybil* and a similar picture emerges from Dickens' *Hard Times*.

In the second half of the nineteenth century attempts were made to discover the reason for the lack of religious fervour amongst the working class. One explanation was that the organization of the Church of England was based on a rural society and that it was difficult to transplant this parochial organization from the countryside to the towns. Many people who moved from the countryside to the towns lost the churchgoing habit. But even if they wished to attend church they were often at a loss as to where to go. The churches did not contain enough seating accommodation. Only 30 per cent of London's population was capable of being seated in church in 1857, and the figure was only 17 per cent in County Durham.

A major factor which kept many members of the working class away from church was that it was connected with the Establishment. It was not unusual, for example, for clergymen to be JPs. In addition, in 1836, of the 23,000 Anglican clergymen, 16,000 were educated at Oxbridge and there was a vast gulf between them and their flock. The working classes often felt that they had no part to play in the churches and that they were not wanted. This feeling of alienation was emphasized by the system of pew rents. If you could not afford to rent a pew you were pushed into the hard, free seats at the back of the church. In addition, several poor people were too ashamed to attend church because their clothes were shabby.

Nonconformists generally had no more appeal to the working classes than the Church of England. They too rented pews. In several of the other Dissenting bodies, such as the Quakers, many people had made fortunes at the time of the industrial revolution and had little in common with the working class. The Congregationalists were very proud of their middle-class roots and they felt that their message was aimed at the middle class. At first the Methodist movement had been directed at the poorer sections of society. However, the virtues of hard work and self-discipline emphasized by the Methodists brought prosperity, and by the mid-nineteenth century there were many middle-class members of Methodist congregations. Only the Roman Catholic church continued to expand steadily in the second half of the nineteenth century amongst the working class.

Religion in Late Victorian Times
The 1851 census stirred up missionary activity in working-class areas where it was realized that building was not enough if the churches were going to stand empty. In London Exeter Hall was taken over to hold mass religious rallies. This missionary zeal is symbolized by the activities of two bishops of London. Bishop Blomfield raised funds and consecrated over 200 new churches, whilst his successor Bishop Tait(1811–82), who was much more evangelical, carried his religious message to as many people as possible. The Nonconformists renewed their revivalism and were helped by an influx of preachers from the United States of America. In 1873 two

American evangelists, Moody and Sankey, travelled the country, preaching and singing hymns. There were attempts to bring the working classes into chapels by holding non-denominational meetings, but with little success.

In 1865 William Booth (1829–1912) and his wife began a mission to the heathen of Britain. They founded the Salvation Army which concentrated on working-class areas of cities and appealed to the people at their own cultural level. Of all the revivalists movements in the second half of the nineteenth century the Salvation Army was the most successful. In 1882 the Church of England created the Church Army in an attempt to have the same influence. By the end of the nineteenth century concern with the lack of church attendance was beginning to die down. Churchmen lost their optimism. They realized that the role of religion in society had contracted. It had become just one aspect of life, not the predominant aspect.

Summary

In 1760 religion played a central role in the life of many individuals and in the life of the nation. By 1914 it had ceased to be a predominant factor in life. Religious practice declined throughout the nineteenth century; only the attendance at Roman Catholic churches increased. There were many attempts to bring religion to the urban mass but none was a resounding success. Attempts by some churches to provide legal aid and saving schemes again did little to improve attendance. When the state began to provide social benefits on a large scale in the twentieth century the churches became even more redundant in the eyes of many people.

Exercises
1. Show the importance of three of the following in the field of religion: John Wesley, William Wilberforce, John Henry Newman, Charles Kingsley, William Booth.
2. Describe and explain the importance of church reform in the 1820s and 1830s.
3. What was the Oxford movement and what effect did it have on the Church of England?
4. Why did so few members of the working class attend church in the mid-nineteenth century?
5. What attempts did organized religion make to increase working-class religious practice in the late nineteenth century?

Museums and Galleries

All the following museums and galleries cater for school parties and many have excellent education departments. Suggestions for visits are given for each chapter and the numbers correspond to the chapter numbers.

1   The National Portrait Gallery, St Martin's Place, London, WC2, houses a national collection of portraits of the famous and infamous in British history.

2   The Museum of English Rural Life, Whiteknights Park, Reading, and Agricultural Museum, Wye, Kent, both house national collections of material relating to agriculture and village life.

3   The Science Museum, South Kensington, London, SW7, and the North Western Museum of Science and Industry, 97 Grosvenor Street, Manchester, house collections relating to industry.

4   The Museum of Costume, Assembly Rooms, Bath, has a world famous collection comprising every aspect of fashion with fine Georgian costumes. West Wycombe Park, Buckinghamshire, the home of Sir Francis Dashwood, with its temples and lake, was frequently visited by John Wilkes.

5   The American Museum, Claverton Manor, near Bath, illustrates aspects of American history. Washington Old Hall, Washington Village, near Sunderland, was the seat of George Washington's ancestors and contains Washington relics.

6   Wilberforce House, High Street, Hull, is the birthplace of the slave emancipator and it houses a slavery collection.

7   The National Maritime Museum, Romney Road, Greenwich, London, SE10, has a Nelson gallery. The Portsmouth Royal Naval Museum is situated near to *HMS Victory* and contains relics of Nelson and his associates.

8   The Wellington Museum, Hyde Park Corner, London, W1, contains many of the Duke's trophies and uniforms. The Public Record Office Museum, Chancery Lane, London, WC2,

contains Wellington's dispatches from Waterloo.

9   There are illustrations of Peterloo in the Manchester City Art Gallery, Mosley Street, Manchester, M2.

10   The Castle Museum, York, includes exhibits relating to prison life and the development of the police force.

11   Mount Stewart House, Newtownards, Co. Down, is the house where Castlereagh grew up and it houses his relics.

12   The Industrial Museum, Moorside Road, Bradford, houses a collection relating to the woollen and worsted industries and factory life. The National Postal Museum, King Edward Street, London, EC1, contains a collection of stamps and relics of the early postal service.

13   The Robert Owen Memorial Museum, Broad Street, Newtown, Powys, contains numerous documents and relics relating to Robert Owen. The Museum and Art Gallery, John Frost Square, Newport, Gwent, houses a collection relating to the Chartist movement.

14   The Ulster-American Folk Park, Omagh, Co. Tyrone, tells the story of the great migrations of Ulster people to the United States.

15   The British Museum, Great Russell Street, London, WC1, contains many of the drawings and cartoons which illustrate Palmerston's career.

16   Claydon House, Middle Claydon Village, near Buckingham, houses a collection of mementoes of Florence Nightingale. Relics from the Crimean War can be seen at Queen Alexandra's Royal Army Nursing Corps Museum, at Aldershot.

17   School parties are welcome at the Palace of Westminster to see how Britain's democracy works.

18   The National Museum of Ireland, Kildare Street, Dublin, contains a collection dealing with life in Ireland in the nineteenth century.

19   Hughendon Manor, High Wycombe, was bought by Disraeli in 1847 and contains many of his relics. There is an interesting Congress of Berlin room.

20   Gladstone's house is at Hawarden Castle; his personal relics are at the Old Rectory, Hawarden, near Chester.

21   The Rhodes Memorial Museum, Bishop Stortford, Hertfordshire, houses a collection illustrating the life of Cecil Rhodes and the history of southern and central Africa.

22   The Museum of London, London Wall, London, EC2, has a collection of items relating to the suffragette movement.

23 The Imperial War Museum, Lambeth Road, London, SE1, has a display on the origins of the First World War.
24 The National Army Museum, Royal Hospital Road, London, SW3, has relics of the Indian mutiny. Maori and Aborigine artefacts can be seen at the Museum of Mankind, Burlington House, London, W1, and at the Commonwealth Institute, Kensington High Street, London, W8.
25 The Museum of the History of Science, Broad Street, Oxford, houses a collection of early scientific instruments. Downe House, Downe, Kent, is the home of Charles Darwin and contains many of his relics.
26 The Carriage Museum, Circus Mews, Bath, contains a collection of stage coaches. The National Railway Museum, York, has a fine collection of nineteenth-century railway engines. The Museum of Transport, Glasgow, has a large collection of ships and ship models.
27 The Museum of Education at Leeds University illustrates the development of British education.
28 Wesley's House and Museum, 47 City Road, London, EC1, contains a large collection of Wesley's relics.

Suggestions for further reading

General Histories
A. Briggs, *The Age of Improvement 1783 – 1867*
D. Thomson, *England in the Nineteenth Century*

Economic and Social Histories
T.S. Ashton, *The Industrial Revolution*
J.D. Chambers, *The Workshop of the World: British Economic History from 1820 to 1880*
G.P. Jones and A.G. Poole, *A Hundred Years of Economic Development*
H. Perkins, *The Origins of Modern English Society 1780 – 1880*
M. Bruce, *The Coming of the Welfare State*

Party Histories

G. Kitson Clark, *Peel and the Conservative Party*
R.B. McCallum, *The Liberal Party from Grey to Asquith*
R. Blake, *The Conservative Party from Peel to Churchill*
H. Pelling, *The Origins of the Labour Party*

Foreign Policy

R.W. Seton Watson, *Britain in Europe 1789–1914*
A. Cecil, *British Foreign Secretaries 1807–1916*
M.S. Anderson, *The Eastern Question*
L.M. Penson, *Foreign Affairs Under the Third Marquis of Salisbury*
N. Mansergh, *The Coming of the First World War*

Ireland

A. Macintyre, *The Liberator: Daniel O'Connell and the Irish party 1830–47*
C. Woodham Smith, *The Great Hunger: Ireland 1845–49*
J.C. Beckett, *The Making of Modern Ireland 1603–1923*
F.S.L. Lyons, *Ireland Since the Famine*
N. Mansergh, *The Irish Question*

Biographies

C.J. Bartlett, *Castlereagh*
P.J.V. Rolo, *George Canning*
J. Ridley, *Lord Palmerston*
Lady G. Cecil, *Life of Robert, Marquis of Salisbury*
R. Jenkins, *Asquith*

Index

Berlin Memorandum, 185
Berlin, Treaty of (1878), 187–90, 196, 207
Bessemer, Henry (1813–98), 21–2
Birkbeck, George (1776–1841), 285
Birmingham, 55, 87, 116, 120, 125–6, 131, 166
Birmingham Political Union, 119, 131
Bismark, Otto von, 154, 173, 186, 240
Black, Joseph (1728–99), 259
Black Dwarf, the, 83
Black Sea, 54, 149, 157–8, 161–2, 174, 186, 207
Blanketeers, 87
Blenkinsop, John (1783–1831), 273
Blomfield, Bishop (1786–1857), 125, 293
Boers, 190, 197, 242, 255
Boer War (1899–1902), 197, 209–13
Bonaparte, Joseph, 75
Bonaparte, Napolean, 61–80
Bonnymuir Riot (1820), 88
Booth, Charles (1840–1916), 231
Booth, William (1829–1912), 294
Borodino, 78
Borstals, 232
Bosnia, 185–90, 244–5
Boston Massacre (1770), 37
Boston Port Act (1774), 37
Boston Tea Party (1773), 37
Bradlaugh, Charles (1833–91), 194–5
Brandreth, Jeremiah (d. 1817), 87
Bridgewater, Duke of (1736–1803), 269
Bridport, Lord (1727–1814), 60
Bright, John (1811–89), 134
Brindley, James (1716–72), 269
Bristol, 3, 16, 120
British Medical Association, 264–5
Brougham, Henry (1778–1868), 85, 98
Bruce, Henry (1815–95), 177–8
Brunel, Isambard Kingdom (1806–59), 276
Bryce, James (1838–1922), 204
Bucharest, Treaty of (1913), 245
Buddle, John (1773–1843), 17
Bulgaria, 156, 185–90, 207
'Bulgarian Horrors', 186
Buller, Charles (1806–48), 257
Bunker Hill, Battle of (1775), 40
Burdett, Sir Francis (1770–1844), 82–3
Burgos, 76
Burgoyne, General John (1722–92), 41, 45
Burials Act (1880), 194
Burke, Edmund (1729–97), 47–8, 55
Burke, Thomas (1829–82), 203
Burma, 207, 250
Burt, Thomas (1837–1922), 221
Bute, Lord (1713–92), 1, 26–30, 37
Butt, Isaac (1813–79), 172, 201
Buxton, Thomas Foxwell (1786–1845), 123

Byron, Lord (1788–1824), 49, 113

Cadiz, 64
Calder, Sir Robert (1754–1818), 64
Cambridge University, 5, 47, 102, 262, 278, 285, 286–7
Cambridge University Act (1856), 287
Campbell, Sir Colin (1792–1863), 251
Campbell, Thomas (1777–1844), 286
Campbell-Bannerman, Henry (1836–1908), 204, 217, 228
Camperdown, 60
Campo-Formio, Treaty of (1797), 60
Canada, 27, 32, 40–1, 44, 74, 154, 255–8
—Canada Act (1791), 53, 257
—Canada Act (1840), 257–8
—Dominion of, 258
Canals, 4, 269–70
Canning, George (1770–1827), 71–2, 93, 97–8, 110–15, 136, 145
Canning, Stratford (1812–62), 251
Cape of Good Hope, 58, 103, 184, 261
Cape St Vincent, 60
Cardigan, Lord (1797–1868), 159
Cardwell, Edward (1813–86), 175–77
Caroline, Queen (1768–1821), 88–9, 111
Cartwright, Rev Edmund (1743–1823), 15
Cartwright, Major John (1740–1824), 82–3, 87, 117, 119
Castlereagh, Viscount (1769–1821), 70, 72, 80–2, 91, 93, 103–10, 145
'Cat and Mouse Act' (1913), 235
Catholics, 288
—Catholic Association, 99–100
—Catholic Emancipation, 62, 68, 69–71, 73, 97–101, 111, 136
—Catholic Relief Act (1829), 100
—Catholic Relief Bill (1778), 31, 52–3
Cato Street Conspiracy, 88
Cavendish, Lord Frederick (1836–82), 203
Cavour, 153
Cawnpore, 251
Ceylon, 58, 62
Chadwick, Edwin (1800–90), 122, 125, 139–40
Chamberlain, Joseph (1830–1914), 193, 204, 216–7
Chartist Movement, 83, 128, 129, 130–32, 165, 218
Children Act (1908), 232
China, 136–7, 149–50, 207–8, 241
Chimney Sweeps, 83, 182
Cholera, 128, 136, 140, 160
Christian Socialists, 224, 291–2
Church of England, 4, 99, 288–94
Churchill, Lord Randolph (1849–94), 194–5, 203